MAINTAINING THE SELF IN COMMUNICATION

Concept and Guidebook

Harold Barrett

Alpha & Omega

A & Ω

Credits

Chapter Two: From *The Prince of Tides.*
Copyright © 1986 by Pat Conroy.
Reprinted by permission of Houghton Mifflin Company.
All rights reserved.

Chapter Six: From "Mending Wall" by Robert Frost.

Publisher's Cataloging-in-Publication (Provided by Quality Books, Inc)

Barrett, Harold
Maintaining the self in communication : concept and guidebook / Harold Barrett. — 1st ed.
p. cm.
Includes bibliographical references and indexes.
Preassigned LCCN: 97-72960
ISBN: 0-9658440-5-6
1. Communication—Psychological aspects. 2. Interpersonal communication. 3. Narcissism. 4. Self-perception. 5. Socialization. I. Title.

BF637.C45B37 1998 302.2'242
QBI97-41155

International Standard Book Number: 0-9658440-5-6
Library of Congress Catalog Card Number: 97-72960
Printed in the United States of America

Cover design by Lake Lizard Graphix
Edited by Karla Huebner
Composition by Page One Graphics/David Nishikawa

Alpha & Omega Book Publishers
P. O. Box 4526
Incline Village, NV 89450

Address orders to:
Alpha & Omega
Publishers Services
P. O. Box 2510
Novato CA 94948

TO THE GOOD AUDIENCE

When they are good, they are very, very good, and when they are bad, they are horrid. Audiences, I mean. This, then, is to salute the GOOD AUDIENCE: the communicator who, with competence, compassion, courage, and civility, cares enough to let us know when we're doing well and when we're not.

ABOUT THE AUTHOR

Harold Barrett, Ph.D., University of Oregon; professor and consultant in communication; Professor for 29 years in the Department of Speech Communication, California State University, Hayward; author of eight books on public speaking, interpersonal communication, civility in rhetoric and communication, and the history of rhetoric; founder of the "Conference in Rhetorical Criticism"; named "Outstanding Professor of the University" by faculty of California State University, Hayward. Harold and wife Carol have four sons, and five grandchildren.

Contents

Preface

This book grows out of studies that I began in the 1970s. Along with studying pertinent theory on human development and behavior, I have collected abundant material on narcissism, defensiveness, and motivation in the communication process. My observations of human behavior—in the United States and abroad—are extensive, as are explorations of relevant novels, plays, movies, and material from assorted media. I have tested certain of the material in courses in interpersonal communication, ordinary rhetorical interaction, and defensiveness in communication. *Rhetoric and Civility: Human Development, Narcissism, and the Good Audience* (Albany: State University of New York Press, 1991), was one product of that effort. This new book is an expansion and closer interpretation of a small part of that book.

One of the earliest influences on my work was the splendid essay, "Rhetorical Sensitivity and Social Interaction," by Roderick P. Hart and Don M. Burks. In it I found direction for a rhetorical understanding of communication, not to mention validation for use of my background in psychology. I would name the following as representative of other excellent mentors, first in the supporting fields of psychology, psychoanalysis, and infant development: Mario Jacoby, Alice Miller, Gregory Rochlin, H.R. Schaffer, Daniel N. Stern, and Donald W. Winnicott. Heinz Kohut's psychoanalytic ideas (and those of kindred theorists) are indispensable to me and fit nicely with established theory of my discipline. Kenneth Burke's rhetorical theory of identification, compatible with those sources, provides bedrock for discussing human interaction. Another provider of bedrock is the Aristotelian rhetorical discipline, and in appreciation of that I shall always be indebted to my major professor, Bower Aly.

I want to believe that the result of this application of rhetorical precepts to the act of communication is a theoretically sound, functional, and compassionate view of our fundamental role as communicators: we who are motivated by our narcissism, and yet are hampered by forms of it—we who, while going forth with the heart of a David, must attend always to protecting the heal of an Achilles. Carried along in daily interaction by our narcissism—both good and troublesome—we make our way, drawing on the power of rhetoric to maintain ourselves.

A number of students and colleagues have contributed significantly to the development of ideas in this book. First, I would like to thank those students of California State University, Hayward, who in the 1980s and 90s also taught the professor, as they involved themselves in his classes and seminars on defensiveness in communication.

Professors Lesley DiMare and Roderick P. Hart read chapters of the book and offered constructive comment. I greatly appreciate their sound counsel.

Jon Sharp, ever the reliable guide, drew from his extensive experience as book publisher to answer innumerable questions on publication of the book.

Karla Huebner read the entire manuscript and found many ways to make it clearer and more readable. She is a "good audience," and I am grateful.

Further, I want specifically to acknowledge the support of Ronald B. Adler, Claire Allphin, Peter A. Andersen, Rick Anderson, Joe Ayres, Wende Black, C.J. Carman, James V. Carroll, Isaac E. Catt, Jensen (Cheng-sheng) Chung, William F. Eadie, Robin Edmonds, Karen Fritts, David Rojas Gaytán, Joseph George, Bubba Hansen, Bob Heffernan, Patrick John, Peggy Kane, Peter Kane, Susan Mainwaring, Megan Marie, Robert C. Martin, Sally Murphy, Stephen R. Nelson, Michael Osborn, Suzanne Osborn, Daniel S. Prentice, Carol S. Rowe, Agha Saeed, Jacob Scott, B.J. Scully, Mike Sebring, Mary Settlemyre, Shellie Stauber-Haygood, Renald Stettler, Patti Walker, and Gale Young.

C.J. Bliss gave the entire manuscript a keen and critical reading and made numerous good suggestions for improvement.

Once more, Jake Barrett served as proofreader and adviser. I thank him for his sharp editorial eye, encouragement, and good heart.

Thanks to Carol, for all she does as my in-house, one-person editorial department. Starting in the 50's, we've read a lot of proof together. This is the fourteenth go-round.

Harold Barrett

INTRODUCTION

Introduction

Looking After The Self

Interpersonal security is currently a common topic in the media. An example is a recent interview with Harvard political scientist Robert D. Putnam. Putnam believes that Americans have lost much of their willingness to trust. A generation ago, when asked if they trusted other people, two-thirds said yes; now two-thirds say no. Americans are untrusting because they don't know each other, Putnam says. Today they are less connected to each other—and less happy.[1]

One result of this lack of connection and trust is a greater dedication to self-protection in communicating with others. Given a condition of insecurity, the solution is predictable: purposeful effort to look after and justify the self. Insecurity and protectiveness have always been a part of human interaction; the issue of the moment is about their increase.

This book is about taking care of ourselves in communication: supporting, sustaining, defending, and justifying. It's about, self-maintenance, an everyday function of our interactions with others.

Self-maintenance behavior arises from some sense of uncertainty with others, from a perception of danger to the self—whether negligible or great, obscure or obvious. Thus we have defense mechanisms, as they are called. Theorist Karl E. Scheibe holds that *defense* mechanisms are so named in psychoanalytic theory because "the ego is considered to be under a more or less constant state of siege."[2] And, I would add, the communicator's response to the siege is *constant.*

It's easy to find testimony to the pervasiveness of insecurity and consequent safeguarding. Psychoanalytic theorist Marshall Edelson holds that defensiveness is "a ubiquitous aspect of human action." (Indeed, *any* use of language is defensive, he believes.)[3] Just yesterday I heard down at my little post office, "Why is everyone so damned defensive these days?"

A FUNCTION OF COMMUNICATION

Gregory Rochlin, whose ideas are reflected on many pages in this book, offers this truth on the self (and self-esteem): "Its defense may bring the highest honors and justify the lowest violence."[4] Defending and thus maintaining the self, an ordinary function of communication, has both good and bad dimensions. Moreover, no mode of conduct is more fascinating in the drama of human interaction, as is apparent in the life stories of communicators, including those whose deeds we celebrate: Washington and Lincoln, Churchill and Roosevelt, Joan of Arc and Susan B. Anthony, Martin Luther and Martin Luther King, Jr.—as well as in those whose deeds we deplore: Joseph Stalin, Richard III, Adolf Hitler, and Joseph McCarthy. All of these notable figures were self-defenders in their communicating. Sigmund Freud said that defenses of the self direct the daily functioning of humankind. That's true, for better or worse.

There's high adventure and peril in communication, a fact that all of us seem to feel. Using athletic talk about teams playing defense ("D"), we can say that in the risky interactive game called communication, we play "D" at every moment. Knowing our ways, advisers urge, "Don't explain, don't complain!" ("Don't be defensive!") That's appealing advice, yet asking us not to look after ourselves is like asking us to give up being human.

Every Communicator's Story

Plots of every communicator's story are built around self-maintenance. Why so? Because self-worth is always at issue in communication; it hurts to be disrespected, dismissed, or disregarded. This may explain why **our persistent and compelling need in communication is to give an account of ourselves.** Intense or minimal, our motivation will never cease; protective messages will continue, whether as simple explanations, subtle excuses, hostile retorts, or anxious retreats. Such is our uneasiness about personal status and safety—apparent now more than ever before. A generation ago, Dean C. Barnlund saw signs of increasing interpersonal vulnerability—if not danger—and noted that a common use of communication is to act on our own behalf: "Communication arises out of the need to reduce uncertainty, to act effectively, to defend or strengthen the ego."[5] Thus, in studying the act of communication, we must include the fundamental needs of self as sources of motivation.

Now, before expanding the discussion, I want to present some concepts in communication that will be basic from this point on.

A Rhetorical Perspective

In this exploration of ordinary human interaction, I am guided by a rhetorical perspective on communication: that we *choose* ways to be with others, always with *purpose,* always seeking to be *effective* with them. That's what it means to be rhetorical in communication. Whether succeeding or failing, our aim is to use self-sustaining methods that will help us be effective. Psychologist Guy E. Swanson, in his scientific study of defenses, holds that defensive strategies of daily life, grounded in social interaction and interdependence, "are justifications tailored to social relations that are in danger and need of preservation." In other words, the goal is to adapt to others and maintain connections to them. In this, the choices are "likely to be determined by the nature of the social relationship concerned."[6] What's useful in maintaining one relationship may not be useful in another.

Characterized by strategic choice in the exchange of messages, the interactive function of communication is rhetorical. **To be rhetorical is to make choices for success.** Consequently, I will always use the word *communication* in a rhetorical sense, i.e., to refer to the symbolic interactions of people *exercising options* in saying things and pursuing their respective *purposes.* The rhetorical function is at the heart of communication, for participants put messages together to secure responses from each other. As we move on through the chapter, these basic ideas will take on greater meaning.

In terms of rhetorical theory, those with whom we relate and communicate are our "audiences." Moreover, as audience-conscious communicators, we're never innocent in our efforts to get a response, for our intent is to "get something"; most fundamentally, it is to secure confirmation of the person we believe we are—or want to be. That's why mindfulness of *self*-status is foremost in communication—*always,* regardless of the occasion or apparent meaning of the message. **We can never be sure of ourselves, especially of the other's attitude toward us or of our capability to relate to that**. Possessed of a vulnerable self and being rhetorically aware, we involve ourselves inventively with relevant ideas and feelings, dealing with issues of the moment, seeking to be successful: we want to identify with audiences and be confirmed by them. In other chapters, I'll have much more to say about interacting to identify, being confirmed, and other basic topics suggested here.

The Rhetorical Imperative

Our strategies of interaction arise from a powerful rhetorical imperative: to affect audiences favorably about ourselves. Most of our self-sustaining measures work fairly well most of the time and with most audiences. Swanson found that defenses "enable us to go on acting in a coherent fashion," promising to "afford us whatever gratification seems possible. In that sense they are adequate—sometimes ingeniously so."[7] Stories of brilliant accomplishment can be traced to this very ingenuity: for example, the eloquence of Winston Churchill.[8] Yet, other stories tell of inadequate self-maintenance strategy: stories of personal failure, strained relations, and communicative disaster.

And remember our internal messages, those we send to ourselves. In an in*tra*personal sense, excuses, denials, rationalizations, and other kinds of validating messages to ourselves about ourselves can help us to feel good with ourselves and to accept ourselves. Being comfortable with ourselves is basic to acting comfortably with others.

SHAME versus GUILT

For a psychological grounding on the nature of the social threat to the self, we can do no better than to consult Heinz Kohut, founder of the school of self psychology. Kohut's study of human behavior led to an important challenge to classical Freudian psychoanalytic thought. Departing from classical theory on the conflict of drives as fundamental to human behavior, Kohut centered instead on humankind's sense of self-defectiveness. In arguing his theory, he contrasted the family environment of Freud's time with that of subsequent generations, finding great differences in influences on child development. He contrasted the close household involvements and constant family stimulation of Freud's Victorian era with conditions of more recent decades. Families now have looser ties. There's much greater emotional distance among members, and one result is understimulation.

In Freudian theory, the *neurosis* is the common psychological complaint; it's tied to guilt and overstimulation from the persistent presence of family members, particularly parents. Guilt results from felt transgression, e.g., in violation of parental or social rule. But more recently, reflecting shame from felt neglect or deprivation, particularly parental, it is *narcissism* that is the common condition.

Shame results from a sense of felt defectiveness. In the absence of optimal parental or social constraint, the self is inadequately responded to, resulting in the narcissistic feelings of emptiness, unfulfillment, and deficiency. Thus, Kohut concluded, this is "the era of the endangered self."[9] The prime motivator of our time is shame. As we strive to protect ourselves against shame, our communicating is affected. This will become clearer as the book unfolds.

From his Freudian grounding, rhetorical theorist Kenneth Burke found guilt to be the primary motivator of human action, including communication. It is in response to felt guilt that people act upon others, seeking to redeem themselves. In interpreting Burke on this point, Stephen W. Littlejohn puts it well: "We communicate to purge our guilt"; that's the primary motive for the act.[10] Burke died at age 96 in 1993, and I like to think that had he been as keen a scholar in the 1980s as he had been into the '60s, he would have become acquainted with writings on self psychology or related works, to discover the dominant place of meeting *shame* as motive for communication.[11]

To counter the shame of personal deficit (felt inadequacy), humans invent modes of maintaining the self: some facilitative, others maladaptive. Of course, shame has always been with us, and the response to it is not a new behavioral act. But now the incidence is much higher, leading to a higher incidence of corrective activity to protect and justify ourselves. Of course guilt continues, but given increased narcissistic injury, e.g., from neglect, shame has become the master emotion. We live in an age of diminished parental presence and authority and in a general culture marked by increased social disregard. Consequently, we are provided with less feedback on connectedness and worth—or less constructive feedback. We are more on our own and more likely to question our adequacy, experience social endangerment, and respond self-protectively. The results—good and bad, hardly noticeable or blatant—appear in all daily communication: at home, on the job, at school—everywhere. Expressions vary. One aim of this book is to trace the influence of shame on strategic choices in ordinary communication. All ideas mentioned here will be developed as we move along in the chapters.

ON CULTURE AND SOCIALIZATION

Consider the following premise and implications for communication: **Rewards of individualism increasingly come into conflict with rewards of community affiliation**. "I want to be *me*, but I need *you*" expresses this personal-interpersonal conflict of our time: Or "It's great to be a person apart from others, but I need things from them." Issues of the conflict can be set out in various subjective terms:

- being gloriously alone and independent versus being safely associated and interdependent
- magnifying personal differences versus acknowledging kinship with others
- keeping distance versus seeking intimacy
- suffering the pain of separation versus enjoying the compensations of communication

The communicator's dilemma is about wanting to rely on self-confirmation versus needing the confirmation of others. It's a question of in*tra*personal (individual) versus in*ter*personal (social) satisfaction. It's an old story but with numerous postmodern twists and significant connections to other conditions of this age.[12] The dilemma is basic to the study of maintaining the self in communication.

East and West

At the outset, let's recognize the fact of cultural diversity in communication patterns. For example, in the United States, there is variance from culture to culture in strategies of self-maintenance—and from family to family, gender to gender, and from region to region. Communicators and students of communication should be aware that differences exist, and should be attentive to specific instances, some of which may influence the character of a moment of communication.

Thus we take the workings of socialization into account when studying variations in communication methods. And though anthropologists occasionally point to an isolated culture in which constraints on infant behavior appear to be minimal, apparently all cultures impose a socialization process on their children, one that moderates expression of their natural and normal narcissism. Certain differences in self-perception observed among Western and Eastern cultures can be traced to variations in the tightness of socialization processes that are imposed, primarily during the first two years or so of life. In some cultures, the social framing of the self is keen, and narcissism is actively suppressed, i.e., expressions of self and self-fulfillment are discouraged. The most familiar examples are collectivistic cultures like those of Asia. In others, such as the traditionally individualistic cultures of North America, greater encouragement is given to development of a self and related behaviors.

We know that in East Asian cultures, shame is a product of ardent socialization and group association. But in North American cultures, socialization is less stringent; the group is less exigent in shaping behavior, less insistent on conformity to norms. In North American cultures, individuals value independence, and they feel shame when they sense personal inadequacy. Thus they seek some kind of exoneration or justification when they perceive themselves to be in violation of their self-concept. Pride, respect, trust, specific kinds of prowess, and other personal mandates are among the major issues. East Asians feel shame when they violate group norms, when their behavior hurts the group.

But note the common property. While forces of socialization differ in intensity, people of every culture and background possess a self that is subject to threat and injury. And all are influenced by a concept of self. For instance, the pain that East Asians feel in bringing discredit to the group comes from knowing that they have violated their concept on group allegiance. Defending against that shame—maintaining or saving face—is necessary because self-worth and continuation of benefits of membership are in the balance.

Broadly speaking, in North American cultures, self-maintenance behavior is motivated by perception of personal *deficit*; in Asia, e.g., Japan, it stems from perception of social *debt*. The Japanese word for this debt is *on*: never-ending social obligation. Among East Asians, rewards from conformity and assuming the social burden are great and in fact vital. Thus, in giving up independence and engaging reciprocally, an Asian experiences the joys of belonging and having a place with others. Though always somewhat probational, one's group status and security continue with conformity.

Self-maintenance communicative strategies in North American cultures arise out of fragmentation of the self, out of one's uncertainty of adequacy: doubt that is ever-operative.[13] In East Asia, it is uncertainty related to one's group status and place that motivates maintenance responses. North Americans, in their individualism, dare to give up the security provided by commitment to group affiliation; they risk being alone—uncared for—and they suffer for it. Freedom is frightening yet cherished; social controls, though needed in community life, are resisted. To be dependent is to be weak; but to be independent is to forego the comforts of association. When East Asians perceive themselves to be in violation of group interest—when given to expressions of individualism, they too suffer, in their loneliness. When deviating from premises of the self-concept, members of both general cultures experience shame. From their respective orientations, they build maintenance strategies to use in communication.[14] These and related issues in two different cultures suggest sources of productive and counterproductive self-maintenance methods.

Common patterns of maintenance communication—from rage to submission—are widely but not equally represented in North America, Asia, and elsewhere. In response to threat, e.g., humiliation, East Asians generally appear to favor the strategies of withdrawal, evasion, and denial. Their non-confrontational rhetorical strategies serve to counter their shame and secure continuation of respectful community membership. Without group acknowledgment—confirmation—the self is without value: alone and vulnerable to the worst embarrassment. In extreme and rare instances, the violator resorts to the ultimate act of self-protective withdrawal: securing the self in suicide.

When interpersonally uncertain or threatened, people on all continents respond protectively. Thus **the great commandment is to maintain the self**.

BEFORE GOING ON TO CHAPTER ONE

Here's a word on the organization of the book. There are six chapters. The first four treat basic topics relating to self-maintenance in communication: e.g., communicative behavior and the self, the communicator's growth from infancy, and theory and strategy in communication. The other two chapters are a guidebook for improvement in communication, directed to you and your growth.

Also, note the large Glossary of Terms. This part of the book will help you to handle terms and ideas, some of which may require clarification. As you read along and come across an unfamiliar term, turn to the Glossary in the back.

CONCEPT

Chapter One

Maintaining the Self in Communication

MAIN THEMES OF THE CHAPTER

- Each of us has a self to keep safe and justify; therefore,
- Self-maintenance is a common human goal.
- We become uneasy when we feel that our well-being is threatened, when we are insecure and concerned about injury to the self.
- All of us have feelings of inadequacy and pride and a need for reassurance, to be taken seriously and respected.
- Consequently, we support, uphold, and defend ourselves—to maintain status as "somebody"—in all scenes of communication and all relationships.
- Productive, creative, and even loving acts benefit from self-maintenance motives that arise out of uncertainty as to safety or status.
- Though we intend our self-maintenance strategies to serve us well, some are intrusive in communication.
- Strategies are both verbal and nonverbal.
- Strategies are expressed outwardly and inwardly.
- Among the major strategic groupings from which we choose—*topoi*, we call them—are *Control, Achievement, Op-*

position, Attribution, Anger, Denial, Withdrawal, and Prevarication.

- Self-maintenance procedures can be understood with common elements of communication theory: "Senders and Receivers," "The Exigence," "Roles," "The Enthymeme," and "Identification."
- The need for confirmation is the "generic" exigence.
- Among key issues in the communicative experience are intimacy and self-disclosure, risk, trust, and reciprocity.

SELF-MAINTENANCE: A COMMON GOAL

Keeping the self together and balanced, functioning successfully in communication, is a primary human goal. In pursuit of the goal, we act to *sustain* ourselves with *safeguards*: to *prove* ourselves worthy, *to uphold, defend, protect,* and *justify* ourselves. Forms of this activity in communication are very closely related, e.g., *protecting* and *justifying*; more often than not, the various forms are indistinguishable in objective. Therefore, I'll use some of them interchangeably. Here's an excerpt from the Glossary to clarify the general process of maintaining the self:

> **self-maintenance** self-care in communication; involves choosing measures to provide for safety in communication, to sustain the self against real or imagined threat of diminishment or injury

To illustrate the ordinary nature of communication in looking after the self, let's take the example of defending.

"Don't be so defensive!" he shouted.
"You're the defensive one!" she shouted back.

Which of the two *is* the defensive one? That's an easy question. The answer is *both* are. In fact, everyone is, in one way or another—more in certain situations than in others, but potentially in *any* situation. **Self-maintenance activity is one of the most characteristic behaviors of humankind.**

Here are some sample expressions of self-maintenance:

"Hey, thanks for calling; I've been meaning to call *you* for a week now. I really have."

"If they cut in on me, I give 'em the finger, baby!"

"I don't want you to think I'm inconsiderate or anything. I'm really not the kind to let people down, but on the night of your party I had to take Mom to see Grandma."

"Hey, how come you want to read *my* essay, anyway? Something wrong with it?"

"So I blew a thousand dollars. I don't care about money."

"If you want something done right, do it yourself; that's the only way to be sure."

"It's not me, man! I didn't screw it up."

"Believe me, I can think of 15 reasons why my little college is better than your *great* public university!"

"I usually don't tell people that I like country music."

"Yes, our family was one of the poorest in the Bronx—and I'm darned proud of it!"

Now, all of the incidents above are direct and verbal statements, but let's remember that sometimes the message to prove or exonerate the self is silent, appearing as a scowl, a determined folding of the arms, or a turning away.

Some Personal Stories—But Nothing Unusual

What's this subject all about? What's the nature of self-supportive communication and defensiveness in the general culture? To get a better understanding of it, let's look at some extended examples. Here are five actual cases as reported by the participants, in their own words.

Derrick's Story

I like to play "Trivial Pursuit," but only in teams. Why? Because on a team there is safety from ridicule and humiliation. I like the comfort of anonymity.

However, the first time I played was individually. My turn came up, and I rolled the dice. I got a political question—a subject on which I was very shaky, as everyone knew. Later, when I got an easy question, they all laughed in relief. But the worst thing that could happen did happen: I didn't know the answer. My face turned red; my pulse beat faster. I felt hot. As I made a wild guess, there was silence. It was wrong.

Play moved on, and I remained in last place, as my self-esteem sank lower and lower. I wanted to hide. "I don't care about being good at this game anyway," I silently lied; "besides, the questions are impossibly hard."

What had happened to me? This much I know: My goals of perfection were being challenged in front of friends; I defended through silence, emotional withdrawal, and rationalization.

I do enjoy the game more now but still prefer playing in teams.

Tara's Story

Todd and I had been going out for six months, and we had built a close, serious relationship. We told each other everything; we loved each other. Then the blow fell. He met me after work one day and to my utter surprise said that he did not want to go with me anymore. I felt deeply wounded—lost, confused, upset, betrayed—totally devastated. But I didn't let him see my inner tears. I hid my true feelings and tried to be objective. I didn't want him to know he had hurt me and how helpless and unsure of myself I was. Of course he knew I was hurt, but if he knew how much, it would have been easy for him to use me to his advantage. He wouldn't get that satisfaction from me! I wanted to show him I was strong and not ruined. It wasn't until I got to my car that I began to cry.

Hiding my true feelings was one of the hardest things I've ever done.

Emily's Story

I almost didn't graduate from college because a course in public speaking was required. People took it in their first or second year, but deathfully afraid, I put it off until my very last term. What agony it was to get up there all alone and in front of twenty pairs of eyes focused on my every movement, not to mention twenty pairs of ears. . . . What's my problem, anyway? I did everything in the book to weasel out. I pleaded to the Dean to take substitute work. No dice. When finally enrolled, I didn't show up for the first major speaking assignment and got an F grade on it. Violating a class rule that all speeches must be given from an outline, I wrote one speech out word for word and gave it that way, hoping to reduce the pressure by hiding in the page. In the last speech, I did fairly well, probably because of my humor that helped to disarm the audience. They say that public speaking is an American's number one terror, but why me? What am I afraid of losing? There's no real hurt in making a speech, right? Wrong!

Melissa's Story

It began last year when I asked my mother for permission to go to San Diego with a group of six friends. I would miss two days of school but would make up all assignments before going. She said "No," arguing that seven girls should not go off on such a trip without an adult. "But we're all seventeen or eighteen now, and we'll watch out for one another," I answered. "There's nothing to worry about, Mom." Then she brought up my bad grades, my father's temper that was sure to flare up, and all sorts of other weak excuses. The real reason was that she did not trust me. Then I went to my room, slammed the door, and threw her photograph under my bed.

Later that evening, I went to my friend's house to tell her that I couldn't go on the trip. I called my mom every bad name I could think of. To my surprise, my friend agreed with everything I said and told me she felt the same way about my mother. Hearing her say bad things about Mom really hurt! I found myself becoming very upset and protective of my mother, even though I had said it all first. I yelled at my friend and told her not to talk about Mom that way: "You've got a lot of nerve saying bad things about my mother."

What I was doing was covering up for the fact that my mom didn't trust me. But I would have been just as upset, if my friend had taken my mom's side.

Rick's Story (really Jim's)

I was in a Reno sports book—a betting place—with my roommate Jim, watching a baseball game between the Cardinals and the Reds, when an emotional thing happened. Earlier that day Jim had bet on the Reds. But I am a Cardinal fan, so when the game ended with the Cardinals winning, I showed my pleasure with a clenched fist held high and an audible "Yes!" Immediately, Jim snapped at me, "You're fucked!"

"Hey, I like the Cardinals," I said (I had forgotten about his bet.)

"You know that I lost money on that game," he screamed; "a real friend never rubs it in when the other loses. You should support your friend, even if it's against your favorite team."

I said that I didn't agree with his gambling philosophy and that I'd back any team I liked. When I accused him of being a bad loser, he threw his racing sheet at me and left the room.

Later we sort of resolved the conflict. We're still friends, but the old trust isn't there anymore, not really.

Of the Highest Order

Self-maintenance activity is more than mere habit; it pursues a major goal and is carried on with structures that have become integral to one's total being. Looking after the self has a place of the highest order in everyone's life.

What's behind messages like Tara's and Jim's? First of all, each of us has a self-concept: a demanding and assertive personal view of who we are and how we want to be seen and taken, of the kind of person we feel ourselves to be or the kind of person we think we *ought* to be. Specific reflections of this insistent self-concept appear in our attitudes, values and ideals, ways of doing, and positions on just about anything that is important to us.

Second, each of us needs to be treated as a worthy person and cared about—at least, to be taken seriously and respected. We need others to support and confirm us in who we are. In a word, self-esteem is a critical personal factor in communicating; it has to do with how you pay attention to my *self* needs and I to yours. **Climates of mutual support—and nonsupport—are created by the two of us together, as we bring our needy and sensitive selves to each other.**

Behavior in the five cases above shows that effort to uphold and justify the self arises from threat to individual well-being—and it appears most obviously in *interpersonal* communication, as we put ourselves in association with others. And the fear of being hurt, offended, disqualified, or diminished in some way can be very strong. When perceiving personal assault or embarrassment, the people in the stories above took specific measures to meet their crises. Their actions, while taking different forms, are not unusual.

The All-Powerful Self-Concept

What do the incidents below suggest about the self-concept and the need to be regarded well? Note the variety of motivating circumstances and how the individuals met ordinary human challenges. The circumstances are in italics.

Offended and wanting revenge, he vowed, "I'm gonna tell everyone what I know about her!"

Pleased with acknowledgment and praise, he modestly admitted, "Well, yes, I was the one who assisted him with CPR."

Unwilling to accept an almost unbearable feeling of defeat, she proclaimed, "I feel great! No problem! None whatever!"

Stinging from a felt attack on her religion, she never said another word during the entire evening.

Jolted by a sudden and loud command to leave the room, she cringed and murmured submissively, "Yes, ma'am."

Consumed with jealousy, he held her shoulders tightly and demanded, "Where in hell were you when I called seventeen times last night?"

Add to these instances all those messages communicated by persons who feel *slighted, put down, praised only faintly, unfairly compared, ridiculed,* or *passed over.* There's pain in *feeling unwanted and rejected, "out of one's element," unappreciated and misunderstood, incompetent*—and *believing oneself to be an imposter, a victim, weak link, traitor to the cause, ugly duckling,* or *an outsider.*

What About You?

Then there's you. Are you ever defensive or anxious to prove your worth? Say "Yes," because I know you are. Like the rest of us, you have a vulnerable self. It's disturbing to you to feel neglected or perceived as less than you think you ought to be. You have pride but also occasional feelings of inadequacy; you need recognition and approval. Feeling insecure at times about your place in life or your status at home, work, or school, you try harder—you're anxious to do better, to feel good about yourself or show that you're somebody. Much of such effort to achieve is beneficial, but it doesn't always come off smoothly. Sometimes there's distracting anger and hostility, criticism of self and others, backing off, and hiding out.

Try This. Recall a recent intense urge to protect yourself: when you felt that "call to action," to justify your background, explain your sexual orientation, stand behind your family, or vindicate your profession or political party or favorite music group. Or think back to how you felt down deep when you sensed that someone was trying to

—manipulate you or boss you around. What was your response to this felt abuse?

—lord it over you, acting in a superior manner. How did you handle that interpersonal wrong?

—impose on you a rigid and unacceptable point of view. What did you do about that?

—be noncommittal with you, remaining adamantly silent and evasive. How did you meet that?

On such occasions, how did you react? With a self-maintenance strategy? Quite likely. If so, what form did it take?

HOW PREVALENT IS THIS BEHAVIOR?

Self-maintenance strategies in communication appear in all relationships and interpersonal events: in friendships, romantic relationships, family systems, professional situations, church organizations, political entities, all school groups, and so forth. Commenting specifically about self-protection, psychoanalytic theorist Harry Guntrip wrote in these terms:

> The multifarious ways in which people are on the defensive against one another, in business, social life, marriage, and parenthood, and even leisure activities, suggests that the one omnipresent fear is the fear of being and appearing weak, inadequate, less of a person than others or less than equal to the demands of the situation, a failure: the fear of letting oneself down and looking the fool in the face of an unsupportive and even hostile world. This fear lies behind all the rationalized self-assertiveness, the subtle exhibitionism, the disguised boasting, the competitiveness or avoidance of competition, the need of praise, reassurance and approval, the safety-first tactics and security-seeking, and a multitude of other defensive reactions to life. . . .[1]

That's one professional person's view of the prevalence of safeguarding the self—the way we act, particularly in our less certain, less confident moments. Who can begin to calculate the vast amount of communicative energy spent in ordinary self-maintenance by one ordinary person in one ordinary day? That's a good question, for it suggests a fact: **A degree of uncertainty about one's social safety or status operates in every message sent: in every conversation, public speech, interview, and discussion**. And it's a part of every display of "attitude," as we call some kinds of scornful behavior or insolence.

Human uncertainty is one of the staple elements of television situation comedies. It's prominent in the lives of characters in novels, stage plays, movies, and comic strips. One of the most lovable insecure comic strip people is Cathy; her self-maintenance strategies are quite true to life. Without conditions of self-doubt and unpredictability on personal status, communication in the Doonesbury and Dilbert strips would be literally unreal. The conditions of characters would be false and the stories unappealing. Can you identify any important character in any well-written piece of fiction who is fully secure? I can't. The characters of *good* fiction are *real* in their self-maintenance activity.

Now, when talking about proving the self, justifying, and so forth, we must acknowledge (and be grateful for) the good results that often occur. Worthy accomplishment, professional success, and good works all have beginnings related to self-maintenance needs, in that all are associated with requirements of security and support—and of choices made to meet those requirements. Thus there are two possible consequences: Our self-protective ways *do* find positive and useful expression, but sometimes they function negatively against our best interests: for example, when they take the shape of neglectfulness or some kind of abuse. It follows that communicative interaction, energized with goals of self-maintenance, ranges from stimulating and constructive dialogue and rewarding interpersonal communication to personal attack and counter-attack. Whether obvious or indistinct, strategies of self-care are ever-present in communication.

ALWAYS WITH PURPOSE

Behavioral studies suggest that we humans interact *with purpose.* In communication, we make *choices* about ways to be with one another, *purposefully* saying this instead of that, *purposefully* speaking out or being silent, and so forth. And we can be only as we are (Who else are we?) But let's delay further exploration of our human nature until the next chapter, when we take up origins of self-maintenance strategies and motivation. Meanwhile, consider this: **Our unswerving aim in communication is to look after ourselves**. It's to keep ourselves intact—

"together"—internally balanced, acting as we want to be perceived, saying what we want to have heard. Some of our guardedness serves us well; some doesn't, ending up as inappropriate, even disastrous. We all know about the bad times, when we "hate ourselves in the morning" after what we said under emotional pressure.

SELF-MAINTENANCE IN COMMUNICATION: EIGHT *TOPOI*

Is there a useful way to categorize self-maintenance resources available for communication? Classically, we have the psychological nomenclature called "defense mechanisms." Remember those? They have names like rationalization, repression, regression, projection, introjection, sublimation, and so forth.

But rather than adopt a list of mental "mechanisms" and end up with nothing but an outline of abstractions, we must find categories that will reflect a sense of the behavioral dynamics of communicative *interaction.* Any practical study of self-maintenance strategies will take account of the potent energy involved, while emphasizing the interactive give-and-take and ever-present fact of personal purpose. Consequently, we need action terms to depict what goes on, to give meaning to the justifying, qualifying, rationalizing, asserting, confronting, bragging, avoiding, excusing, soft-pedaling, soothing, supporting, and so forth of ordinary communicating. To this end, I have identified eight strategic groupings. They are expressed as common purposes: to control, achieve, oppose, attribute, express anger, deny, withdraw, and prevaricate.[2] Each of the eight *topoi* is a package, a collection of related options. Incidentally, *topoi* is a Greek word for topics. Aristotle used it. I like the word because it conveys the idea of *purposeful action* and connotes *strategic choice in interaction* and *variety of choice and opportunity in interaction.* Let me now introduce each *topos* (singular) briefly; I'll refer to each again in other chapters. As you look over the eight categories, note those that seem to have appeared in your recent communications with others. You hear and see them every day.

1. Control

Needs of security and certainty move communicators to regulate events, to find strategies for making things happen favorably. The need to control may be compelling or casual, and specific behaviors are numerous. Aims relate to ordinary communicative effectiveness, e.g., in being ready to handle unwelcome surprises or shocks as they might arise. But the goal may extend beyond seeking ordinary communicative control and effectiveness. For example, contrast the simple act of a person's choosing appropriate telephone language in placing a catalog order (necessarily exercising some control) to the extreme of a parent's determination to regulate an adult child's social activities. Likewise, at work, one employee may be rather easygoing, getting the routine communicative jobs done without excessive exertion (though there's always *some* management of events in communication), while another person will act to gain complete personal dominance of all functions related to on-the-job interactions. The latter mode might be considered "more defensive" than the former. Yet another example is the individualistic, iron-handed executive who seems unable to delegate authority to others or make use of cooperative problem-solving methods.

2. Achievement

Achievement needs frequently lie behind acts like self-justification. Related strategies often operate at a sensible and relaxed level: for example, that of doing a job adequately and feeling good about it. But contrast that with a level of functioning that is tremendously intense—when the communicator is determined to be absolutely right or brilliant or unchallengeable—anxious to stand out over others. Behavior of this extreme type is commonly called "perfectionism."

An example of the extreme is the vice president whose quarterly reports consistently and unnecessarily double the length of other vps' reports. This person's fervent drive to achieve—and get credit for it—requires great expenditure of time and energy.

3. Opposition

Protection of the self is a purpose of messages using the *topos* of *Opposition.* In this instance, a communicator assumes a contrary stance in communication with others, e.g., in "standing up for oneself." It may be expressed in some cases as disagreement or disapproval and in other cases as abject repugnance or contempt. *Opposition,* whether taken as ordinary dissent, rebuttal, stubbornness, resistance, challenge, nonconformity, derision, obstinacy, negativity, or scorn—whether seen as spirited support of one's position or as fierce denunciation or counteraction—is prevalent in all quarters of daily life.

4. Attribution

Attribution is common in communication to maintain the self. Communicators frequently face "How did this happen?" issues and matters of cause, responsibility, fault, or blame. In "getting to the bottom of things," one may name someone responsible—or oneself. Whether the communicator's spirit is constructive or malicious, the motivation is often one of self-protection, from a need to ascribe blame or accountability, and so forth. In this way the communicator attempts to maintain personal equilibrium and satisfactory communication.

Examples include the employee who realizes his computation error and consequently accepts responsibility; an older brother who blames his little sister when he trips on the stairs; the baseball batter whose habit is to scowl at the umpire when he takes a called third strike; the well-intentioned soul who needs to know whom to *absolve*; and the person who is motivated to solve "Who dunnit?" puzzles of relationships, whether concerned with a minor disagreement or a serious interpersonal conflict. A recent major example is that of a high-level government official who, involved in illegally selling arms to a hostile nation, pointed the finger of guilt at one of his colleagues.

5. Anger

If or when one is inclined toward sustaining the self through

Anger, one will express strong displeasure or perhaps resort to violent verbal attacks. Like all *topoi*, *Anger* may be either beneficial or harmful. Others may view the behavior as useful passion, righteous indignation, bad temper, sullenness, belligerence, wrath, resentment, or great furor.

One example is two drivers' heated exchange after racing to occupy that empty space in the parking lot. What's at the root of such expression? Fairness is an issue, as is self-worth. Thus do self-maintenance needs of these communicators enter in: They feel a need to stand up for themselves and protect their "rights." That's one reason why some businesses install a "Take-a-Number" system to facilitate fair turn-taking at the counter. Customers who become preoccupied with protecting themselves may be less likely to return than customers who feel secure.

6. Denial

When choosing *Denial* as a method of self-care, one seeks to dodge an unpleasant or threatening reality, whether with a customary strategy or a the spur-of-the-moment choice. Such communication involves inventing a method to protect against facing the "truth" or the "facts." In refusing to perceive something that's psychologically menacing, the communicator attempts to insulate the self from it by negating reality.

For example, a person may deny the fact of someone's death and thus provide cushioning against loss. Another example is the middle-aged woman who prefers teenage-style clothes, thereby revealing both her self-perception and her protective regression. Then there's the father who, unwilling to accept his son's rather ordinary athletic ability, criticizes the coach for not nominating his boy to the all-star team.

7. Withdrawal

If maintaining the self through *Withdrawal*, one will shun a certain event or individual, retreat from a threatening scene, maintain silence and mental distance, assume a passive posture, repress thoughts or feelings, resist disclosure of feelings, or in any number of other ways protect against the dangers and discomforts of social participation or judgment.

8. Prevarication

Prevarication is self-protection involving falsehood, excuse-making, justification of personal beliefs or actions, inhibition, deceptive statement, evasion, and so forth. As with all *topoi,* the strategic aim is to uphold the self: the self-concept, self-esteem, or sense of worth. Other modes of *Prevarication* are equivocation, euphemizing, use of passive voice, and "waffling."

An example of *Prevarication* is the socially useful "white lie." Another is shown in the case of the project coordinator who when asked for a progress report responded evasively, "Everybody's working real hard on this one, Chief—yes sir. I'll have more to tell you at mid-week." In this case, what needs of the self is the communicator seeking to care for?

Selecting Useful *Topoi*

In the process of communication, one isn't restricted to drawing from only one of the eight *topoi.*[3] Some of us find ourselves using them all at various times. Also interesting is the view that choice of *topos* may depend on personality type. For instance, extroverts may favor expressions of *Anger,* while introverts may favor *Withdrawal.*[4] But our social consciousness dictates that our choice of *topos* will be influenced by our perception of the situation and conditions. Audience characteristics are particularly significant in communication. That is, we fashion our messages in accord with the likely reactions of others. Why? Because we humans are *rhetorical* creatures: practical, purposeful, and adaptable. That's a point not to be forgotten by communicators!

To enhance your grasp of these maintenance methods, go back to the earliest pages of the chapter and classify the numerous examples of safeguarding communication found there. Are they strategies of *Achievement,* or *Attribution,* or *Anger,* or one of the other *topoi?*

Try This. Here's a quiz for you. In the conversation below, Friend #2 seems to be defensive about something. What threat does he feel? In your opinion, from which *topos* did he draw?

Friend #1: So you had your picture taken.

Friend #2: Yeh, the company asked me to.

Friend #1: And you ordered a few for yourself?

Friend #2: Heck no; my wife did!

As you review the eight *topoi*, you may want to add to the list. Can you think of other types?

MAINTENANCE COMMUNICATION: VERBAL AND NON-VERBAL LANGUAGE

One way to increase our understanding of protective strategies is to recognize them as verbal or nonverbal or as combinations of the two. Strategies of protection expressed with words alone—rather rare—are verbal; all others are nonverbal or a combination. Paul, who wants Jennifer to know why he won't be able to see her tonight, explains on the telephone: "It isn't my fault." She hears his defensive message: his words, the sounds of his breathing, and variations in his voice. Now, if they were in face-to-face conversation, Jennifer would simultaneously *see* things: Paul's averted eyes, his frown and lowered head, and so forth. Paul would then see proud Jennifer walking away swiftly, making a nonverbal and silent, final self-supportive statement.

All verbal and nonverbal parts of messages contribute significantly to meaning. Some kind of nonverbal accompaniment always will be there with the words, except perhaps in such media as books with no pictures—and even then, variations in font, punctuation, and underlining affect meaning. But, regarding face-to-face communication, the great majority of self-maintenance content in any message is suggested nonverbally. Nonverbal message symbols are as short as a wink or as long as a speech in full pantomime, if you can imagine such a creation. Note that Jennifer sent a message with her walking away from Paul (a self-supportive "speech" of a minute or so, as long as he watched).

Even the tone in Paul's telephone voice is notable. Numerous other forms of nonverbal language will always be a part of his messages—and ours: high or low pitch, increased vocal intensity, accent on a given word, and so forth. A listener hears these bits and pieces, gives them meaning, and puts together a total message. Thus most statements are made up of more than words. To understand protective communication, we must be aware of both verbal and nonverbal strategies and how they function together, for both help shape the message and influence its effect on the audience.

MAINTENANCE COMMUNICATION: OUTWARD AND INWARD

Another important way to study self-supporting behaviors is to think of how they are expressed: outwardly, inwardly, or in combination. Of course, outward forms are the more obvious, seen as statements sent *to* or *at* another. They are the messages that show up in hand gestures and other bodily movements, shy glances, glares, direct verbal explanations and accusations, requests, and clear acts of affection or resentment.

The inward forms are more subtle and largely in*tra*personal (as with talking to yourself) and often not perceived by others.[5] In in*tra*personal communication, usually silent, people reflect on what they think about themselves; they make self-assessments, pondering self-concepts, ideals, and how they ought to act; they mull over personal goals, quandaries, role-taking patterns, accomplishments, and personal shortcomings. We all know these well. Such ruminations occur both when one is alone and while one is communicating with others. They frequently involve comparisons of self to others, calculations on safety and risk in communication, and so forth. Among the kinds of self-maintenance messages that may be expressed inwardly are self-criticism, determination to control an event, decision-making regarding evading a perceived threat, plans for putting together a winning presence, and all sorts of other strategic choices on communicating effectively.

But regarding interpersonal and intrapersonal activity, it can be said that in any social scene *all* behaviors have in*ter*personal implications because **people in association with others are in a**

constant posture of adaptation: in their awareness of others and in their responses to others' messages. In a real sense, *the others are always on our minds.* Consider also the influence of those indistinct behaviors that seem to have no immediate purpose. For instance, a message influenced by a feeling of depression, though inward and vague, may be clear to another and have a real impact. Additional examples are perceived aloofness, indifference, suppression of animosity, and states of sadness. Can you tell when she is "guarding her tongue" or "crying on the inside?" And how are you affected? **The symbolic act of communication is to influence and to be influenced.** Look for the subtle signs.

SELF-MAINTENANCE AND COMMUNICATION PROCESSES

Before going to the next chapter for a discussion of beginnings and origins of a person's self-maintenance strategies in communication, we need to determine what constitutes success (and failure) in communication. An understanding of that topic will give us a solid base from which to extend our exploration into the ramifications of sustaining the self. I'll explain several related processes in communication and tie them together in a frame for examining the dynamics of communicative interaction. The first element is "Senders and Receivers," the second, "The Exigence," and the third, "Roles." All three are modern conceptions. The fourth is about the enthymeme (pronounced EN-thuh-meem), an old reliable idea. The fifth, on "Identification," is a comprehensive idea of all time that will bring the other processes together into one unified and useful theory.

Senders and Receivers

In most textbooks, communication is diagrammed as a transactional process of people exchanging messages comprised of both words and nonverbal language (such as body movements, eye activity, and vocal variations). Senders encode messages with language symbols, and receivers decode them ("read" and interpret them). Each person sends and receives messages simultaneously: While one communicator is saying something, the other smiles or frowns or interrupts, and in so doing, returns a message called *feedback*. Each is involved constantly: initiating messages and providing feedback, adjusting content and making decisions on how to respond. Among significant elements in this vital process are the place and time of the communicative event, the status and feelings of the persons involved. Also relevant are the channels members use: that is, whether they are communicating face to face, from backyard to kitchen, over the telephone, or via E-mail.

The curse of communicators is the "noise" that enters into their joint ventures. *Noise* is the name for any kind of interference, whether physical, psychological, cultural, or political. For example, a room temperature of 45 degrees might be a "noisy" distraction, as might playground activity outside, a participant's preoccupation with a marital problem, participants' unreconciled ethnic conflict, or a participant's indifferent attitude. **Intrusive maintenance strategies in communication constitute noise.**

The Exigence

An exigence is what sparks an interaction, what gets it going. In Lloyd F. Bitzer's words, an exigence "is an imperfection marked by urgency; it is a defect, an obstacle, something waiting to be done, a thing which is other than it should be."[6] It's something that requires a communicative response. For example, a child's throwing mud on the family car may prompt (or require) the mother or father to scold the child. Parents take the mud-throwing as an exigence for communication. As they perceive it, the event—the defect "marked by urgency"—requires corrective action. Recognition of a parking problem at the city hall may trigger the city council's deliberation; council members agree on the existence of a condition to which they must respond, an exigence. Apparent student confusion about an assignment is observed by the instructor, and, recognizing through this feedback an exigence for communication, she decides to clarify the assignment. Employee unrest over a new company policy is eased by an alert executive's recognition of a rhetorical exigence and then his convincing explanation to employees. Consider the case of a husband who, feeling that his wife's glare was meant as criticism, exploded with great anger. He perceived an exigence, and he felt he had to respond. Powerful emotions led to his perception of her behavior as a demand on him to thrust forth that hostile self-defensive message. Another husband in a similar situation might not feel threatened. **What one person acts on as exigence may be "no big deal" to another**. Who cares about lack of parking spaces at the city hall? Why worry about a child's mud-throwing? Some do care and speak up; some don't.

Roles

In a communicative sense, roles are strategic behaviors that we acquire in the process of growing and learning to relate to others. Reflective of who we are, as parts of our identity, they are personal resources to use in all interactions. Behavioral roles are forms of self-representation: They are built up, rehearsed, and made ready to be applied in communication as effective means of dealing with exigencies. Collectively, they comprise one's repertoire of public selves or personas—parts of the self that communicators put "out front" in their interactions.

Place yourself in a given situation, one in which you determine that something must be said; that is, you perceive an exigence. In responding to it, you adopt a role—one of many available to you. Let's make it a time when a friend confides that she just had a bitter argument with her boyfriend. In an instant, you find yourself responding, this time conveying your thinking and feeling by assuming the role of "Comforter." Why "Comforter"? Because that was what your purpose at that critical interpersonal moment suggested to you. That's the way you chose to be with her. On a different occasion, or with a different person in different circumstances, you might sense it appropriate to call up the part of you that is "Cautioner" or "Therapist" or "Judge." Of course, it's not too often in interacting that we consciously think about whether to select this role or that. We just do it, in accord with our purpose of that instant. In any event, role-taking is one way to explain our choice in what we say and how we say it, in any kind of situation. Given their rhetorical function, roles are intertwined with messages.

In these terms, our communications involve us in seeking confirmation or acceptance of our roles. Success will be revealed in the role the other person assumes in response. Confirmation of our "Therapist" role may be evidenced in the other person coming back in the role of "Client" (a person willing and ready to accept therapy). That was what we seemed to be asking for. But if the "Therapist" persona is rejected—that is, if the other doesn't want to be treated therapeutically—we'll probably sense that and switch to another role.

In the dynamics of communicative interaction, role selection will change with each perceived change in exigence—sometimes from moment to moment. At one moment, your "Financial Consultant" may appear. Or maybe the exigence will call for "Prosecuting Attorney" or "Cheerleader." As we relate to friends, co-workers, family, and others, we seek ways of being effective through selected roles—as do others with us. Thus purpose and message composition are enforced by the agency of role.

The Enthymeme (EN-thuh-meem)

An enthymeme is a kind of basic thought that a communicator selects, wanting the audience to *listen* to and find *meaning* in. Think of any main idea of any speech. Any thought or premise of a sender is a raw and personal notion conceived by that individual, and only when it has meaning for the receiver will it be communicated. Thus the sender needs to act strategically to influence the receiver to get involved in the process of creating and completing meaning. When Brent shouted to roommate James, "Hey, it's started to rain hard," he was doing more than making a weather announcement. His purpose became clearer when he added, "And if we don't bring our books in from the patio, they'll get drenched." That's the content of Brent's enthymeme, and quick to appreciate the good sense in Brent's message, James jumped up to help bring the books inside. Brent found James' meaning persuasive; he adopted the enthymeme and responded accordingly. If, on another occasion, Brent were to say something like "A nice guy is one who'll run right down and get a pizza for his hungry roommate," James might not be as willing to become engaged in creating an enthymeme. Why participate in a meeting of minds if there's no chance to share meaning. Sometimes communicators fail because they ask too much.

Enthymemes are represented in the main ideas or frames of thought that a communicator presents. If promising, they invite involvement. When an enthymeme is welcomed by the listener—judged acceptable or intriguing—she may choose to help complete it. Thus, the competent communicator, adequately acquainted with her thinking on his topic, adapts to that thinking (acknowledges common interest), seeking to enlist a partner in the communicative enterprise. Successful communication is a partnership.

We must keep in mind, said Aristotle, that the audience—the other, the receiver, the listener—is the central figure in human interaction. That is, the audience has the final say on a message, deciding whether to listen or tune it out, whether to reject it or stay on and work with it.

Ever-purposeful, we interact with audiences as we find them—as they are—discovering ways of preparing messages that make sense and interest them. **Caring and skillful communicators are those who know how to invite their listeners to participate in the communicative process: to share in the construction of enthymemes.** Though conceived 2,500 years ago as a line of reasoning in a public speech, the enthymeme has application in all communication, including the most intimate. In practical terms, it's one unit of a communicator's total message (sometimes the entire message). Here's an example: "If you want to move up in this company, always remember our deadlines." That's the frame, but much more may be said in elaboration. Here are two more enthymemes, basic parts of what could become extended messages: "She hasn't had trigonometry yet; we can't expect her to solve that engineering problem" and "Clearly, he's either a pitcher or a third baseman, and I know he doesn't hit well enough to play third for the Armadillos."

Note the incompleteness in the three enthymemes above. In the first, the one on deadlines, the sender assumes that the receiver wants to move up in the company; in the second, the sender assumes that the receiver agrees that a course in trigonometry is needed. The unstated assumptions are premises that the two must agree upon, to communicate. In the third enthymeme, the unstated and pivotal premise assumes (silently affirms) that a third baseman has to be a good hitter.

In successful communication, listeners accept and complete the open or unspecified portions of a well-formed enthymeme. Sender and receiver function together in the creation of understanding. Communication, therefore, is *cooperatively transactional*, with speakers and listeners interacting *together.*[7] Remember, too, as we'll see in subsequent chapters, that enthymemes may have at least as much emotional as rational content.

Here's a story about an enthymeme in communication. It's a case history of one person's attempt to discover shared meaning with another, something we all do all the time. Tina wants Pat, a man inexperienced in dressing for winter conditions, to understand that good boots should be worn when going off to hike in the snow. The enthymeme—the practical line of thinking—that Tina has *in her mind* is conceived with very reasonable premises. Note, too, that her enthymeme, while making good sense in terms of the reasonable probabilities, also reflects her *feeling* and concern for Pat's welfare. Look inside her head now, to see the entire formulation of her enthymeme (or practical, rhetorical syllogism, as Aristotle called it) with three premises:

> When going off to hike in the snow, a person should wear good boots to protect the feet.
>
> Pat is going off to hike in the snow.
>
> Therefore, Pat should wear good boots to protect his feet.

That's the complete basis for her belief and feeling on the subject—but it's hardly ready to express to Pat. Why? Because it sounds rather silly in its academic phraseology. It's schoolteacherish and impersonal, and if Pat were to hear it like that, he might feel that Tina looks on him as a child. Yes, Tina's thinking is sound, but it's not rhetorical, not ready for sending; it's doomed to failure. So the interpersonally aware Tina converts her valid but overly formal reasoning into acceptably worded good sense, saying,

> Hey Pat, remember that you'll need good boots when hiking in the snow.

In essence—as adjusted by Tina for receptivity—what we have now are the final two premises of Tina's logic. Wisely, she abandoned the "lesson" of the major premise: that parental "a person should" premise that might be objectionable to Pat the adult. Moreover, the major premise is not necessary in this communication, for Pat will catch on without hearing it from her. Only with children could Tina (then in the role of teacher) get away with the preachy statement as she first visualized it. But she has shown herself to be a smart communicator; she knows how to shape enthymemes *with* her audience. She knows when to use a peer role instead of a parental role, aware that the enthymeme of one role will be received differently from the other.

This discussion of the enthymeme "in action" outlines the fundamental process in this transactional theory of communication. It shows the use of an enthymeme in guiding communicators in acknowledging exigencies—and in inventing ideas and influencing others to listen and participate. It's also useful in analyzing the communicative activity of others. **To perceive a sender's enthymeme is to grasp the message, including the role that helps to convey it.** Whether the listener or analyzer focuses on the receiver's enthymeme or apparent role, the first goal is to understand the message.

Let me add this on communicative effectiveness: Given her basic enthymeme and the message that she created with it, Tina's success in communicating with Pat will depend on her credibility; that is, it depends on his trusting her on the subject of boots. Aristotle believed that credibility, *ethos,* as he called it, very likely is the most critical factor in an interaction. Being a credible, trustworthy person—is tremendously important in communication. **Nothing carries more weight than *ethos.***

Identification

The essential goal of any communicator is *to identify with the other,* to find some kind of kinship or connectedness or point of unity. What's the basis of that statement? For an answer, let's go to the ideas of Kenneth Burke,[8] whose profound writings have had extraordinary influence on our thinking about rhetorical dynamics in communication. Burke advised that in approaching the study of people interacting, we must appreciate the condition of their estrangement from each other: the fact that **separation marks the human condition**. Given our many kinds of distinctness and difference, we are divided; we are people apart from others, and deeply conscious of it. But finding this condition unacceptable, we are moved to interact, to take steps to bridge the gaps and bring ourselves closer through communication. The condition is natural. **If, however, we humans were not separated by our differentness and differences, we wouldn't be moved to communicate**. There would be no need to seek a comparable identity or position, for we would already be together. We'd already be *in communication.* No motivation is more basic than that which pushes us to seek interpersonal harmony, to *identify* with others. All such reaching out and relating—communicating—is to influence; it's rhetorical activity, purposefully entered into to achieve union with our audience, whether of one or many. Participants in communicative transactions seek to discover grounds of similarity and rapport on which to create understanding and be effective with each other. Identification is a process of communication: being *with* others.[9] Identification is also a *goal* of the process; that is, the sought result. In identifying with others, we connect with them (identify with them) and come to "be somebody" with them (identified with them). Process and result are the same.

A word that's close in meaning to identification is *attunement,* a condition of interpersonal harmony. Daniel N. Stern, writer on infant development and infant communication, uses the term attunement that way.[10] To Stern, attunement is the performance of behaviors that express the quality of shared feelings: the sharing of *internal* states (what's behind the outward actions), what participants feel inside—and, I must add, what they *think.* It's an intersubjective experience, created in communication *with* the other(s). By the way, the word attunement was first used in the 19th century by a philosopher named Alger, in reference to "the healthy attunement of the discordant faculties and forces of the soul." We in this century are very much aware of discord and of forces of the soul that separate us and with which we must contend as we seek attunement. **The major discordant force lies in interpersonal distance and the fear of relating closely with others: a fear that acts against the force for attunement or identification.** In the next chapter, we'll continue our discussion of the dynamics of those forces in conflict.

An Example of the Process of Identification

Let's say that Carol wants you to believe, with her, that free education from kindergarten through four years of college should be made available to all Americans. But she knows that in communicating with you on this topic, there's an obstacle. For while you do value education, you think the financial burden imposed by Carol's proposal would be too great for the nation to bear. Knowing of your concerns, she appeals to you with a *shared* value, arguing that in educating all youth in this nation—a *mutually held* objective—we may have to sacrifice something. Or she may argue that her plan will save money in the long run. She wants you to see it her way, to accept or *identify with* her point of view—and *identify with* her (which will depend on her *ethos* or credibility). To succeed, Carol must know *your* frame of reference and acknowledge *your* position, for she seeks *common* ground. It's not unnatural for you two to be divided, but it's vital to Carol that she succeed in getting together with you on the education issue. It disturbs her very much to be separated from you. She wants to be *attuned* with you. And that's the wellspring of her motivation: to meet the division—to wipe out or treat the difference—and *be with* you. **To be apart unhappily is to be "no where" for both of you—for all of us!** The last thing to lose in communication is our base of contact, our grounds for relating. That's what happens when people are "out of communication." That's what it means to be alone.

Always we are strategists—out to influence each other and bring ourselves together, even at those times when not giving much conscious thought to what we're saying. The behavioral theme of our *human* nature is the same wherever we are with others: It's a searching for common "stuff"—ideas, habits, feelings, beliefs, interests, customs, backgrounds, et cetera—with which we can conduct a relationship of a minute or of a lifetime. **We want real attunement, if we can get it.**

Confirmation, Identification, and the Master Exigence

Consider the insistent human need of confirmation. Where does the absorbing quest for confirmation fit into the process of communication? It's the communicator's basic move in the act of *identification.* To be confirmed by another person means to be recognized. And that's the initial experience in the identification of sender and receiver, the basis of what's to follow: e.g., role validation as super student, reliable worker, able athlete, good mother, world traveler, or whatever.[11]

What are the interpersonal consequences of all this? In confirmation, another person is accorded status. To be so treated is to be acknowledged and linked to someone. It's a process of mutual satisfaction through reduction of distance. I want to be somebody, and to be identified with you is to be somebody. That's why I want to be identified with you, to be somebody who is heard and given a response. **The urgency to be confirmed by another is the most basic exigence: Call it the generic exigence**. And as the motivation behind the initiation of all communication, **it's the master exigence**. Confirmation is the gateway to attunement, and that's what you and I *need.* That's why we interact.

KEY ISSUES

To understand the dynamics of one person identifying with another is to appreciate key issues of communicative interaction: especially *intimacy* and *disclosure of self, risk, trust,* and *reciprocity.* Let's look at these.

Identification is an intimate act, necessarily. With their purposefully chosen verbal and nonverbal language patterns, participants in communication bring themselves together, to reach and affect each other. Without their positive, active effort, they would remain as they were, out of touch—safely but unsatisfyingly apart. I say *safely* for good reason: **Intimacy involves risk, taking a chance with others.** It's trusting others with one's feelings, giving up a measure of control and power as an individual, or putting oneself in the position of being "found out" or appearing to be arrogant, phony, dumb, unworthy, unmanly, unfeminine, or whatever.

Risk is a requirement in communication, for without it, without disclosure of substantial dimensions of the self, you can achieve no more than superficial identification. Yes, there are real dangers in risking the self with another person. "If I open up, how do I know I won't be manipulated by her?" "What if she's indifferent to me, or hostile or critical?" "If she doesn't feel good about herself, how can she feel good about me?"

But the point is, **unless you can trust enough to make yourself open and available for interaction with her, there'll be nothing to connect to except your "nothingness," your "reservedness"—your being as a person defensively holding back.** Therefore, good communication is dependent on knowing and respecting your audience. If she doesn't want to be known—that is, if she won't be intimate sufficient to the point of taking a chance on sharing something significant of herself with you, your communication with her will be limited and wanting.

From this, we can see how trust is basic to the sharing of selves and ideas in the act of communication. Moreover, it's not enough for one person to be trusting, while the other resists intimacy. *Reciprocity*, with each person adapting to the other and contributing generously (generously enough), makes it a promising transaction with the probable result of true attunement. These are the conditions for *functional* communication.

BIG DECISIONS

In communication, senders and receivers make critical choices on encoding and decoding, while remaining alert to eliminating "noise" whenever possible. Their purpose is to facilitate cooperation in structuring enthymemes and carrying off roles, with the goal of reaching each other and maintaining their connection. Without a rhetorically fitting perception of exigence and discovery of grounds of identification, the communicators will not succeed.

Remember the case of Tina and Pat? Tina took a chance on acknowledging an exigence; that is, when she decided that she ought to speak up and offer Pat some guidance on proper shoes in the snow. She risked acting as "Adviser" (while hoping to maintain "Peer" status), and in so doing, wanted him to respond as "Willing Learner" (and "Peer"), to confirm her role. She went about it maturely and intelligently. Her expressed enthymeme had a good chance of keeping contact with Pat and influencing him to interact cooperatively, yet she had to work at it. To alienate was the last thing she wanted to do, for **alienation is the antithesis of communication.** She knew that and used her head in shaping an enthymeme that would induce Pat to join with her in the ultimate creation of meaning. She wanted him to listen to her, to trust her and participate in her reasoning. She didn't want a reaction of distracting defensiveness from him. In this instance, that would have hampered communication.

In the chapters that follow, we'll find important use for the ideas on communication discussed in this chapter: sending and receiving, acknowledging exigencies, choosing roles, building enthymemes, and confirming and identifying.

Try This. From the twenty-five OCCASIONS FOR SELF-MAINTENANCE COMMUNICATION listed below, select one that relates to an experience you've had. Recall the occasion, and do the following:

1. Tell how in an insecure moment you came to perceive an exigence (some condition that required a response).
2. From which of the eight *topoi* did you draw for a strategic response? Was it one of the eight that I have discussed above? If not, what's your name for it?
3. Briefly stated, what message did you want to send? To whom did you send the message? What kinds of inward—intrapersonal—messages were a part of the process? Distinguish

between verbal and nonverbal elements of the message. What result and feedback (response) did you want?

4. Shape your self-maintenance message as an enthymeme, indicating the part supplied by the other(s) in the communicative interplay.

5. Describe dynamics of the interaction, using the theory of identification. How critical in the exchange were conditions of confirmation and disconfirmation? In your analysis, include issues of intimacy, risk, trust, self-disclosure, and reciprocity, as experienced by the participants.

OCCASIONS FOR SELF-MAINTENANCE COMMUNICATION

When you . . .

- respond to the charge of damaging another's property
- are embarrassed after making a social error
- try to handle the boss's dissatisfaction with a job you've done
- seek satisfaction after an acquaintance spreads a false story
- feel hurt in not being invited to the party
- sense public criticism of your behavior
- take a comment as threatening to your self-image
- feel shunned by a friend
- feel slighted in a group activity
- don't want to face the facts or your true feelings
- hear a comment that seems to be critical of your race, religion, sex, family, or school
- are jolted by a loud command of a coach, parent, or other
- feel down deep that you do not believe yourself to be qualified, e.g., to be in college or a given profession ("I'm just an imposter.")

- feel apprehensive about a surprising change in company policy or a relationship
- have a feeling of not belonging in a certain group
- are jealous
- are unsure of your personal status with someone or some group
- feel socially awkward in a specific situation
- fear speaking up in class
- are denied an expected honor or reward
- sense diminishment of your reputation in the family or other group
- feel wronged by a boyfriend or girlfriend
- feel that you deserve better treatment from someone on whom you depend for confirmation
- feel incompetent as a writer, athlete, cook, mother, etc.
- feel lacking in good looks

Chapter Two

The Communicator's Biography

MAIN THEMES OF THE CHAPTER

- We relate to others in accord with the ways we see ourselves, communicating an identity and seeking a positive response to it.
- With security and self-worth at issue, our natural choice in communication is to guard against violation of self.
- Vulnerable and dependent, developing infants are subjected to too little and too much stimulation, and thereby sustain injuries and losses.
- As infants become socialized, they acquire maintenance strategies for use in communication.
- Self-maintenance strategies are the products of favorable and unfavorable narcissism, with the great power of shame at the core.
- In shaping an identity, infants are influenced by family members and family systems, the general culture, and specific cultural forces.
- Confirming others and identifying with them require enough personal security for the communicator to risk respecting perceived differences.
- A fearful and immature reaction to perceived differences in others creates the single biggest obstacle to our communicating.

- In our development, we come to adopt a personal ideology: "bundles" of beliefs, principles, values, and convictions.
- The self-concept, inseparable from other parts of our ideology, includes premises about ideals and personal expectations, self-worth, and gender.
- Influenced by ideology, we meet exigencies in self-maintenance communication—building enthymemes and assuming roles—all to the end of identifying with others and being confirmed by them.
- We are known to others—our audiences—as we maintain ourselves in communication with them.
- Success in communication is defined by our audiences, as they confirm us—and by us, as we confirm them.

THE TRUTH ABOUT US

This chapter is our true biography. It's about who we are and how we got that way. It's about the motivation of our triumphs and creative achievements as well as our mistakes and failures. Our story is about developing that sterling human resource called *power in communication*; it's also about limitations in that resource. **Ability and disability in relating to others arise from common sources, as we shall see**.

To provide a backdrop for our discussion of the ways we function as communicators, let's peek into the lives of three people. People like them live in your town and in mine; they live in every town. Though some of their behaviors are more useful than others, my aim here is not to praise or blame, but to describe how it is with them.

Tom

We find Tom as a student in a college sociology class. When the professor called on him to define "demography," he said, slightly embarrassed, "Oh, yeah, I remember seeing that word in our reading." Smiling, he added, "But I guess I don't remember what it means." He would have felt better knowing the answer, yet he took the matter in stride, deciding then and there to check out the word—and all other new words appearing in future reading assignments. Though accepting his deficiency of the moment, he didn't want to be caught like that again. And there was a test coming up! I'll call his case one of healthful narcissistic motivation. More on that later.

Janet

Janet is a woman of twenty-eight who works in middle management at Transcon Oil Company. Smart and well-trained, she's a very responsible employee and highly motivated. One of her chief personal goals as a manager is to "keep on top of things." She makes a special effort to direct the work of her staff; micro-managing, some call it. Janet is around a lot, "looking over shoulders" and following up. She realizes that not everyone in the office welcomes her close supervision, but as she once explained to a friend at lunch, "You know, Kelsey, I'm the one who has to report to the VP up on the 5th floor; besides, I want our group here to be the best. Is there anything wrong with wanting credit from upstairs?"

Well, she gets a lot of credit upstairs; she's a successful, valued employee. But what's the cost to her? Time is one cost: Many evenings are devoted to company work—and weekends, too. Moreover, the job is stressful, in part from the way she defines it, what with her high standards and keen aim to prove herself and be rated tops! She's always under self-imposed orders to be the paragon of executives—Superwoman, as some put it. Yesterday, late in the afternoon of a very trying day, when her boss casually asked her how the reorganization of customer service was coming along, she just *knew* that he was being critical—but she chose to hold her feelings in. Janet's unexpressed message—the one that no one there has ever heard—was, "Why take it out on me, Big Shot? After all, I'm only one person, you know." She conceives of herself as a loyal soldier. Janet has many more good moments and good days than bad; her good-but-not-always-good narcissistic motivation isn't unusual in the world of work.

Dennis

Dennis is a man of twenty. He's alert, good-looking, and often quite friendly. But yesterday he was released from employment at a furniture rental business, the third job he's had this year. Last night, he told his girlfriend about it, the same old story: "Those bastards down there don't know how to handle their employees; I know they'll be calling me back when they see their mistake. I've got twice as much experience as most of them there. . . . You, know, I really feel like telling 'em all off. . . . And, by the way, Darlene, what the shit does that look on *your* face mean, anyway?" Dennis' narcissistic motivation, or at least what we see of it here, is not healthful.

Nothing Extraordinary

These are three familiar patterns of self-maintenance behavior. Tom took his uncomfortable classroom experience lightly, without undue personal alarm. Though embarrassed at not having the answer for the professor, he handled his momentary imbalance by accepting his slip-up, without loss of self-respect. Janet is a marvelous achiever in everyone's eyes, on her way up the corporate ladder. She has many strong points. Yes, she has self-doubts, and she tends to keep her feelings bottled up. Striving as she does to avoid "bad marks," she puts a big burden on herself. And Dennis' defensiveness is clearly his vocational and interpersonal downfall, his weak spot as seen by others.

Personal Perceptions of Self

What do we find in these everyday cases? Note that they involve individuals with personal perceptions of self to be maintained. Each has a special sense of being *someone,* and in social interaction wants that image to be acknowledged. That's the way it is with all of us. Our self-perception is a key factor in communication with others. **We relate to others in accord with the ways we see ourselves, and we want a positive response to that identity**. For example, if you believe that being physically strong is essential to your self-esteem, you may become defensive if someone intimates that you're weak.

In relating to others, we communicate using chosen facets of our identity. We put parts of our selves out there, and we want the right feedback. "Confirm me!" is everyone's underlying plea. "Tell me I'm OK." No personal message is more primary or insistent—with any of us. Sometimes we're confirmed in our self-perceptions: for example, when a friend says, "Hey, nice going!" Sometimes we're disconfirmed, for example, when we're asked, "Are you the one who messed this up?" **It's for confirmation of a valued self-perception or against its disconfirmation that we take much of our protective action.** Sensed or anticipated violation of self can be too much to let go by. Motivation to avoid or answer the hurt is extremely powerful!

Violation of Self

You've noticed that I used the term "narcissistic motivation" in discussing each of the cases above. Those three people are narcissistic, and so are you and I. Everyone has a self to protect against violation, and rumbling behind our actions and inactions are individual senses of self: pride, personal status, and varying degrees of self-esteem. **With personal selves to reckon with and live with—to embrace and reject, improve or neglect—we are narcissistically motivated.** To talk about the self—about wanting respect, being hurt, striving to be liked, and needing support—is to talk about narcissism. As perceived by others, our narcissism is our *selfness.* It's an extremely critical factor in communication. No factor is more critical, as you'll see throughout the book.

To be sure, a prime goal in living and relating is to guard against violation of self. It's almost a law of human nature that embarrassment and humiliation—conditions that we take as self-diminishments—are to be countered. Tom reacts with a self-assured resolve to do better. Janet, in response to her pressures, adapts by calling up long-established self-maintenance processes. She has obvious performance capability, as well as specific tools ready for ordinary use and for any emergency that may arise. That's common in achievers. Then there's

Dennis. Overwhelmed by low self-esteem, he struggles with himself daily—almost every minute—and dysfunctionally some of the time. Though it's surely no consolation to him, there are worse cases of dysfunctional defending.

A Natural Choice

When self-worth is at issue, safeguarding is a natural choice: to justify one's feeling or decision, to put up a barrier against threat or actual attack on one's background, identity, belief, appearance, or any other area of sensitivity.

From a sense of being slighted, misunderstood, judged wrongly, or not being accepted or given proper credit, we communicators determine an exigence for making a statement: a qualification, explanation, denial, attack, evasion, or even a peace offering. Acts of self-maintenance also include shouting or hitting, hiding or crying, leaving or bragging, and many more.

Maintenance Patterns

From characteristic verbal/nonverbal and inward/outward expressions come patterns: structures that represent the dynamics of protective ways of being. Each person has acquired a unique collage of safeguards, but let's try to identify some basic patterns to serve as models. Recall again the cases of Tom, Janet, and Dennis. Do you see patterns represented in their behavior? Here are some I see.

Pattern #1

Tom ordinarily communicates rather self-confidently. He took his classroom embarrassment positively and learned a lesson without feeling deep shame. Let's take his strong self-regard as a model to suggest a pattern of maturity. Foremost here are self-assuredness in reaction to minor failure, with adaptation, self-correction, and recovery behavior appearing to be graceful and relatively easy.[1] Tom's narcissism is useful in motivation: That is, his self-investment or self-interest is productive and conducive to growth. His maintenance strategies serve him well, facilitating communication rather than detracting from it.

Pattern #2

Janet, in the middle range, is concerned about others' evaluations, while imposing on herself a strict standard of performance. Her accomplishments are significant, but given the expenditure of personal energy in doing her job and proving herself to others, she is not always entirely "her own person." But who is? Who is fully and consistently congruent to his or her so-called "true self"? No one. Communicative adaptability requires concessions; others must be accommodated. Janet's case will suggest to us the second pattern: one of high motivation but with reduced ease and self-assurance.

Thus, in Janet's case, we see adaptability and a mastery of productive maintenance behaviors. The good results are achieved at a personal price; success is realized by a certain amount of strain and control (often conscious). Adoption of a suitable presence in functioning seems to demand Janet's regular attention. But, as in Tom's case, Janet's narcissism is useful.

Pattern #3

Dennis operates with a real disability—with an interpersonal "broken wing." His self-maintenance strategies constitute a serious problem in employment and in social activity. His case will suggest to us the third pattern: deep fears and insecurity—and resulting anger and bitterness—yielding intrusive defenses and interpersonal dysfunction. Communicative adaptations are poor, infrequent, or declining. Insecure, socially incapacitated, and unfavorably narcissistic, Dennis often enters communicative situations with less than favorable chances on identifying satisfactorily with others.

CARING FOR THE SELF

What motivates self-maintenance? *Insecurity*—a little or a lot.

Why does a person feel insecure? Because the person feels *vulnerable*—somewhat or very.

What does vulnerable mean? It means *being open to experienc-*

ing hurt. It may mean feeling *helpless* or *exposed* or *weak* or *overly dependent.* Clearly, there's something of a cause-and-effect sequence here. When the feeling is acute enough, the person who feels insecure and vulnerable and fearful will take either *direct* self-sustaining action, such as telling a lie or *indirect* action, such as leaving the scene.

Individuality in Interpretation of Messages

Given our individuality, we receivers find personal meanings in incoming messages, at times without regard to the senders' intents. Some of us will find a given message threatening; others will not. That is, every perceived statement offers a kind of Rorschach test. "What is he saying? What do those words and movements mean?" we ask down deep. If reasonably content with ourselves—possessed of a well-grounded self-concept, we may find no cause for alarm as we interpret his message. Thus, a favorable response has a chance to occur. If fearful and unsure of our personal adequacy in dealing with a given sender and message, we may sense a threat and feel an intense need to bring up weapons of attack or run for cover. We have a self to maintain.

When a major metropolitan newspaper published a political cartoon depicting current economic needs of an ethnic group in the community, members of the group perceived the cartoon as implying group weakness, and they were outraged. The newspaper claimed that it only wanted to advocate economic support for the group. The newspaper may have erred in its editorial art; the group may have erred in its interpretation. In any event, both became defensive.

Recognizing the existence of insecurity, vulnerability, helplessness, fear, and so forth, we can begin to understand the bases of most self-maintenance strategies. Large questions are to be asked and answered. Why do we feel insecure and vulnerable? Insecure about what? Vulnerable to what? What kind of fear is this? What does it mean to be helpless, and why does helplessness occur? How is shame related to upholding and justifying ourselves? What parts do family and cultural influences play in our choices of maintenance patterns? Since we sometimes feel at odds with others when we're involved in caring for ourselves in communication, can self-maintenance be connected to social distance, especially as it relates to how we perceive differences in others?

In looking for answers, let's begin at the beginning.

In the Beginning[2]

Though each human is born with unique biological attributes and with all sorts of tendencies that will affect growth, the shaping of our self-maintenance patterns begins at birth: with our arrival into an unfamiliar and demanding, possibly distressing, social environment. Taking the baby's position, we can visualize it as a rough and noisy setting—a place of sudden jolts and shocks, unmodulated voices and other loud sounds, quick bodily movements, and so forth. And occasionally, conditions are quite the opposite—and just as uncomfortable: that is, when there's no vocalization or touching or other reassuring and orienting activity, when there's minimal contact and no felt closeness or warmth. In every infant's life, there are moments of too much stimulation and too little stimulation. Both have an effect on growth: for instance, in regard to development of a sense of personal control and effectiveness.

Infants are naturally vulnerable and dependent. They're open to all surrounding influences. They depend on others being there with sustenance and softness. They depend on signs of caring, messages that say "You belong!"—on being provided with the most vital environmental condition: *security*. "The abiding lesson of the first year of life," says Willard Gaylin, "is that he who is loved is safe."[3] Oh, to feel *safe*! **Babies who feel safe, who sense that they belong and are wanted, have an edge in the process of becoming healthy people and good communicators**. To be loved is to know that you're *good*—approved of and accepted. You're spared undue fear and ready to become a confident and competent social being. The fact is that adequate nurturing is the most critical factor in development of a healthy self, for it determines the level of security in the social environment and the formulation of the infant's patterns of self-maintenance. That formulation gives substance to the communicative identity.

First Lessons

Facing environmental exigencies (reacting to stimuli), infants soon learn to invent and use coping strategies. When overstimulated, for instance, they'll learn to handle the pressure by looking away or making facial expressions that signal their feelings of tension or discomfort. In situations of great stress, some infants will go limp, suggestive of the defense of withdrawal that is not uncommon in adults. As time goes on, infants build their repertoires of simple maintenance strategies, both active kinds and the more passive. Of course, crying is one safeguard that's always been there. Continuing their development, infants refine and adapt their strategies as they meet new, overly stimulating situations.

Then there's understimulation. Child development authority Daniel N. Stern describes the case of Joey, a fictional infant of four and one-half months.[4] The story begins with the mother not making eye contact with Joey; her mind is elsewhere, and her face is expressionless. Joey, who has become very well acquainted and comfortable with her facial features and movements, wants her to attend to him. He looks for familiar signs, recalling what she usually does with him.

> Her remaining expressionless, even for a moment, when face to face and gazing at him is unusual, although it happens now and again. And it disturbs Joey that her face is "still and flat," its features motionless. This flatness must be eerie to Joey, who is immersed in her face as his immediate and entire world of stimulation. He feels that she—her vitality—is absent, and he wonders where she went.

Such blankness is perplexing to infants and tends to provoke crying, frowning, and other gestures intended to secure a reaction. Indeed, blankness may be perplexing to people at any time in life, even adulthood. I recall one experience while teaching when I apparently responded with a blank expression to a student's comment. For some reason, perhaps waiting for her to say more, I chose not to give verbal or nonverbal acknowledgment of her comment. Immediately I saw a look of puzzlement on her face, and then she said, "What are you telling me?" My neutral face, my "nothing" message, had distressed her—probably frightened her a bit—and she needed to know where she stood with me and if I were being critical or what. Babies and adults depend on others' reactions, the absence of which can be confusing and frightening. I'll have more to say on the topic of so-called "noncommunicativeness" later in the chapter, when treating infants' fear of strangers.

Consider other ordinary examples in the infant's day: when there's a sharp break in gratification, as the soothing activity of a caregiver is interrupted by adult business; when the parent is absent for a period and the baby feels abandoned; when nursing or changing is postponed, or when the baby's neurological system picks up emotional tensions in the household.

LOSSES AND DEFICITS

The first two years or so are the most critical in a person's life. It's during this period that outlines of character and identity are established. There will be problems; there will be pain. No one can escape the trauma that's part of building a self, of becoming somebody. As we know, no infant enjoys a perfect growth environment. There can be no heaven on earth in which all needs are met instantly and fully, even if that kind of heaven were desirable (which it isn't, for the sake of balanced growth). No, we must accept the fact that every baby is wounded, whether from overstimulation or understimulation. **Even the best environment has lacks, and the most conscientious caregiver is fallible; infant frustration is inevitable**. And much of it is OK, as we shall see.

But to succeed, infants must learn behaviors for dealing with upsetting social, psychological, cultural, and physical conditions. They must take care of their wounds, as they form a self. **It's in those early interactions with others—in events of ordinary communication during those decisive first two years—that infants structure components of identity and adopt primary modes of self-maintenance**. For the fortunate ones, the acquired deficits are optimal and productive; that is, they are useful in motivation, conducive to the building of personal strength and interpersonal readiness. For the less fortunate, the problems may be too severe to be handled adequately, and for them the consequences are reduced levels of security and maladaptation. Some narcissistic patterns of the less fortunate will very likely be oppressive, and many of their adopted self-maintenance behaviors adverse. The less fortunate will know more psychological pain, and others will be affected by their pain; communicatively, they will be less functional.

Narcissistic Motivation

In laying out the ground on development of the self, I've mentioned the influence of narcissism, that "great force of self."[5] Now, let's go more deeply into this important topic.

As we grow within family and culture, experiencing varying levels of stimulation and support—some good, some bad—our patterns of narcissism take shape. Differing from person to person and from scene to scene, narcissism determines all self-maintenance activity.[6] It's insistent narcissism that requires creation of communicative strategies to comfort and sustain a needy—normally wounded and normally deficient—self. **Behind the perception of an exigence of self-maintenance lies narcissism, urging communicative action to meet the need.**

Favorable narcissism, as seen in healthy patterns of behavior, influences us toward accomplishment, stability, and satisfaction of many kinds. Unfavorable narcissism promotes opposite sorts of results. The quality of one's narcissism is revealed in one's self-maintenance behaviors.

As one psychoanalyst notes, "Narcissism is a reflection of the sense of one's safety in the world," and "Much of what we call narcissism is really a system for self preservation." Others are in agreement, calling it "the concern of the self with defending the self."[7] Given our *human* nature, our nature as possessors of a precious and endangered self, it's not difficult to understand why self-preservation, not to mention deep yearnings for self-expression and a never-satisfied hunger to be effective with others, requires so much energy in our communicating. In the process, narcissism puts potent behaviors to work. Clearly, our discussion here is about something extraordinarily significant: the roots of *motivation.* Narcissistic motivation is fundamental to our daily dealings and very existence—to all our communicating.

Some common instances of self-maintenance arising from narcissistic motivation are the various justifications for being late, explanations for not paying the gas bill, and reasons for forgetting an anniversary. Suppressing a disappointment, cheating, and throwing a tantrum are so motivated, as are kinds of apologizing and evading of hostile questions. In some situations, so is escaping to bed. All of these arise from degrees of personal insecurity (which the individual may not be able to understand or may deny) and are strategies for "saving" oneself or "clearing one's name." These measures are activated to protect a self felt to be at social risk. Narcissistic motivation—whether clearly beneficial or possibly detrimental—affects all human behavior. Preeminent motivational elements of narcissism—recognition, self-affirmation, power, and self-esteem, all served by self-maintenance activity—are basic themes in our lives, perhaps even more basic than sex.[8] Though Sigmund Freud would probably find reason to disagree with that conclusion, he did recognize the great power of narcissism.

SHAME

You may have noticed that I've made some reference to shame.[9] Now let's give it the prominence it deserves. If you act in a way that's contrary to your perception of how you've come to think you *ought* to act (contrary to a personal ideal), you're very likely to feel shame. Shame arises from feelings of self-deficiency (perhaps traceable to an early wounding). It provides the power of narcissism that I've been describing and the driving force for strategic readiness in communication.

Most people feel shame and take action to counter it. The injuries and losses of our infancy are experienced as a sense of shame. Unlike guilt which develops from violation of a social rule or moral law, shame comes from felt inadequacy. A teenage boy may feel guilty when he deviates from a family rule that he internalized in childhood: for example, when he ignores his parents' lesson on use of alcohol. But it's shame that he feels when he doesn't show himself "man enough" to drink beer with the guys, or when he doesn't stand up to a bully's threat on the playground. To know humiliation or embarrassment—when felt weakness or inadequacy are exposed—is to know shame. That hurts! At the bottom of the hurt is reduced self-esteem.

We must act on our shame! Self-maintenance responses to feelings of shame may be reflected in supreme artistic accomplishment, athletic achievement, good works in the community, or myriad other self-reassuring, productive performances or life patterns. In such instances, shame is positive motivation.[10] But negatively, shame may be an instrumental factor in bitter interpersonal conflict, interruptive withdrawal, and many other counterproductive behaviors.

Shame and Loss of Innocence

During the second year or so, children become aware that they are distinct individuals, separate from their parents and others. From then on they must reckon with their individuality, a wonderful blessing but at times a curse. In our culture, **individuality always plays a part in communicative invention; bound up with shame, it influences our choices of safeguarding strategies.**

Jerry

Let's take the hypothetical case of little Jerry. Beginnings of his sense of shame can be traced back to infancy. When Jerry became aware of his individuality—his distinct selfness—and of the fact that others responded to *his* messages, he began to sense his interpersonal influence and effectiveness. That is, he came to sense that he was *somebody* with others. Realizing that he had the power to please and displease, he reached a unique and happy/sad moment in life: He no longer enjoyed the innocence of selflessness and ineffectuality. He became aware that he counted for something and could affect outcomes of interpersonal events, and he began to feel interpersonal obligation and responsibility. That's when he started to know both pride and shame: for example, when he found himself proudly able to delight his mother—and shamefully able to disappoint her. Here we see a connection of shame to empowerment.

In that formative period, Jerry began to get some conception of who he was because caregivers—parents and others—indirectly told him about himself, as they responded in particular ways to his behaviors. Their messages, as he interpreted them, often said something about his status and self-worth. For instance, he felt troubled when in displeasure they would communicate with him in an insensitive, unempathic way. He received those messages as "You do not please us, Jerry." When he sensed that their messages demanded that he defer to *them* and meet *their* insistent narcissistic needs, he felt a heavy role. Under the weight of parental patterns, he eventually experienced the emotion called shame.

But the other side was glorious. When their messages provided the soothing acceptance and comfort that he needed, Jerry felt secure in his blossoming power and individuality, assured that he could continue to risk asserting himself as somebody. He would grow as a communicator.

That's how Jerry began to learn of interpersonal power and about the burdens of relating to others, about the consequences of empowerment. Before his second birthday, he learned that certain of his actions were those of a "good boy" and others were of a "bad boy." Whenever the newly empowered Jerry sensed neglect or lack of warmth and acceptance, he felt unlovable and unworthy, that he didn't measure up. He felt shame. His sense of shame would be a factor in all the days of his life. Parental handling of this developing selfness and potential effectiveness with others lies at the bottom of everyone's sense of shame, positive or negative. **And dealing with a sense of shame is the function of self-maintenance in communication.**

Shame, Disclosure, and Attunement

Self-maintenance strategies range from controlling to withdrawing—all to the end of avoiding or managing shame. Day by day, as we respond to communicative exigencies, we show facets of who we are, even at times when we don't want to show much. We must disclose something of ourselves in order to communicate. So, calling on available rhetorical resources, we try to generate methods for adaptation *and* caring for ourselves. **To meet dual purposes—covering felt uncertainty**

about ourselves while staying attuned to audiences—we muster our creative communicative power.

MORE ABOUT THE INFANT'S WORLD

Let's extend our discussion of the momentous forces that are at work in the infant's world. Start with the people in the immediate surroundings, those already settled there: the parents, various family members, and influential others who appear. These people, with their distinct characteristics and ways of communicating with the infant—their active or passive presence or physical absence—play big parts in the baby's daily experience and growth. They vary in age, habit, aspiration, and level of narcissistic need. The last variable is reflected in degrees of stability and sensitivity, kindness and interest in others, and personal goals. All members affect that impressionable and dependent infant's contouring of a self. Some people will be a more significant influence than others, of course.

The "Establishment"

Members of the "establishment," those with settled places in the family group, will make numerous adjustments to the new person coming into their environment. Some will make big changes in their patterns of living. Others will adjust very little. But the point to acknowledge here is that these established "oldtimers"—kids as well as adults—have been involved for some time, maybe years, in setting things up for themselves: in organizing their lives, acquiring habits, and adopting personal strategies for getting on. Individualistic doings have been central in their existence. The *new* entrant into the group, the baby, must learn to fit in around those others as they go about their business.

It's in this effort of using natural abilities to adapt to given conditions that the infant shapes a self and discovers strategies for functioning with others—learning how to get along and communicate with them. Given a baby's amazing resilience and responsiveness to circumstance, adaptations are almost limitless. But the baby's great adjustability also has a down side. Let's look at both the good and the bad consequences of adaptation.

Socialization and Learning to Cope

How do infants put together the resources to cope with the others? First of all, we know that babies are born with some social readiness. Then, in relating to significant people in their lives, they learn expected behavioral patterns. Infants adopt modes of behavior as influenced by parental model and wish. If not immediately, they soon sense what parents or other caregivers want and need: reassurance that their babies will fit in and conform to held values and norms, that the babies will confirm them and their ways. Dependent on others' care, the little ones learn to make connection to others as they find them. In practical terms, infants seek to keep their status, a goal that requires accommodation. The vital process of attunement with parental figures is basic to their growth and success.

Thus from fundamental need, infants learn to adjust and live up to others' designs: "striking bargains" and doing and being "what's called for." Their learning to adapt involves invention and mastery of self-protective personas for functioning successfully with other influential people who come along later on.

Socialization is learning "the system," how to get along with others in the world. Among the lessons are those of right versus wrong, rules to follow in relating to others, rhetorical exigencies to acknowledge or deny, and roles to adopt for successful interaction with audiences. The process is conducted through parental and cultural constraint, through the influence of those significant others with *their* demanding individual needs. Parental figures, with *their* values and dedication to *their* goals, normally will be able to satisfy the prime needs of their infants too and thereby promote sound growth. They'll do well with their babies and help them to become socially effective and civil in their self-maintenance activity, *if* they themselves are reasonably stable, mature, and self-respecting people and thus able to attend to and care for a child. **The self-maintenance patterns acquired from parental authority will be clearly reflected in the child's developing strategies of communication.** But . . .

When Parental Narcissism Obtrudes . . .

When powerful parental figures who in *their* unfavorable narcissistic strivings are overly occupied with *their own* needs of self—and *who are like children* in doing only for *themselves* and without adequate benefit to the infant, the ordinary result is neglect of the little one's developmental needs. A mother who was seriously deprived of loving support early in life and who now carries a deep narcissistic injury may well look to her *child* for the gratification and soothing that she never received. She may be moved to use the child for *her* personal purposes. In this event, the infant is constrained to "come to *her*"—to "be there for *Mommie*." With a very pressing need to be convinced of the mother's love and be confirmed by her, the infant will bend the self to serve her.[11]

In his novel, *Prince of Tides*, Pat Conroy gives us an illuminating example of this kind of injury to a child in the formulation of a self. Listen to the observations of the main character, an adult male:

> My parents had succeeded in making me a stranger to myself. They had turned me into the exact image of what they needed at the time, and because there was something essentially complaisant and orthodox in my nature, I allowed then to knead and shape me into the smooth lineaments of their nonpareil child. I adhered to the measurements of their vision. They whistled and I danced like a spaniel in their yard. They wanted a courteous boy and the old southern courtesies flowed out of me in a ceaseless flood. . . . I longed for their approval, their applause, their pure uncomplicated love for me, and I looked for it years after I realized that they were not even capable of letting me have it. . . . I needed to reconnect to something I had lost. Somewhere I had lost touch with the kind of man I had the potential of being. I needed to effect a reconciliation with that unborn man and try to coax him gently toward his maturity.

Given the power of their shame and peculiar narcissistic need, this character's parents imposed a rigid set of idealized expectations on him: their cultural vision of a proper southern boy. Needing their esteem, he responded as they willed, of course. Thus he denied himself, gave up what he might have become. He came to define himself as was demanded. That's the story of his socialization.

In normal growth, infants make accommodation to parental constraint and are influenced beneficially. As a result, their social behaviors are constructive. Yet when the infant in this process is caused to make excessive and inappropriate accommodation to a mother or father's unmet needs, progress toward maturity in those critical formative years is thwarted. In ministering to oppressive narcissistic parental requirements and thereby forming a self that is *for others* the child never gets to incorporate promising and vital parts of the self for *himself* or *herself*.[12]

In communicative terms, we can say that some babies are forced to process premises of desperate parental need. In their compliance, they yield to coercive enthymemes constructed by Mom or Dad for *their* personal satisfactions. The offspring will take on roles enforced by heavy parental narcissism. This is a rhetorical way of putting it, and such is the unhappy result of a reversal of dependency roles. For the sake of the child's development, it should be the other way around, with parental premises adapted to urgencies of the child and parental sensitivity to the *child's* development of roles and promising enthymemes.

When parental figures can't love—when they're over-burdened in attempting to take care of themselves, they are unable to do what's necessary to help their children feel secure. Unassured, the children find themselves questioning their self-worth—and feeling too shameful about perceived inadequacies. Then comes the all-out effort to cover shame. This involves adoption and continuing refinement of means to show themselves as worthy, along with great effort to conceal the selves that they don't want seen. Some of these supportive measures will be useful, but others will be counterproductive, such as those alluded to in the excerpt from *Prince of Tides*. Implications for communication are enormous.

Family Systems

The boy in *Prince of Tides* grew up as part of a dysfunctional *system.* All families construct and operate systems; over time, family members set up and organize certain "codes" and "laws" of their living unit. Families determine definite behavioral routes and patterns; indeed, many of their ways become fully ritualized. Included among the fixed elements are certain customs that are to be acknowledged, secrets that must be kept, and "games to be played." Members learn how they're supposed to be in that group, how to act in this situation or that, and when to say what ought to be said. They learn whether it's OK to come right out and call Aunt Doris' "old problem" alcoholism, whether to ask why Tim never shows up for Thanksgiving, and whether saving money is more appropriate than spending it on nice clothes. They learn if conflicts are to be avoided at all costs or if they may be discussed openly, if a given sexual orientation is to be ridiculed or if it is to be respected, and so forth.

Sex and Gender

New members of a family acquire understandings on sex and gender, including customs related to specific behaviors, patterns that are more applicable to one or the other sex, and, possibly, rules to which each sex is expected to adhere. When family systems prescribe an inflexible structuring of sex roles, the child's development of self-maintenance strategies will be affected accordingly. They will incorporate premises on what men and women ought to be and do.

Children in other systems will come under more flexible influence, leading to acquisition and acceptance of gender traits that generally transcend biological identity. These more fortunate children will grow up as communicators who respect their own and others' gender plurality and appreciate traits like softness in men and forthrightness in women.

Let's briefly mention cultural influence here as it pertains to sex and gender, keeping in mind that relevant dynamics can become quite complex. Though family systems most significantly affect a child's structuring of concepts on sex and gender, cultural forces also contribute. While some cultural forces support family concepts, others may contradict them and produce conflict as a child develops a perception of self. For instance, when a family lesson says "No" and cultural values say "It's OK," the stage is set for internal confusion, frustration, and acquisition of self-maintenance behaviors that reflect the conflict.

In Review of Systems

Families have ready-made, relied-upon, systems into which children are born. They are made of the kinds of self-care and protection suggested above; for example, those to do with rules, roles, secrets, money, and various norms and social values. As precepts, they influence infants in their learning strategies of looking after the self: for example, about how to be "good," keep control, be an achiever, blame others, and deny unpleasant facts. The child, influenced in growth by a complex system of family support structures, soon becomes aware of which behaviors work for him or her and which will not and which are fitting at home but not elsewhere.

Powerful family models operate in the system, and deep, deep dependencies get set up. Thus is the infant's adoption of maintenance strategies influenced. Their value outside the family unit and for the future will depend on many factors. The question is whether family forces contribute to interpersonal strength or to repression and frustration. Here are some specific questions.

- Does the home seem to be adequate as a caring, loving, and secure place?
- Generally, what's the level of stimulation? Is it appropriate? Too little? Too much? Are caregivers too close? Too distant? Overly passive? Overly active?
- Are family members affected positively or negatively by others' narcissistic needs?
- Is it a closed family system or one allowing for new thought and "fresh air"?

- Do the many forces at work in the family seem to contribute to adaptability? To rigidity?
- Which forces seem to foster mature, positive self-concepts and which foster perceptions likely to result in continuation of childlike behaviors and unhealthful dependencies?

These questions indicate some of the issues that bear on development of patterns of communication—on the origins of those self-maintenance strategies that we acquire and use in sending other people messages about ourselves.

CULTURAL INFLUENCES

A child's self-sustaining attributes are molded positively or negatively through nurture, including conditions of culture. Thus we have another variable affecting the structuring of an individual's identity as a communicator: relevant cultural forces. For just as with family influences, a culture—the collective beliefs, values, and behaviors of larger cohesive units of society—has considerable impact on members' development.

Each of us puts together a repertoire of life stories, all with threads reflecting strategies on caring for ourselves. The process begins at home. Parents and other caregivers are of their culture; they are in it and tied to it. Families enforce cultural conditions; they are the primary influence on children's adoption of cultural standards and values, providing lessons, goals, models, and checks that usually continue to have effect throughout a lifetime. Families are pronouncers of many cultural "ought's" and "should's." In some instances, in what may be viewed as dysfunctional homes, standards may be negative in their influence on growth and on development of competence in communication. And often it's impossible to tell whether a parent's influence on a child derives from individual need or cultural forces. Does the father's indifference to his daughter's despair arise from his narcissistic callousness or from some cultural norm relating to suppression of feelings?

Added to the great cultural structures that prevail in caregivers' homes are outside cultural influences. The school is a primary source. The media will make major cultural marks on the growing child, some of which will be beneficial or merely innocuous, and others of which will add to and worsen unfavorable conditions of the home situation. Media can generate bases for useful bonding *and* for unfavorable defensiveness.

Cultural Scripts

Gershen Kaufman reports on three major cultural scripts that prevail in contemporary American society: the success ethic, independence and self-sufficiency, and the pressure to be popular and conform.[13] The force of these scripts is not negative, per se. As sources of productive motivation, their value is obvious. Any negative aspect relates to the character of its power and reception, whether its rule is absolute or reasonable. Let's examine the scripts, with an eye to their probable influence on development of strategies to maintain the self in communication. I'll illustrate with good and bad premises of enthymemes.

The *success ethic* of our culture impels members to strive, to compete vigorously, to achieve. It can put intense pressure on us to do better than others, to "score." In the pursuit of success, we find it necessary to demonstrate personal adequacy. To a reasonable extent, motivation of this nature is healthful. But when one makes accomplishment—whether in business, athletics, or the arts—the only way to gauge his or her worth, a low evaluation of personal performance will lead to reduced self-regard and self-criticism. Thus shame is experienced, followed by self-protectiveness that may be distractive. Communicators who assume patterns stressing extremes in achievement send a message that being average is a curse.

The premise of an enthymeme derived from the success ethic may suggest good communicative potential, e.g., "The satisfaction of doing a job well helps me as I relate to co-workers." But some enthymemes do not have good potential: "If I don't do it better than everybody, I'm nobody."

Then there's the urging to be *independent and self-sufficient.* This is the call to individualism, being on one's own, denying dependency, not requiring anyone for support: the principle of standing alone and tall. That's one of the American ways to prove adequacy. "Don't be a crybaby," we say. "Hey, I'm the only one who can take care of me!" Occasionally this cultural prescription seems to declare that being *humanly dependent* is absolutely shameful!

The premise of an enthymeme derived from the independence ethic may suggest good communicative potential: e.g., "It's OK to consult others on personal problems, but eventually I must make the big decisions." Or it may have dubious potential: "Any time you have to lean on somebody else, you're liable to find yourself on the floor."

Third is the cultural command to be *popular and to conform.* In this culture, we are pressured to pay extraordinary attention to peer evaluation, fashionableness, and on "being in" and "with it." Feeling oneself not liked or not belonging may be to perceive oneself as deficient—and that, too, is shameful.

The premise of an enthymeme derived from the popularity/conformity ethic may suggest good communicative potential: e.g., "A person has to be reasonably agreeable or there'll be little chance for identifying with others." Or it may have questionable potential: "Whether in politics or sales or love, they'll fall all over you if you wear the right clothes and tell 'em what they want to hear."

At a later point, I'll sharpen connections between the forces of culture and strategies of self-maintenance. But before we leave this topic, note potential value conflicts; for example, between individuality and conformity. Imagine the frustration and then the defensive scrambling that might result from attempts to resolve such a conflict: specifically, when one insistent cultural voice demands, "Do your own thing!" and another demands, "Do as others do!" or "Do what's good for the group!"

A Multicultural Perspective

Though all infants are involved in the general culture, those of ethnic families come under additional cultural influence. After Euro-Americans, major North American groups are African American, Asian-Pacific, Middle Eastern, Hispanic, and Native American.

Ethnic forces constrain conceptions of self. The group, as it adheres to established norms, social values, and parentally taught behaviors, exerts profound influence on the infant's development. As an influence on growth of attitudes and behavioral patterns, the group's cultural character functions significantly in affecting the infant's perception of exigencies: the sense of whether to speak up or not—and how. Further, cultural factors affect the choices made in communicating. As a result, **the infant's system of maintenance in communication will take on a unique form, reflective of the culture**. Even when cultural melding occurs, the internalized ethnic structures of most children will continue to influence character and identity.

As in family systems, cultures have built-in behavioral modes that affect communication. For example, many Asian-American children, given the probable influence of Confucianism and Buddhism, are inclined toward social strategies that are less direct and confrontational than those of the wider, general culture. An Asian background emphasizes social accord and downplays expressions of individuality. Traditionally, children reared from an Asian model are taught interpersonal harmony and interdependence: that it's good to avoid friction in a group and to be like the others rather than different. Dependence, restraint in self-assertion, and compliance assure one a number of significant benefits, not the least of which is security in relating to others.

Takie Sugiyama Lebra discusses five principal patterns of social interaction in Japan: belongingness (including identity in group affiliation), empathy in communication, dependency on others (a normal need for support), occupancy of the proper place (and achieving status therefrom), and satisfaction in reciprocity ("tit for tat"). Suggesting obligations that are as clearly prescribed as the benefits, these patterns of social relativism differ sharply from patterns of individualistic Western cultures.[14] As you might guess, maintenance structures of avoidance, withdrawal, personal control, and self-blame (especially, through confession and public apology) seem to be characteristic of Asian cultures, in contrast to more direct Western strategies. Of course, these references to Asian tendencies should not suggest that protective behavior among Asians is never overt (or even violent) or that prevarication, withdrawal, self-control, or self-blame are not common self-maintenance patterns in Western cultures. Only in relative terms do these differences exist.

Another example of behavior related to culture is *machismo,* a strong or exaggerated sense of manhood, in which attributes such as virility, strength, and entitlement are promoted. *Machismo* flourishes in Latin American cultures and in certain other parts of the world. Forms appear in behavior of people in the United States and Canada. Behind traditional *machismo* lies a culturally imbedded defensive code, a set of unwritten rules found in perceptions of honor, power, status, and morality.

Similarly, the dominant defensive imperative of Italians is *non farsi far fesso*: not to be made a fool of.[15] Reminiscent of this guideline is the American goal not to become a sucker. Americans have many words for sucker, like "pigeon," "easy mark," "dupe," "pushover," "boob," "patsy," "goat," "chump," and many more. When parting, Americans may warn a friend, "Don't take any wooden nickels!" And they protect ourselves against showing vulnerability to trickery by saying, "I wasn't born yesterday." In a recent newspaper article, journalist William Raspberry commented on how Americans these days have become defensive when persuaders appeal to their interest in the "common good." They fear being duped. "It isn't that Americans no longer care about the common good but that they have lost faith in mutuality. They're afraid of being played for suckers."[16]

Philotimo of the Greek culture also relates to avoiding the role of sucker, but emphasizes success in competitive activity, maintenance of pride, shunning ridicule, and keeping one's balance in all social interaction. Among Greeks, self-regulation of behavior is very important. For example, to drink alcoholic beverages to the point of losing control of one's actions is to risk social penalty and perhaps financial loss.

Given all the trading, rivalries, and warring in the Mediterranean region over thousands of years—extensive interplay in travels back and forth from port to port and island to island—

one can imagine how directives on self-protection and maintenance of reputation and dignity could be built up and become culturally imbedded in Greece, Italy, and their neighbors.

An example of behavior that might be traced back to cultural forces turned up last January in the "Ask the People" section of the newspaper. The question put to interviewees was "Which New Year's resolutions have you broken already?" One man of Euro-American background answered, "I haven't made any resolutions because I try not to allow myself to be put in a position where I would disappoint myself." Without making any judgment of it, we recognize his philosophy as a self-protective, one of guarding against self-loss. We can accept that. But how did he come to such a position? Is there a cultural precept behind it? Quite possibly.

Cultural Interface

A major problem in intercultural communication stems from lack of understanding another group's acquired methods of communicating their thoughts and feelings. Clashes sometimes flare up in heterogenous communities when one culture's "self-maintenance baggage" comes into conflict with other group's. A typical consequence is a defensive response, which may interfere with communication.

The frustration and conflict can be explained with elements of communication theory. Recall from Chapter One the theory of exigencies, roles, the enthymeme, and identification/confirmation. Can we expect a message sender/receiver from one culture to be able to think together and build enthymemes with a receiver/sender from another culture, if they are at odds over values? Remember that communicators express or suggest their values in the major premises of their enthymemes. In what circumstances can we expect persons of differing cultures to identify with and confirm one another—to endorse the premises of each other's enthymemes? And what if their respective values (fortified by narcissistic need) lead to stereotyping? Since respect and success in communication require some level of mutual endorsement, these are big questions.

Fernando and Saul

Take the case of two men of different ethnic backgrounds. Fernando's parents were born in Mexico. Saul's parents were born in Canada. His grandparents came to North America from Germany in 1938 to escape oppression under Hitler.

Eventually, these two settled with their families in the same town and came to be next-door neighbors. One Sunday morning, Fernando borrowed a garden rake from Saul and promised "to return it soon." But his meaning of "soon" differed from Saul's. On Tuesday afternoon Saul decided it was time to retrieve the rake and called across to Fernando, "Say, I'd like to borrow that rake back, Fernando." Fernando replied, "Didn't I return that? I'm sure I did. I'll check. Got an important job there, have you?" Saul answered, "Yeh, a little yard work."

That evening, Fernando told his wife about the incident—how Saul "embarrassed him" as he put it. "What's with those guys and their possessions!" he declared. And over in his house, Saul told his wife about how he had to ask for his rake back: "With Fernando, you can never be sure he'll do as he says." In each man's mind were annoyances made to fit the other's ethnicity. From feelings of the moment, each was moved to make trite and mean generalizations about the other's cultural traits. Inventing from malicious classifications can occur when people are hurt, when they feel humiliation or disrespect.

Saul's background influenced his defining the word "soon," to mean sometime that same day. And to get the rake back in his shed where it belonged, he *had* to do something. Thus, he lied about needing it immediately, and that hurt him inside. From his background, the more casual Fernando didn't share Saul's well-defined specifications on timeliness on returning something borrowed. But sensing Saul's irritation, he quickly felt required to protect himself, hence his disbelief about not returning the rake. This was not like lying, in his view: just an innocent word to save face. These are people of their cultural heritages—usually good neighbors—whose stress of the moment led them to mishandle an event. In their pain they put sharp points on individual differences and fell into stereotyping. Repairing the breach will take time and mature communication.

A Few Observations

Communication is easier when people discover similarities with others. As George Vaillant notes, ". . . the presence of people whose personalities, values, and language match our own, and who enhance our sense of safety and our self-esteem" increases "our capacity to interpret conflict, to respond maturely, and to deploy the less distorting (that is, more mature) defenses."[17] Here are some perspectives that apply to the biographies of all communicators:

First, we all need the confirmation of others. Very often, all we require is a gesture of acknowledgment and acceptance. Moreover, **the more we hold the other person significant, the greater we need confirmation from that person** (The primary example is the child's need of parental acknowledgement.) Our neighbors, who are constantly right beside us, can be quite significant in our lives. And sometimes their cultural backgrounds differ markedly from ours. To err in perceiving others is to chance triggering the other's uncertainties. Without validation of who we are or think ourselves to be, almost any of us can become depressed, critical, or even downright unbearable. Peculiarities of our self-concepts explain why we work hard at self-maintenance in communication, including self-justification.

Second, confirmation takes place through communication: acknowledging and being sensitive to points of contact, sharing elements of thought and feeling—experiencing attunement.

Third, **unless we communicators are secure enough—mature enough—to risk appreciation of differences, we'll be unable to confirm others and identify with them.** We'll neither confirm nor be confirmed. We'll remain apart.

FEAR OF UNFAMILIAR PERSONS

The case of Fernando and Saul gives us a hint of the kinds of self-maintenance activity that can result when communicators choose to make something of their differences. To learn more about it, let's look into the topic of unfamiliarity among people. We'll start with ordinary conditions of infancy, noting that at about seven or eight months, infants begin to show a fear of unfamiliar people. But this apprehension fades in a few months, and most child development researchers don't believe that this fear—xenophobia, fear of strangers—is innate.

According to sociobiologist Richard D. Alexander,[18] infants probably come to fear strangers or strangeness in people as a result of early contacts with people whose faces convey confusing or perplexing messages. *Familiar* people who seem unresponsive, whose facial presence is vacant and felt to be mysterious, bewilder infants. Alexander refers to such confusing messages as "noncommunicative" or "paradoxical"—meaning indefinite and self-contradictory. The child, mystified by blankness and facial inconsistency, doesn't know what to make of it all. One reason is that the messages seem not to be directed specifically at the infant. Though coming from relatives and familiar others, these indistinct and vague facial presentations provide all of the *experiential background* necessary for the infant to learn to be fearful of strangers.

Here are three applications of Alexander's theory. First is the vital process of confirmation. When caregivers become "noncommunicative," and thereby withhold needed confirmation, most infants will be shaken by the "nothingness" they receive. This can be a terrible experience, one that leaves the receiver nowhere—neglected, in limbo, without assurance on safety. It's no wonder that fear can accompany all future experiences with people who appear different, e.g., are of another cultural. For many persons, that feeling will be instrumental in the invention of self-maintenance strategies, often the type devoted to defense of the self.

Second is the strength of nonverbal message content. You may have noted that Alexander's explanation suggests the great power of nonverbal communication. This tells us once again that to limit observations on communication to words alone is to miss the message, sometimes entirely. As we investigate acquisition of self-maintenance communication strategies, we must remember the importance of the nonverbal.

Third is the function of stimulation in infant-caregiver interaction. Clearly, the so-called noncommunicative phenomenon that Alexander explores can be related to understimulation. Remember the case of Joey and his encounter with his expressionless mother? Her momentary blankness in countenance, while not unusual, is an instance of confusion in expression and intent. It was a distressing surprise to Joey, not what he expected or needed from her. That sort of "noncommunicative" shock could, if repeated continually, set up a xenophobic background for Joey (a basis for fearing strangers). The stimuli for developing fears of unfamiliar persons appear in all infants' everyday lives. In some persons they become acute enough to thwart sound development. And when they meet strangers or any others whose countenances are noncommunicative or confusing, they experience fear and react with an unfavorable strategy of defense such as hostility or prejudicial behavior. Alexander suggests that an adult's fearful reactions to differences such as facial characteristics and skin color might be explained solely by the kind of early conditioning we've been discussing.

The readiness of an adult to react fearfully to others whose countenances are perceived as disturbingly different seems to be regressive. It's provoked from the "remains" of infancy, from unhealthful lessons of old. Further, since it's of limited communicative value, we should treat it as a problem. The mature person is able to deal successfully with structures of infancy and to progress in unlearning the least promising. A first order in communicating is distinguishing between potentially favorable and unfavorable choices.

Perceived Differences: The Bottom Line

Something explicit must be added to Alexander's theory: **People in their insecurity protectively sense that those whom they see as critically different from themselves cannot supply the confirmation that they so desperately need.** "Yes, I want in the *worst way* for you to see things as I do—to be like me. But if you can't—and I realize that, there's no way you and I can communicate in any real sense." Thus speaks frustration arising from perception of difference and the assumption that to be different is to be preoccupied with self and not available to "me."

This may begin to explain why some people feel uncomfortable around those of another culture. And what of those whom they distinguish as "disabled" (or "old" or "uneducated," et cetera)? To some extent, their discomfort and focus on differences stem from a kind of sensed vulnerability and self-doubt. Take the case of Melinda and a disabled woman named Nellie. Melinda is apprehensive of what she perceives as Nellie's persistent craving for a relationship; she sees Nellie as narcissistically insatiable and needy, one who will ask too much of her. Thus, Melinda is unsure of herself in the presence of Nellie, afraid of being overtaxed socially—of being grabbed onto and forced into an attachment. Assuming that Nellie requires commiseration, Melinda feels helpless to meet that need. Unable to regulate Nellie's behavior or change her to fit her own peculiar narcissistic requirements, Melinda usually must choose between avoiding Nellie and, as she puts it, "Staying on and going through the motions with meaningless yak yak." Those are the choices of one alienated communicator.[19]

Not free to identify with Nellie in any way, Melinda comes to feel ineffective. That leads to lowered self-esteem (wrapped up with shame), which will likely lead to resentment of Nellie—whom Melinda may claim to be the "cause" of her own feelings of inadequacy (Observe how dwelling on difference has led to blaming.) And why should Melinda want to relate to someone who "makes her" feel helpless, reminding her of her "weakness"? Besides, the self-absorbed Nellie *can't confirm her!*

Thus Melinda refuses to give of herself. At bottom is her perception of differences, sense of personal endangerment, and feelings of inadequacy and shame—all of which impair her rhetorical functioning, blocking her freedom to invent useful strategies to confirm Nellie (which one day might be reciprocated). Thus one narcissistic seeker of interpersonal validation comes to discount another's value as potential provider of validation. In looking after herself as she does, with great intensity and zeal, Melinda loses some of her power as a communicator.

Ordinary and Less Ordinary

You might try using elements of Melinda's case to analyze other instances of fear arising from ordinary perceptions of difference: of the old woman you know who reminds you of your mortality, the president of the company who reminds you of your insignificance, the street beggars who threaten you with nonverbal reminders of your tenuous privileged status, beauty queens who remind you of your ordinary physical endowments, or politicians of your own craftiness.

When hounded by unexamined interpersonal fear and helplessness—in roles ruled by reaction to others' peculiarities rather than the will to discover common attributes—and feeling safe only with the familiar and known, some folk readily resort to heavy self-insulation. Below is a composite biographical sketch suggesting a form of alienation that foretells disturbance in communication. While probably never voicing it, down deep the helpless and fearful one feels that

> Only kindred souls are equipped to give me the sense of safety, the true mirroring—the feedback and assurance on identity—that I need! What I need—acknowledgment of me as I want to be acknowledged—is not available from those unlike me. I cannot be assured that it is *in* them to reach out and guarantee that they are able to *really know—me.* It is a matter of trust and respect. People who do not share my identity cannot be there for me, not really. Do they feel the same separation from me? Probably. They are of their separate selves and places. And knowing that, I cannot risk my *self* with them. They have nothing for *me.* And they can hurt me, because in their cultural, generational, occupational, linguistic, ethnic, attitudinal, racial, religious, physical, sexual, gender, class, experiential, or other peculiarity, they cannot communicate with *me.* **Whenever any two humans are face to face, facts of their differences are always in both of their minds.** Oh yes, we do talk a little, when necessary, but it does not mean much! So, do not ask me for anything more than toleration.

When interpersonally fearful and possessed of narcissistic misgivings on self, one can become communicatively crippled by perceptions of difference and distance, forced apart from others—separate and untouched. This condition might be called loss of communicative rationality. Since we need each other so, the loss can be tragic.

This analysis shows why some people experience serious relational conflict; why they become uncivil and invent ill-fated self-maintenance strategies. Knowing this, we must face up to the truth that **critical, raw, and untreated perceptions of difference sustain human distance and yield the most severe and obtrusive defensive behaviors. That's our single biggest obstacle to productive communication.**

But what of the toleration that was mentioned above. "Ordinarily, isn't it enough to be tolerant?" we might ask; "Are closeness and cohesion that necessary, really?" While it's true that cursory communication may be adequate upon occasion, toleration—which is usually no more than putting up with another—is not an acceptable model. To succeed in the pursuit of happiness, it's necessary that we achieve closeness and cohesion. The kinds of communication that individuals often need and society must have require more than just putting up with others; adequate communication is built on trust, reliable information about others, and willingness to find unity and a true meeting of minds—a sharing of purpose and spirit. When self-maintenance measures encourage fragmentation, they work against the good of individuals and the community, sometimes disastrously. Such is the nature of the condition that we face here, and such is the basis of the communicative scourge that we call incivility. And that is one of humankind's biggest problems today.

What About You?

As a human being with much communicative experience, you know a good deal about the endangered self. Can you explain the kind of funk that brings out your unsocial feelings and when a bad mood forces an uncivil reaction to differentness in others? Is helplessness a part of it? What about resentment of some sort? Can you sense these things? If so, have you come to know the warning signals and learned to use them in monitoring and understanding yourself as a communicator? In my observations, **the best communicators are those who can account for their fears and antagonisms in relating to others with unfamiliar backgrounds, attributes, and tastes.** Please think about that.

IDEOLOGY

To round out this discussion of the communicator's development, let's add a vital factor from the realm of ideas. An essential process in each human's growth is the ongoing construction of a basic body of concepts, beliefs, moral philosophies, points of view, and the like. These are the ideological foundations of our being. Along with other dimensions of growth of the self, individual ideological development occurs in social interaction and is influenced by family and cultural elements. As with every human process, numerous forces come into play in the formulation of an ideology. These include the psychological and social, as we shall see.

What does it mean to talk about ideology? Think of ideology in terms of orientations on issues, of values, principles, and ideals: the structures of our mind or soul that constrain the direction of our perceptions and judgments—and therefore our relating to others. **Components of an ideology are the fundamental lines of thinking that we bring to every act of communication, in the invention of every enthymeme and role.** Among these are abstractions like goodness, truth, beauty, justice, pleasure, right and wrong, altruism, loyalty, peace, patriotism, freedom, and so forth. Personal standards and points of view on these vary among people. While you and I share many philosophical beliefs, we differ on others. Our respective cultures influence us; ideas from Confucius or Buddhism may appear in enthymemes of Asians, including many Asians of North America. And the thinking of anyone reared in Europe or the Americas has been influenced greatly by the ancient Greeks.

Other relevant subjects are achievement and success, optimism, equality of opportunity, self-discipline, self-control, honesty, social status, generosity, responsibility, efficiency, and fairness. Most of these are *issues* (ideas that suggest debatable propositions: e.g., "Is honesty always the best policy?"), and many are also *values* (ideas suggesting conceptions of what we consider good: e.g., efficiency, progress, and social harmony).

What items would you add to the list of issues and values? Among the many that might be added are those that relate to money, fame, conformity, authority, pride, honor, parental respect, love, self-sacrifice, practicality, faith, time, gender, race, assertiveness, individuality versus community, and safety. This is just a sampling of ideas representing the stuff of our selves as thinkers: ideological elements about which we have perceptions, make judgments and interpretations, assume attitudes, and come to decisions—and from which we put messages together. Needless to say, some appear as prejudices and some as myths: e.g., poets do poorly in business or knowledge of the truth is sufficient to its triumph or English food is terrible.

Variety

But why is there variance in ideology among individuals? Specifically, why does your collection of premises and principles differ somewhat from mine? Why can't all ideas be objective? To begin your answer, think about the various family and cultural influences on our respective patterns of development. Remember, too, that individuals have varying inborn attributes or potential. But generally it seems safe to say that inborn mental powers have less influence on ideological development than conditions after birth. Thus, along with our native endowments, we must recognize the effect of environmental influences on the formation of ideology: on nurturing as it affects each person's acquisition of principles, conceptions, doctrines, philosophies, rationales, notions, tenets, and so forth.

Subjectivity

No held idea is a "pure" idea; there are always subjective traces. No one's thoughts or fundamental beliefs are distinct from feelings. Our beliefs on *anything* are always tinctured by emotion and self-interest. Narcissistic sensitivity always accompanies the "rational" structures in one's ideology. Thus ideas are tied to personal insecurities; reasoning is tied to self-maintenance.

This means that narcissism—the great force of self—is ever a factor in formulating thought and its communication. Indeed, our collection of narcissistic needs—needs of the self—act as the grand marshal of ideological development and expression of ideas.

"Comforting Convictions"

Writer Bertrand Russell said that "Every man, wherever he goes, is encompassed by a cloud of comforting convictions, which move with him like flies on a summer day." How true! Those comforting personal convictions, those keen ideas—including fantasies and biases—that we have adopted as "true" or "right" for us constitute our ideology. Whether "with a bang or whimper," chosen samples of that ideology appear in every message we express. The same is true of our receivers' ideologies and *their responses to our messages.*

A communicator's personal ideology is ever-ready for active service: It gives purpose and meaning to a message and supports self-maintenance activity. And while it might be said that at one moment emotion seems to dominate and at another moment reason dominates, they appear together in any message. **Woven of threads of thought and tinged by narcissism, ideology is the fabric of all communication.** All *topoi* incorporate structures of ideology.

In Shaping Enthymemes and Roles

To put together an ideology is to build a supply of premises for enthymemes. We draw on that supply when communicating: in conversation, debate, public speaking, interviewing, expressing love, and all other kinds of interacting. An enthymeme, you remember, is a frame of thought used in communication. Here's a sample abstract of an enthymeme drawn from a position that someone acquired along the way in life: "Since X political candidate has consistently refused to support a strengthening of the air force, I cannot vote for him." Somehow that thinking on national needs became fixed in the person's mind and was made ready for retrieval and expansion into a conversation at election time. Here's an enthymeme of different origins. "Please don't ask me to say who left the cash drawer open; a guy doesn't tell on a co-worker."

His resolve not be a "snitch" seems to be firmly held. Where do we get such concepts?

Include role selection here, too. The guy who refuses to tell on someone, chooses not to be a snitch. To be otherwise would be to take a role that's against his ideology—against a moral precept, an ideal, or a basic value. Moreover, to tell would be to damage his *ethos*, his credibility in the eyes of significant persons in his life.

What are some of your "comforting convictions"—prized notions that have become major premises of your enthymemes and have shaped the character of your favorite roles? Can you recall a few? Think of those that have appeared in your communicating today? Consider, for example, the basis of your stand on expanding the local library or the position that you've taken on street begging or your point of view on the need for new career opportunities—or a prejudice that appears now and then in your conversations.

Note, too, your ideological conflicts and their entry into your communicating. For instance, a belief in freedom of expression may be tested when the issue of sexually explicit material on the internet is debated.

Some Introspection

Try This. Take time here for some introspection. Single out one of your comforting convictions—a familiar or satisfying principle, value, or belief, and then analyze it. Include a try at tracing its origins in your development (how you came to adopt that bit of ideology), its prevalence in your communicating, its rational versus narcissistic content (but which in strict terms cannot be separated), and its usefulness to you in communication (pluses and minuses). Conducting such an exercise will help you to understand yourself as a communicator, for your ideology is a large part of your identity and your *ethos:* you as perceived by others.

Before moving on, we should remind ourselves of a worrisome fact about ideology. Any given element of ideology will yield strategies that are either useful in communication or counterproductive. Recall my earlier reference to rigidity in the self-concept and intense preoccupation with what one ought to be or do and ought not to be or do. There are times when an inflexible ideology, disallowing helpful compromise, can be an obstacle to good communication, as well as a hindrance to social progress generally. In this regard, what did President Clinton mean in his 1994 State of the Union address when he remarked that to achieve the nation's goals, we must "put our ideological armor aside"? From his point of view, legislators' use of ideology as a defensive shield can run counter to national good.

SELF-CONCEPT AS A STRUCTURE OF IDEOLOGY

The self-concept is ideological. It's a set of self-principles that we generate in the course of personal development and which is ultimately represented in all of our thinking, feeling, and communicating. When he says, "I do have principles, you know; I won't beg her for the $300" or asks, "Wear that tie? Who do you think I am, some kind of weirdo?" he speaks from principles of his self-concept; rules that place requirements on his actions. His statements reveal bits of personal ideology, which in his terms are about "who I try to be" and "how I ought to be." Here, as always, we see narcissism at work, the ever-active and persuasive agency of self.

Knowing the function of narcissism in daily life, it's easy to understand that dimensions of the self-concept permeate our general ideology. All principles of an ideology are colored by an individual's perceptions about personal identity. This is to say, for instance, that our beliefs and values regarding military preparedness, child-rearing, and air traffic control reflect in some way our concepts of self. We are *whole* beings, with inseparable parts.

The self-concept is rigid in some of us, less so in others. It may amount to a healthful and realistic view of our personal identity, or it may be a code that is heavily marbled with burdensome "ought to be" premises and obstructive questions on self-worth—the influence of overbearing narcissism. As you can see, *perfection* is often a central issue in the self-concept and the workings of narcissism. On the positive side, a favorable pattern of such narcissism can be the prime mover of satisfying accomplishment. But unrealistic perceptions on achievement may function as excessively "perfectionistic," and ultimately self-defeating, idealizations. Since self-expectations have considerable control over our thoughts and actions, imagining ourselves as able to be perfect will lead to problems in communication.

Gender and Self-Concept

What of gender? Doesn't it relate to self-concept? Yes, it does. Everyone communicates in accord with a perception of self, and gender is a part of that perception. Thus, any discussion of the communicator's biography must include the acquisition and development of so-called "feminine" and "masculine" attributes. In an ideology, beliefs and attitudes on gender questions stand as principles about our self-concepts. "Men don't cry in public" is one familiar rule. Then we have "It is not feminine to like erotic literature" and "Women are expected to be more gossipy than men." You may want to raise questions about these, but read on.

Sex-based rules or principles, like those in the examples above, set up a framework of opposites: Men are this way and women are that way; women can do this but men cannot; it's OK for her to speak like that but it's not for him. Biological conditions have been used to dictate specific roles for people in every kind of communicative situation.

But in recent years, we've seen certain changes in the old rules. We've become less focused on physical and biological characteristics and more on the existence of gender characteristics. The emphasis now is less on determination of role by sex—male versus female—and more on awareness of gender plurality in an individual's nature. This is the *androgynous perspective,* acknowledging the incorporation in one's makeup of both male and female components, regardless of one's sex. Thus the idea that everyone's makeup includes traits of both genders is becoming more and more acceptable and useful. We know that a trait such as sensitivity to others' feelings (sometimes viewed as a feminine trait) will help both sexes succeed in communication, as may assertiveness (masculine), acceptance of controversy and debate (masculine), and a willingness to conform or please (feminine). Whether or not these gender classifications are entirely accurate is not the point. The point is that each of us has various gender inclinations, which, in general terms, we name as feminine or masculine. How we perceive our gender leanings and how they're perceived by others are critical in our interactions. That's why we need to be aware of them. As Deborah Tannen argues, the "risk of ignoring differences is greater than the danger of naming them."[20]

This may be the place to mention the practice of stereotyping by sex or sex roles. Not only is it wrong, it's distracting in communication. That's why we find it more useful to identify gender traits among communicators: to visualize a masculine-feminine continuum on which to place tendencies relating to dependence/independence, willingness to disclose feelings/reservedness, directness/avoidance, competitiveness/cooperativeness, and excitability/calmness. From this frame of reference, we can envision a coherent and serviceable model, one formed from an *integration* of traits as we may perceive them in ourselves and in those with whom we communicate.[21]

Freedom of Role

As we know, girls traditionally have been raised—socialized—to incorporate principles of domesticity into their personal ideologies, in preparation to fulfill the roles of caring wife and mother. Traditionally, men have been raised as providers, to be independent and in charge. But with the relaxation of family and cultural injunctions on fixed roles has come greater freedom of choice. And, as is usually the case, when rules are relaxed, people tend to become less certain about "how to be." That's because clear definitions provide a sense of security; established guidelines give consequent sense of place and ease. To the extent that a woman's traditional family and culture were effective in socializing her to form a concept of proper roles, deviations resulted in guilt.[22] And the same can be applied to a man, in his deviation from the model of strong man in control as provider and protector.

With adjustments of our self-concepts and greater freedom in choosing how to be, we are more on our own, so to speak. Our debt to family and society has decreased, while our debt to ourselves has increased (a narcissistic debt). But enjoyment of new options in social functioning comes at a price. To be an individual—conforming to a self-concept as built under relaxed rules, being more alone and self-directed—can be disquieting to a communicator. Such lessening in the force of social principles, while decreasing guilt, contributes to the power of shame: e.g., when we're unable to be as our self-concept would have us. The character of our narcissism and patterns of self-maintenance are influenced accordingly. Strategies of communicators in our time reflect rule changes—as well as the . . .

Persistence of Some Old Rules.

Though the androgynous perspective is an intrinsically compelling model, it is not universally endorsed. Nor is any other guide to behavior, regardless of value; older ways—unambiguous and comfortable—persist. In our culture's communication patterns there remains ample evidence of demarcation by sex. We must remember this as we communicate with diverse others. **Know thy audience is a first law of communication.** This dictum certainly applies to ideologies of audiences.

A Sense of Justice

As vital as gender, a sense of personal justice lies at the very core of idealizations in the self-concept. I cannot imagine any more powerful value than justice—nor any more prevalent issue in interpersonal communication. Experiencing normal states of imbalance and uncertainty, growing human beings structure sets of standards by which to measure and process their felt grievances: claims of personal entitlement, feelings of neglect, comparisons of how they are treated, expectations of rewards, and other concerns of equality and fairness. Narcissistic need and personal security influence the shaping of a sense of justice and specific codes of right and wrong, merit and reward, deservedness, and so forth. The following premises of enthymemes suggest common ideas of justice. What feelings and principles lie behind them? How would you analyze each?

"It's *wrong* to blame me for my sister's behavior."

"How did they get *an extra allotment*?"

"*What a lousy call*! To me, second place is no place!"

"We've *paid our dues; now it's payday* for us."

"It's *only right* that she be admitted to the University.

"Yes, senior citizens do *deserve* cost of living increases."

"I think veterans have *something coming* from the country."

"The judge only slapped his wrist; he *still owes* society.

"They'll get their *comeuppance*, and *it serves them right*!"

Sensitive to issues of justice, people want a "square deal," to receive "credit" for their effort, to get "what's owed" them—what they're "entitled," to be assured that procedures are followed "according to Hoyle," to have "wrongs redressed," to get a "fair shake" and be treated with an "even hand," to be assured that others "reap what they've sown."

What about *your* premises on justice? What's the content of your ideology in this regard? Specifically, what enthymemes on justice do you seek to communicate? Two of the best known premises are "All people are created equal" and "A person is innocent until proved guilty." Name two or three that guide you daily. How about "All I want is what everyone else gets" or "A favor should be returned"? Recall this defensive fragment of an enthymeme from the 1970s: "I am not a crook!" Can you see the connection between such communication premises and your moral self and character? By moral self and character, I mean the core of your ideological self: your philosophy of life, inner nature, outlook, and more precisely, your ideology on right and wrong.

In maturity, we learn that fairness is not distributed evenly in this imperfect world, that right does not automatically win out over wrong. We meet such imperfection by formulating individual codes of judgment and functional processes. We act to balance the scales, in accordance with our perceptions of imbalance. The premises of our enthymemes on justice reflect the operations of our justice system. In this activity, we're *self*-involved, seeking justice and seeking to justify ourselves and our behavior.[23] When unable to meet the levels we've set, we suffer shame.

Remember that shame arises from doubts about ourselves, about perceived failure to reach our personal standards: ideological premises of the self-concept. Though changing as we grow, these pressing requirements continue, for self-esteem is on the line in all interactions. Uncertainty on status of the self and deservedness, is reflected in insecurity and potential for feeling shame. From that, you can see how the power of shame contributes to a code of justice and how questions about legitimacy and adequacy lead to self-justification and other forms of self-maintenance. **To the extent that a doctrine of self-doubt dominates the self-concept, shame will exert great force in communication.** While strategies vary, we act to protect ourselves against the shame of questionable *ethos* and related narcissistic concerns. Even in health, the self is never "proven beyond doubt"—never fully safe.

IDEOLOGY AND SELF-MAINTENANCE

Combinations of our ideas and narcissistic energy function together in self-sustaining communication. Proportions of narcissistic vigor at play among ideas—and ratios of the two—vary enormously from person to person, leading to significant differences in personality, communicative strategies, and results of communication. Can you see the connection between premises of your ideology and your *self-maintenance ethos*?

And what of conflicts of principle? For example, when you must decide between "telling it as it really is" and avoiding the "truth." How will you care for yourself in that instance? Your patterns in maintaining yourself in communication, inseparable from your very soul, have connection to all parts of your being. And central to your ideology, those patterns mark *your* self as distinct.

Again, the contribution of ideology to self-maintenance is clear. Take the function of defending the self. Author Kenneth Boulding makes a good point in this regard. He notes that our ideology is our image of the world and part of our identity. Consequently, it's something of peculiar value to us: a part that we are "concerned to defend and propagate." Given its centrality to our very being, ideology creates roles for us to play in representing ourselves to the world.[24] Choosing roles to defend and propagate an ideology is a vital function of all daily communicating.

Some Instances

In coming up behind a car with a bumpersticker, have you ever wondered what kind of person put it there? In our terms here, we might ask what role the sender seems to be assuming. What is the person "concerned to defend and propagate"? And what's the self-maintenance function of the message?

Take a bumper message, the one that urges us to "Question authority!" The role seems demanding and assertive. Is it assumed confidently or is there self-doubt behind it? What values are suggested in the message? Economic? Moral? Social? Individual security? Do you sense a narcissistic dimension? Specifically, does it seem to show self-needs, e.g., as pertaining to diminished power, safety, or dignity? What, if any, threat to the individual is revealed?

Think about the message that implores us to "Save the Redwoods." How would you characterize the sender's role? What issues lie behind the statement? Economic? Aesthetic? Issues of right and wrong? Do you imagine that narcissistic injury plays a part in this communication? What does the sender expect to lose if the redwoods aren't saved? What kind of self-maintenance need motivates the sender?

Why do bumpersticker communicators want to propagate ideologies like "Love your babies" or "Tail-gaters will die in hell!"? Which of those two premises is more rational? Which has more meaning to you? Why? Because you are able to join with the author in building the enthymeme? Of those you've seen recently, what bumpersticker speaks best for you? What does that choice say about your sense of justice? About levels of your security? About any part of your ideology? About your self-maintenance needs? What do you get from reading a bumpersticker that speaks your mind?

On Another Level

Clearly, ideology permeates the events of daily life. But it also permeates major world events. On a grand scale, we often see the high drama of ideology as a major factor in social change. The histories of many peoples and nations are stories of the influence of ideas and ideals, of momentous efforts to achieve improvement in condition or status. The narcissism generated by individuals' deeply felt senses of justice and threatened self-concepts animates great movements across the world. Self-need underlies ideological conflict and activates the arguments in fervent debates on all manner of subjects: religious issues, inter-ethnic relations, taxation policy, rights of states and provinces, racial equality in the workplace, gun control, immigration, terrorism, and so on.[25]

When principles of self-concepts become motives to preserve cultural, religious, or national interest, many people are willing to face death in self-defense. Though a seeming absurdity, that's a truth. Communicators' ideological passions and apparent certainty dominate their messages. But so often it's uncertainty—the zealots' uncertain situation, standing, or acceptability—that prompts the rhetorical action (and sometimes violence) to advance the cause and maintain the group. The vigor behind the defense of ideals and doctrine on self owes as much to insecurity and doubt as to any other source.

IN REVIEW

Coming into the world with social potential but immediately subjected to injuries and losses from too much and too little stimulation, infants shape a self. Thus a self is defective and troubled by a measure of uncertainty and fear. If this were not true, there would be normal people with no shame—fully intact and secure, with nothing to defend. And there are no such people!

Also, nearly all of us communicate with some sense of unfulfillment and personal inadequacy—with self-doubt. Beneath the doubt is the ever-active sense of shame: the source of narcissistic motivation to maintain the self, to make use of the best *topoi* to achieve that purpose.

Our self-maintenance strategies—enthymemes and roles—not only work to protect and justify ourselves when we deal with others, they also give others a view of our identity: reflections of our ideology and our concept of who we are and want to be. Thus it is that our self-essence is defined by our audiences as they *selectively process* the self-sustaining information we communicate to them. Some of the information about us—reflecting emotions, values, beliefs, and conceptions—enables our audiences to experience unity and attunement with us, and of course, some of the information will influence them to resist identifying with us. They perceive what they are disposed to perceive.

Thus

We are known to our audiences as we maintain ourselves in communication with them,

and

They respond accordingly, defining success as they confirm us,

and

We their audiences, do the same with them.

These are basic facts of our biography as communicators.

Try This. How do you explain what's behind the incidents below? Why, in your opinion, did they say or do that? Find one term or phrase to fit all ten.

- A student of mine, an amateur boxer, declared, "I'd rather go five rounds with the heavyweight champion than give a public speech."
- Mr. Smith drove around for forty minutes looking for a certain street, instead of stopping to ask someone for directions.
- Andre refused to wear his work clothes to the shopping mall.
- After her college football team was defeated two years in a row by their arch rival, Sherri asked, "Why did I go to this dumb school?"

- After the examination, Ted said, "Actually, I knew all that stuff, but the teacher gave me trick questions."
- Sally commented, "I really didn't want the scholarship anyway; now, I won't have to worry about keeping up my GPA."
- When a less experienced person was promoted over her, Mary said, "She'll last about three weeks up there."
- When John ignored him that morning, Bill was sarcastic with Sara a half-hour later—and she was harsh with the kids at 5:30.
- Vigorous, cheerful, and popular Sam, who was forced to leave the company at mandatory retirement age, fell into a pattern of inactivity, gained too much weight, and became cranky and depressed.
- "You won't have Richard Nixon to kick around anymore."

How would you describe each person's self-concept?
Can you add a couple of related incidents to the list?

1. ____

2. ____

Chapter Three

Ordinary Communication: Good and Bad

MAIN THEMES OF THE CHAPTER

- Communicators, with selves that are accessible to others' selves, are aware of possible narcissistic injury and shame and will go to unbelievable lengths to care for their selves.
- Narcissistic insecurity, normal and natural, is reflected in communication.
- Self-maintenance strategies, found in all communicating, are normal, universal, and chosen to sustain the self.
- Strategies from "soft" narcissism, those positive responses to shame, facilitate feelings of adequacy in communication and produce good results.
- Strategies from "hard" narcissism, maladaptive responses to shame, are communicatively counterproductive.
- The rhetorically sensitive and mature communicator is more mindful of discovery of common ground than male-female distinctions.
- All self-maintenance behaviors, "good" and "bad," can be categorized by *topoi.*
- Fiction offers realistic examples of self-defeating personal maintenance: of people communicating *at* others, *away* from others, or *with* them *too much.*

- Those whose need of reassuring communication is the most desperate may be the least able to get it.

OUR EXTRA SOMETHING

Visits to the zoo or aquarium provide ample evidence that all life forms have acquired defenses in order to survive. Sharp claws, a deep growl, and bigness or smallness are a few defenses. Some of the more exotic examples include the pursued octopus that hides in its ink cloud; the porcupine with its protruding quills; the oak tree that meets a parasite's infestation by growing a ball around the sore spot; the chameleon that tries to be inconspicuous by changing color. We human animals also have defenses against physical attack.

All animals are disposed to look after and protect themselves. But we are different; we maintain ourselves in additional ways—upholding, defending, and justifying—because we have something extra. Besides a body, we have a delicate *self* to keep together: *We can be hurt narcissistically,* as well as physically. We may *feel* demolished after being berated by someone, yet the body remains untouched. The hurt is to the self. We are sophisticated and complex creatures, and our self-awareness and sensitivity may very well be what distinguish us most strikingly from animals with much simpler response mechanisms. More than any other, we are a *self*-conscious species.

Given that peculiarity of our species, we are ever mindful that this fragile self is accessible to the selves of others around us, and thus exposed and vulnerable. Therefore, in interpersonal interaction we are conscious of the possibility of injury. This self-consciousness affects us while we communicate with others; we never strip away all of our carefully wrought cover. In light of interpersonal realities, sensitivities, and occasional lacks in social sensitivity, there's a chance in almost any exchange that one or another of us will experience shame or at least expect to feel it at a given moment. Then what? The result is an instantaneous marshaling of maintenance measures: actions—obvious or not—against diminishment or discredit to the self. It's a human commandment that we seek to meet or transcend shame, to take care of ourselves. In our existence, as we have seen, shame is an extremely powerful emotional state that reflects concerns about self-worth and status. People will go to unbelievable lengths to avoid or handle feelings of shame. Mark Twain may have been correct when he said, "Man is the only animal that blushes. Or needs to"—the only animal to know shame. Necessarily, shame is a major factor in communication.

AN IMPERATIVE: UNIVERSAL AND NECESSARY

Each person has a unique portfolio of self-capital—venture capital that's at risk—that needs guarding, justifying, and watching over. No, that commodity is not money, but it's even more valuable. It's that immaterial, bodiless, "something" called self-worth. Though varied in kind and degree, narcissistic insecurity is universal among us. And also universal is the counteractivity that follows threat to the self, as represented in the strategies to keep it intact.

It's a great force that so directs human behavior. Revealing its force in all of our communications, it acts as a mighty *imperative,* motivating effectiveness in interaction with others. Behind it is the compelling need not to be alone. Response from others must be secured. Confirmation must be achieved. "To *be with* others—identified with . . . and through others to receive evidence of one's being and personal power is an irrepressible and constant goal."[1] Such is the narcissistic motivation for communicative activity. In happy moments, the fire of narcissism is favorable, representing a healthy self in normal need of recompense.

But the subjective truth of our personal limitation is terribly frightening. And in our most solipsistic moments—when tightly wrapped in ourselves, self-occupied—we operate as if the truth about our worth exists only as we produce it in action. In untold scenes, as we sense self-deficiency and anticipate loss of personal worth, we take self-justifying action: attending to personal requirements and urgencies in work, play, or creative activity. **In scenes of communication, our self-supporting actions are integral to all invented messages. Their aim is strategic and purposeful: to keep the self together and functioning successfully with others.**

BOTH BOON AND BANE

Given our *human* nature, we are susceptible to narcissistic pain. As we have seen, most infants will be taken care of well enough in their vital early development. But for the less-favorably situated, the losses or emotional damage will be too severe to be handled adequately later on, and the consequences will appear as reduced levels of social effectiveness and adoption of *adverse* maintenance structures. Many of the unfortunate little ones will be less functional in future communicative activity. Some will find the help needed for growth, but the road can be rocky.

Now remember that some infant compromise is essential to good social learning; adequate relating requires that a measure of individuality must be sacrificed (Recall from Chapter Two, the useful suppression of individuality in Asian cultures.) Narcissistic compromise is necessary to growing, respecting others, and acquiring a sense of community. From that dynamic scene of infancy, **when conditions are good enough, the yield will be a functional self with an adequate maintenance system—one characteristically marked by adaptability, civility and accommodation to others, interpersonal sensitivity, and communicative success.**

Soft Narcissism

Ordinary narcissism is essential to a happy life. It provides the "push" to create, to accomplish tasks, and function socially. Rewards of healthful self-investment—the products of "soft" narcissism—are to be gained in all areas of life: learning, earning money, having fun, making speeches, and so forth. Narcissism empowers strategies of self-care; it motivates one to "be on top of things," to work at goals, and to deal satisfactorily with problems that inevitably will arise. The spirit of narcissism leads to good interpersonal relationships—founded as they are on self-respect, trust, reciprocity, openness, courage, and other important elements. In a word, **favorable narcissism provides soundness and vigor that constitute well-being and a bright outlook on communication.**

One positive expression of soft narcissism is striving to be in command of a situation and to exercise a degree of control over events. Graceful social assertiveness gives personal satisfaction and often returns a message of appreciation from others (confirmation). In this regard, have you ever thought of what it means to be "ambitious"? Are you an ambitious person? Are you one whose self-concept prescribes tasks that you absolutely must get done: You just have to do these things, and you will not give yourself peace until you do! In other words, you operate with a degree of discomfort when things are undone: the banking to do, a relative to visit, the shopping to take care of, that report to write, that telephone call to make, and the piece of work that must be finished. You're motivated; you're a producer. This pattern represents the lives of many. Moreover, it seems OK for them, *and*, it may be OK for those of us who associate with them and benefit from their motivation (their worthwhile maintenance systems). Our fictitious Janet of Chapter Two, the successful manager with an oil company, had this sort of narcissistic motivation.

But look at the other side. While many people with productive self-needs are able to function with moderate narcissistic distraction, those with counterproductive systems pay dearly for what they get out of life. Detrimental compromises—those resulting from neglect in infancy or the requirements of insensitive parental needs—lead to suppression or disadvantageous direction of the infant's vital expressions of self.[2] The result is frustration in meeting potential, the inability to become all that might have been possible. As we shall see in more detail when we examine dysfunctional self-supportive strategies, inadequacy in communication is directly connected to problems in identifying with others: for example, when caused by excesses of pride or arrogance, or other distracting narcissism.

NO EXCEPTIONS

Isn't there some way to avoid this human predicament, to become "non-narcissistic" or "narcissistically neutral"? No, there is not. No one has ever escaped influences of narcissism, not even the briefly innocent Adam and Eve. As that story is told, when they lost their innocence, they became the first people with narcissistic need and consequently the first to take protective action: the first to experience the urgency to shield themselves (In biblical literature, that urgency was the original exigence for defense of self!) Remember their pain and how they fashioned fig leaves to cover their exposed selves? They who were the first to know shame! In the same story, their son Cain, consumed by sibling rivalry, was the first person to exhibit violent defensiveness. All of this in the first three pages!

That's one view of our predicament. That old biblical story can be used to illustrate defensiveness in our time: for instance, in the words of an award-winning novelist who, while surely benefitting from his narcissism in the production of excellent literature, could be embarrassed by it upon occasion. That novelist, Saul Bellow, once told of facing possible rejection of his writing: "You pray at least that rejection will not throw you into a rage and turn you into a Cain." Saul Bellow is human; he, too, requires confirmation. Yes, it's both asset and liability, this vulnerable, sensitive self.

But Are We Normal?

Even though you understand shame and the workings of narcissism and are willing to conceive of our human nature as functional, you may still want to raise the question, "Is that condition—and the defending or justifying that goes with it—really normal?" If normal means "common," the answer is an unequivocal yes. If normal refers to standard or natural behavior, again the answer would be yes, ordinarily. I say "ordinarily" because as I've suggested, and as we'll see later on, some forms of self-maintenance are maladaptive, deviations from the norm.

The "Self-Actualized"

Regardless of the quality of early experience, each person will carry into adulthood various self-doubts and insecurities. But what about those people whom Abraham H. Maslow called "self-actualized"?[3] You may know of his study of people who were notably flexible and adaptable, independent, humane, interpersonally competent, creative, able to transcend national and cultural identity, and so forth. In our culture and time, Maslow claimed to have had great difficulty locating persons with these sterling qualities. He dismissed young persons entirely, finding that they (presumably those who had not reached their middle twenties) "are unsure of themselves, not yet formed, uneasy because of their minority position with their peers." In his research, Maslow found that less than 1% of the adult population qualified as self-actualized.

Moreover, he found that even the self-actualized are not without flaws (which is not surprising). "They can be boring, stubborn, irritating. They are by no means free from a rather superficial vanity, pride, partiality to their own productions, family, friends, and children. Temper outbursts are not rare." They can be cold, unsocial, selfish, depressed, ruthless, and heartless. They can experience guilt, anxiety, self-criticism, and internal conflict. While Maslow qualifies that their experiences or states arise out of "nonneurotic sources," clearly the sources are narcissistic, some problematic. As Maslow declares, "There are no perfect human beings." In our terms, there are no fully secure and fully sustained human beings. With normal and ordinary insecurities, all of us by nature come to rely on patterns of support and protection. In the communications of these self-actualized people—these humanly imperfect people—one will find all eight of our self-maintenance *topoi.*

Ordinary Expression

In some individuals, narcissistic traits will be outwardly expressed and easily recognized. In others, traits will be unexpressed and unsensed, lodged at a deep unconscious level of the mind. But even if ordinarily unperceived, many will appear sooner or later in some form or other. When? When a threat arises that's strong enough to set off the alarm system that calls for the protection of the self: when the sting of humiliation reaches an unbearable intensity, when the will to win becomes an irrepressible need, or when the loss of confirmation becomes too much to endure. Individuals start readying themselves for these unbalancing moments from the beginning of life, building from innate resources.

Over time, we learn to adjust: making preparations to handle the fears set off by perceptions of menacing situations and the personas and actions of others. We must learn to take care of the *self,* to furnish for ourselves a repertoire of self-maintenance strategies. That's what each and every one of us has had to do—normally and naturally.

Cases

Remember Tom? He's the student who was slightly embarrassed in class when he didn't know the word "demography." I used him as a model of pattern #1, of *soft* self-protection—the kind that comes from just a touch of shame. The force of his narcissism is just right, perhaps ideal. After his public experience of shame, the undiminished Tom was motivated to be ready next time. Janet, too, is normally protective, although she carries a greater narcissistic burden of control and perfection.

The following are a few vignettes of gainful narcissism as seen in the lives of hypothetical people. They are cases of normal creativity, accomplishment and advancement, useful ambition, good works, and quests for satisfaction in living; all illustrate constructive behaviors that might be traced back to certain injuries or deficits of infancy. In the process of "recovery" from early deficit, each created something good. Each found value in adversity. Out of disillusionment and frustration—narcissistic injury—came functional behaviors, gratification, and pleasure. This is the point that Gregory Rochlin makes so convincingly and to which he devotes a large portion of his book, *Griefs and Discontents*: ". . . loss is always followed by attempts at restitution." Our achievements are goaded by our discontents.[4] The desirable result is beneficial self-backing. As you read each case and note evidence of the self-concept making demands—that's narcissistic motivation—try imagining other typical self-maintenance behaviors of theirs.

Martin

This man is a student, a twenty-year-old biology major. Though willing to share information and help others with assignments and willing to accept help from others, Martin is academically competitive. At exam time, he wants to be the one who scores highest among his friends in the Department. That's his narcissism showing, and it's OK. While not what some would call an over-achiever, he studies hard, rewrites and carefully edits his papers and reports, and takes pride in doing a job well. He's also proud of his social skills and finds himself able to maintain good relations with the professors and students.

Ella

Ella's a thirty-five-year-old single mother with a pretty good job, but she's decided to go back to school and get a B.A. degree. That'll take two years, she figures. To accomplish this, she'll work part-time. She knows that she'll have to make sacrifices; for example, she loves clothes, but there won't be new ones for awhile. Also, she won't be able to take those trips—that she also loves. Life would be a lot easier if her parents were "not so tight with their damned money. After all, they can't take it with them." Ella's long-range goal—to which she's fully dedicated—is to operate a nursery school.

Roberto

This young man lives for weekends, when he joins other people of various ages and backgrounds on the high school field for a game of soccer. For him, there's no greater thrill than faking out a defender and bringing his foot into the rolling ball at just the right place: Zing! Into the net it goes, like a bullet! He scored twice last Saturday and, while elated about that, he can't wait to get out there next weekend. Once he went three weeks without scoring. He was really down on himself for awhile, and maybe that explains his becoming involved in a shouting match in one game. He does take the game seriously, but after a flare-up, he's able to bounce back to his usual confident self. Performing well is important to him.

Charles

Charles likes to make things for kids in his neighborhood. Since moving there with his family eleven years ago, he recalls that he's made three swing sets, two coaster wagons, two rocking horses, and numerous other toys. Though not exactly an outgoing person, he's known as one who goes out of his way to help others, both youngsters and adults. It gives him tremendous pleasure to do and make things and see others enjoy what he creates. Why is Charles bent this way? How did he choose this type of creative activity instead of sports or painting or writing? And wasn't he a bit disappointed when the family up the street neglected to thank him for keeping their dog two weekends ago? Yes, he was. But then he went into his shop and got involved in a new project; at ease again, he dismissed the bad feeling from his mind, for the moment.

Kathy

Kathy goes to at least one party a week, never turning down an invitation. If no one's having a party, she'll have one. She's a regular "party animal," as one of her friends put it. It pleases Kathy to realize that she enjoys people and has excellent interpersonal skills. But privately she's able to admit that she has to work at it sometimes: for example, when her grumpy brother gets so hypercritical at family gatherings. Kathy seems to accept nearly everyone and never has a harsh word for anybody. Once, just before going to sleep, she began to wonder why she didn't have a hobby. "What's wrong with me?" she asked herself. But then came the flash: "Hey, people are my hobby."

Ann

Ann is a woman with a husband and four grown children. A notable attribute is her problem-solving ability; she's unusually good at it, whether in groups or on her own. For instance, she likes a logistical challenge. If Bob needs to be at the airport at the same time tomorrow as Dan must report to work and Jeff also needs to go somewhere later but Matt has one of the cars up on jacks, how can all of them get to their destinations? Eventually Ann will come up with a plan, often after doing some thinking about it while lying awake during the night. Once, as a member of a committee of parents, she outlined an improved method of school class scheduling that eventually was adopted by the administration. No one had thought of it before. How does she do it? Well, it's true that she's smart, but there's more to it than that. As a girl at home, she was encouraged to explore alternatives to predicaments and was given credit for success in thinking things out. At an early age, as expected by her pleased and exacting father, she came to identify herself as a problem-solver, and consequently that became one of her "claims to fame," a part of her self-concept. She's very proud of her ability.

Kent

Kent loves to shop for bargains, even more than his sister, Deborah. When a department store is having a big sale, he'll be there on the first day, as the doors open in the morning. Sometimes he'll drive across town to save a dollar on a purchase. "Don't you know it probably costs at least two dollars to drive to East Mall and back?" his roommate Peter asks. "Who cares!" Kent replies. "The satisfaction of getting a good deal is worth it." Now, Kent doesn't have unlimited money, and making ends meet isn't always easy. Well then, what is it with his fantasy on bargains? He calls it a kind of "self-fulfillment."

These cases are common, revealing ordinary self-concepts and expectations. They show something we can't deny: **We all have self needs that set off behaviors to care for and justify ourselves.**

Men and Women

Are there differences between the sexes in choice of self-guarding strategies in communication? Yes, to some extent, as affirmed in contemporary books such as Deborah Tannen's *You Just Don't Understand: Men and Women in Conversation.* But, as with gender traits, no communicative strategy belongs exclusively to one sex or the other. This is not to say that communicators themselves don't stereotype behaviors by sex. Some do of course, but they do so from individual perceptions and purposes, not from the observance of any unbreakable "law" on inherency of sex characteristics. Communicators' ways of apprehending messages differ. And in a practical and rhetorical sense, no trait will be received as self-protective (e.g., as submissive or aggressive or whatever) unless the receiver is disposed to perceive it as such. Communicators are guided by their perceptions and relate accordingly; what they perceive influences their invention of messages. Personal ideology, at the center of perception, is ever operative in communication.

While unable to get absolute answers on male versus female behaviors, we find ourselves coming back to basic truths. We can count on the following:

- All men and women seek to look after themselves; that's because all men and women in their narcissistic vulnerability know social fear and other insecurities of self.
- All men and women have self-concepts that prod them on issues of self-worth and how they "ought to be"—on feelings of deficiency and shame.
- All men and women experience some degree of uncertainty about gender traits, asking themselves "Who am I?" and "How should I be?" *and,* regarding gender traits in others, "Who is she? Who is he?"
- All men and women communicate from perceptions of their own and others' gender traits; mature perceptions overrule biology as a variable in self-maintenance.

Though men and women share traits, some of their protective strategies may differ along female-male lines. For instance, some men who question their virility will be motivated to invent self-justifying messages. A woman's doubts about her fertility quite possibly will motivate self-protection. We can't rule out Freud's observations on these issues. But **the big question in communication is "What does the receiver perceive?"** Only what's perceived is communicated. As always, audience perception is the key to message content.

Here's a final provocative truth about female and male persons in communication: All men and women are dependent on others for confirmation of self. Full recognition by communicators of that shared condition can serve to obliterate most distracting differences: We need each other very much. Seeking *common* ground, we start the process of identification. **Mature and rhetorically sensitive communicators pay more attention to attunement than difference in sex.**

WHEN ALL GOES WELL ENOUGH

When all goes well enough in formative years, those that follow are likely to be marked by readiness in communication: with exigencies perceived clearly and realistically, with senders and receivers understanding each other as they act together in forming and promoting their enthymemes—identifying with each other. "Noise"—ideological, psychological, or cultural, or other types—is minimal; cooperation is optimal. There's unity in thought and feeling. Though *self-interest* is always there in the roles and other strategies of healthy communicators as they act together, *adaptability* is essential. Thus are the best hopes of communicators realized.

While the quality of development in childhood is indeed critical, we should acknowledge here that **other conditions can compete with the best laid foundations.** Temporary or prolonged setbacks enter into the happiest of lives and threaten security. One's professional surroundings may become unfriendly; a dear person may move away; a valued relationship may wither; one's physical condition may fail, and so forth. Such are the times when unfavorable—maladaptive—maintenance strategies are tempting expedients. Slips happen to everyone.

Contrasting Modes

Let's examine a sampling of markedly opposed conditions traceable to narcissistic injury or loss in infancy. Of course, the factor of shame is in there, too, as you'll detect. The first of each pair I would call advantageous self-maintenance; the opposed is disadvantageous.

- Productive pride *as opposed to* excessive grandiosity (for example, acting as a superior being)

- Healthy self-regard *as opposed to* fanciful feelings of entitlement (for example, a feeling that the world owes me something special)
- Respectful interest in affecting others *as opposed to* a need to manipulate them
- Mature motives for success in work and play *as opposed to* intense and unrelieved competitiveness
- Ordinary and creative discipline *as opposed to* rigid perfectionism
- Sensible acceptance of reality *as opposed to* ill-advised denial of reality
- Freely chosen social activity *as opposed to* questionable avoidance and evasion
- Balanced needs on self-assurance *as opposed to* insatiability in the quest for confirmation and praise
- Civil behavior *as opposed to* counterproductive rage and violence
- Freedom in humor and play *as opposed to* interactive restraints of melancholy and fear

Ideas and Narcissistic Need

As you study these fascinating behaviors—both functional and otherwise—do not overlook ideological foundations of our systems of self-maintenance. For good and ill, we as individuals acquire ideologies and build elaborate and complex systems to provide security against anticipated unwelcome surprises and interpersonal dangers. These systems of support and defense do not arise out of the blue. They arise from idealizations, from concepts and notions, e.g., from concepts of one's *self*, from perceptions of issues like personal entitlement and justice. The point is that these ideological structures become cohesive combinations of idea and narcissistic need—bulwarks adapted for rhetorical use. That's our substance, the "philosophic" groundwork of our behaviors. Much angry behavior, for example, can be traced to helplessness in securing an entitlement, something urgently required but yet unattained. Much controlling behavior can be traced to a doctrine of individualism coupled with feelings of insecurity. Any maintenance apparatus is welded of both idea and narcissistic demand; the elements are inseparable.

Literally, we spare no effort in getting a workable protective system together. Those of us who are able enough, do pretty well with our act most of the time. But others, those whose self-sustaining apparatus blocks attainment of stability and enjoyment of the good life, find the old patterns exceedingly resistant to change. Usually their start in life wasn't adequate, or early conditions weren't favorable; for them, the adventure is less happy. They seek but do not find.

MALADAPTIVE SYSTEMS

Acknowledging the fact of unhappiness takes us to a closer look at maladaptive maintenance systems. First, what sort of strategy would be maladaptive? **A self-maintenance strategy is maladaptive if it disturbs communicative functioning**, if it puts noise into the circuits of communication. Driven by intense shame, maladaptive self-support calls attention to itself, or offends others, or otherwise keeps audiences at a distance. It may be a rare problem or a daily occurrence.

Here are some snapshots of incidents in various settings that may indicate interpersonal trouble. Note signs of insecurity and reduced self-assurance—all suggesting limitations in rhetorical functioning.

- "Look, Snooty's on her 'high horse' again; how should we try to communicate with her today?"
- "You've got an appointment with Blamin' Blair? Get ready, my friend!"
- "He's so noncommittal; I never know what he's really thinking."
- "You know, Trish, I sense a real strain in my relationship with Ben, but whenever I bring it up, he says, 'Everything's fine; we're doing great; no problem, kid.'"

- "Yeah, I tried getting a word in with the boss, but I'm sure that our great leader wasn't listening. How do you deal with a guy who's got to run the whole show?"
- "Honestly, I don't know what's in her head right now. She's in one of those 'blue moods' and really not here."
- "Poor Faultless Frank: after he misspelled 'receive' in that memo to New York, he was unapproachable for a week. Poor *us*!"
- "No," said the Watergate witness, "I know nothing about the eighteen minutes of erased tape."
- After he hit her, he left; then and she cried. When he returned, she brought forth her "I'm Sorry" voice, asking, "What did I do wrong, Honey?"
- "No matter what you say to him or how you say it, he'll claim you're not respecting him. There's no way to be nice to some people!"

Extreme Expressions

The situations above remind me of the contents of many popular books on improving relations with others, those about getting along with insensitive bosses or how to deal with "difficult people." We've all experienced annoying self-protectiveness: inordinate rage, childish evasions, bitter retorts, explosiveness, excessive accommodation, anxious retreat and withdrawal, hopelessness, recurrent lying, and sundry abusiveness. As bad or worse are use of scapegoats, persecution of so-called "oddballs" or exclusion of anyone who is perceived as strange or "different," and acts of discrimination. One interesting form—though usually not as harmful—is reliance on ambiguity and passive voice in speaking, so as to avoid being pinned down: for example, in saying, "I suppose it was done in some haste" instead of coming right out and saying, "I acted too fast." Or, the dodge, "I am not entirely sympathetic with your point of view" instead of "I do not like your point of view."

Hard Narcissism All Around Us

Television broadcasts and newspapers are filled with examples of incidents reflecting narcissistic injury and maladaptive self-maintenance: "hard narcissism." You'll find examples in TV news and every section of the newspaper. One newspaper recently reported the case of an 18-year-old man in California, who shot and killed a 15-year-old girl, a close friend, because "she would not have sex with me." It hurt when she said no to him in his deep, deep need to be accepted and confirmed as a real man. The hurt was enough to make him kill the rejecting person. In another city, a group of happy teenage girls were out riding one night and noticed that the motorist ahead of them was driving with his lights out. When they honked the horn and waved, trying to tell him about it, he responded with gunfire, killing one of the girls. Upon his arrest, he said that he thought they were making fun of him. In this instance of communicative interaction, one insecure person's terrible urgency to save his self from sensed humiliation ended in an act of horrible violence. Such was the feedback to an innocent message.

Lower down the scale of ugliness—maybe—I heard about a person who carries a supply of golf balls in his car to toss at other motorists who "infringe on his rights": for instance, when they cut in front of him. On the road and elsewhere, many people do feel invaded when someone cuts in or gets too close for their comfort. Though throwing golf balls at cars is an extreme and dangerous form of communication, other kinds of interaction out on the road are not uncommon: for example, expressing feelings with the car horn, middle finger, or loud voice. And I wonder if tailgaters know how close they may come to inciting violent responses to their "pushy" messages.

Last year, a woman rented billboard space to announce to the world, "My husband Bill is unfaithful. Signed, Angela." Obviously, Angela was hurt, and her satisfaction-seeking strategy was to hurt Bill with a public announcement.

A prominent professional baseball player is now a contract hold-out, not for the money, he says, but for "more respect." According to sportswriters, he's been responding to management's disconfirmation by "dogging it" on the field—by not playing up to his ability. That's one of his defensive strategies, something like pouting. Fans of the team are becoming upset with his behavior, and other players on the team are grumbling. Right or wrong in his pay dispute, he feels shame (It's not really a *pay* dispute.) Being in the public eye, he puts his hurt out there for all to see. And of course, he's well aware that the public sees it, for they are parties to the communication, in one role or another.

Though many maintenance procedures may seem petty to us, they aren't to those who choose them. People don't choose to defend or vindicate themselves on matters that are unimportant to them. In this sense they don't lean on their horns or retreat to their rooms when their well-being isn't felt to be in jeopardy. Both *fight* and *flight* behaviors are about the self and its necessary protection. Self-protection is not a petty issue; in a sense, it's a value issue. Notice that *one's self as a value* is to be found in every major premise of a protector's enthymeme. Try checking that out. Here's the major premise of a self-supportive enthymeme to use as a model in your analysis: "If a situation is humiliating, ya gotta do something about it!"

Struggling

Those who struggle daily with their unfavorable narcissism probably have more pain than pleasure—at least as we would think of it. These maintainers have grown to be afraid; they find themselves alone. Many have come to feel helpless; most are moved to favor uses of anger, which may alternate with depression.

Periods of Life

In the struggle for self-maintenance, certain times of life are more difficult than others:

- In adolescence, when big questions press hard, like "Who am I?" and "How can I prove myself?"

- In middle age, when one realizes that time is passing fast, and "I better make up for lost time."
- In old age, when one hears an inner voice saying, "Hey, Senior, you're becoming less able, you know—needier and not as important to others. And it can only get worse."

Conditions of Life

In any period of the struggle, certain conditions are major variables that affect self-concept and communicative functioning:

- In sickness, one faces weakness: frightened by debilitation and feeling woefully dependent (True to her self-concept, she cries, "I'm a woman who's always done for myself!")
- The death of someone precious diminishes a person. ("Why did you do that to me? What am I going to do now?")
- The loss of employment can hurt dreadfully—financially *and* narcissistically! ("I like to work; I *need* to work!")
- Commonly, divorce and other crises in relationships will painfully affect self-esteem. ("What's *wrong* with me?" or "I'll get even!")

Four Key Circumstances: The Big "A's"

Alone. Alex, known as something of a "loner," tends to isolate himself from others. He's awkward working in groups, dislikes it, and is not successful at it. Cynical Cynthia, too, knows about being alone: "When the chips are down," as she puts it, "all you've really got is yourself for better or worse—usually worse." A related feeling underlies Sally's hating the holiday season "when everybody's so damned social and jovial—when I feel awful, so utterly lonely."

Afraid. It was social fear that ruled Terry as he "blew" his interview for that terrific scholarship—and that kept Barbara from even applying for the one she wanted. Both have their uncertainty to contend with, which is tied to low self-esteem and appears as fear of others' judgments or general indifference. One of the explanations of so much unfavorable defensiveness lies in these words: **people are cautious around people seen as unable to care and provide confirmation or likely to withhold it.**

Aidless (helpless).[5] Jacqueline, though known as a smart person, often feels at the mercy of forces beyond her control; call it helplessness. Thinking that her actions don't make a difference, she suffers a loss of energy in communication. Bart, too, dwells on his inability to control events, but few see that in him. What people do see is a man striving to be in charge in all situations: ever in pursuit of certainty, freedom from error, and precision. In Carolyn they see a pattern of backing off, of not standing up for herself.

Angry. Why, in co-workers' words, is Monique so "pissed off" all the time, letting everyone know it? Why is Mark the same way, while trying to keep others from knowing it? Why do people in that family next door fight all the time? Does that guy down the street really mean what he says: "Don't get mad, get even!"? If he does, I pity those around him!

Included in one or more of these four categories of self-protective struggle are all other tendencies related to negative self-maintenance. Among them are accusation, arrogance, manipulation, and untruthfulness.

AT OTHERS - *AWAY FROM* THEM - *WITH* THEM *TOO MUCH*

At Others

The results of serious injury to the self are represented most graphically in the catastrophic rage, violence, and bigotry that are evident in our society. These are overt maladaptive behaviors, showing severe limitation in growth. They are anti-social and self-defeating acts of the helpless and the impotent as they cry out or struggle to prove their worth, or disprove their worthlessness. Neglected, deprived of real pride, and possessed of undernourished souls, these men and women have scant social interest but an oversupply of resentment. And as we note daily in ugly newspaper headlines, they are motivated to spend the energy generated by their shame and narcissistic scarring. Typically, the roots of their conditions are traceable to childhood.

Excessive grandiosity, not entirely separable from rage, is another protective stance that may bring negative results. This is the condition of self-aggrandizement seen in know-it-all behaviors, lying about accomplishments, pompousness, imperious feelings of entitlement, zealous identification with powerful figures, arrogance, and intrusive attention-seeking. Disturbance from ego inflation is a term sometimes used to label this cluster of unfortunate self-maintenance activities.

Away From Others

Perhaps as tragic, but not displayed as dramatically, is the plight of those drawn inward. "There aren't many places where I really belong," said a man named Jim whose defense was to back away from social scenes. Cary exclaimed, "Yes, I quit the team," and then silently said to himself, "There's nobody in that group I care about—or who cares about me." These are words of loneliness, hopelessness, and despair.

Depression

At this point, we need to look at depression. Some forms of depression may be explained in narcissistic terms. One such form is dysphoria. It's a condition of low spirits, characterized by "a generalized feeling of lack of well-being . . . discontent, anxiety, or physical discomfort." Dysphoria is a major contributor to interpersonal discord.[6]

When we're depressed, we "feel bad" and not up to dealing with routines and events of daily life. Overwhelmed by low self-esteem, afraid and self-critical, the hurting self has the option to withdraw, to seek an intrapersonal haven by retreating into itself and operating alone.

Evident in the workings of depression, often connected to the shame of not being "what one ought to be," are melancholy and passive misery, nothingness or emptiness, procrastination and avoidance of responsibility, and blankness. While one's tendency is not to venture out and about, the choice may be to get up and go out but to be there only physically and not in any meaningful interactive sense. The strategy is to relieve oneself from the demands of interpersonal communication, an unwelcome reality. When the only social capability is in expression of a "heavy and weary heart" or a contrived "happy" message, the communication will be heavily affected by one's narcissistic impairment and will have very little to do with audience interests.

I mentioned earlier that protective grandiosity and rage can't be disconnected; the same is true of grandiosity and depression. Explaining such linkages and defensive functions, Alice Miller makes an interesting point: "grandiosity is the defense against depression, and depression is the defense against the deep pain over the loss of self."[7] Needless to say, communicative dysfunction often reflects these invasive narcissistic dynamics.

With Them *Too Much*

You've probably heard of *co-dependence*, the kind of relationship in which the members are excessively dependent upon each other and in their providing for each other keep each other from growing. In a closed system, content with their mutual confirmation, and not able to be individuals in their own right, they have no real interpersonal freedom. It's a very comfortable situation but with sharply curtailed opportunities for strengthening the self. Together, as co-dependents are, their principal communicative strategies are to reinforce the condition they've chosen, providing each other continuing reassurance. Refreshing enthymemes—lines of thought built from expansiveness, free communication on their relationship, and realistic perspectives—rarely come into play in co-dependence. This is narcissistic collusion, what some therapists and analysts call symbiosis. The communicators' identification is constant and easy, but in this instance, it's too much. It's dysfunctional identification.

An example is the relationship of a mother and daughter who build their lives too closely together, yielding to a need for the presence and confirmation of one another. They're reciprocally dependent, and therefore excessively restrained. Afraid to go it alone, they defend themselves with the construction of a self-contained, mutually sustained, interpersonal fortress—forgoing normal social exchanges. A consequence of this regressive choice is their giving up on personal freedom and individuation. Their potential for growth is limited because they're not inclined individually to seek supplementary and healthful communication. They are bound to each other's needs.

EIGHT HARD *TOPOI*

Recall from Chapter One the classifications of self-maintenance strategies as *topoi*: Each *topos* is a grouping of related resources from which we chose in answering exigencies and meeting rhetorical conditions. The *topoi* provide choices of communication strategies. As invented to sustain the self against the experience of shame, most strategies can be judged as normal and constructive—the "soft" kind.

But now it's time to look closely at the "hard" strategies drawn from the *topoi*: attempts at self-maintenance that work against adequacy in communication, doing more harm than good.

Incidentally, as you read on, very likely you'll find yourself thinking primarily of bold or noisy actions and highly visible behavior, like rage. But what's necessary to understand here is a basic truth of communication: Much self-maintenance activity is neither loud nor showy. Though the overt, outward signs of self-support are easier to recognize, try to pick up the subtle indicators. Listen for the quiet or unvocalized evidences of *Anger, Denial, Prevarication, Withdrawal,* or *Control.* The barely disclosed strategies—many nonverbal—are the most prevalent in communication, if we can but discern them.

1. *Control.* Hard *Control* is about extremes in exercising power over behaviors and events. As with all other *topoi,* we invent from *Control* to do right by the self. But too often, the result is overly close self-management and personal control—rigid command over our actions: taking extraordinary care to organize things in set ways. This energy derives

from an unrelenting need to assume directing and governing roles. As a defense, this kind of regulation is evident in manipulation, persistent and dogged measures to rule, keen attempts to gain supremacy in a group, unwillingness to share power, "running too tight a personal ship," over-organizing, use of a power position for personal advantage or exploitation, and the like.

But sometimes the exercise of heavy power is more subtle or indirect, achieving its effect ironically: for example, through use of real or feigned illness, unresponsiveness and indifference, or extremes of altruism and solicitousness. You've heard of "killing [or ruling] with kindness" or "controlling with compliments."

Regardless of the form, the need—and goal—is to be in control, to protect against the expected shame-arousing bombshell, personal error, or other event that might reveal insecurity and vulnerability or set off an erosion of self-esteem. "Since in every new encounter you face a compromise, I play 'em all close to the belt," the unsure one declares. And "If you want a job done right, you have to do it yourself," says the untrustful one.

Interestingly, those who allow themselves to be controlled, may in *their* way be seekers of power; while seemingly controlled, they control. We often see this in co-dependency.

2. *Achievement.* Hard *Achievement* is about protecting the self through pursuit of perfection or infallibility. It's a response to felt deficiency; it's intense striving to overcome feelings of weakness, doubt, and narcissistic disability. Perfectionism means needing to be best in the eyes of those we consider judges and opinion leaders: to "look good" at all times for the critics, teachers, moralists, father figures, and other standard setters. It's to be perpetually right, brilliant, impeccable, trendy, or snobbish—and never satisfied.

It's to be the "winner" or "chosen one." The hard defenses of extreme individualism, tyrannical exactness, and elitism are included in this *topos.* Interestingly, while to one observer the values suggested by a given case of perfectionism may seem commendable and indicative of notable strength in pursuit of faultlessness, to another observer they may appear as a sign of self-deception and a lack of strength. **Acceptability and communicative adequacy are in "the eye of the beholder," the receiver.** Audience response is the most critical variable in communication.

3. *Opposition.* Hard *Opposition* is about sustaining the self through antagonism: opposing with repugnance. It involves specializing in uncivil confrontation and combat, putting others down. It's maladaptive contempt, revealed in disparaging attitudes, disdainful behaviors, holding others in disregard, looking for weakness, scorning and rejecting. As Gershen Kaufman notes, "To the degree that others are looked down upon, found lacking, or seen as somehow lesser or inferior beings, a once-wounded self becomes more securely insulated against further shame, but only at the expense of distorted relationships with others."[8] **There's always a price in hard defending.**

4. *Attribution.* Different from hard *Opposition,* this *topos* is about sustaining or protecting the self by discrediting others' choices (or one's own), blaming others (or oneself). It's attempting to defend the self by transferring responsibility for an error or mishap. The source chosen for damnation may be a convenient scapegoat or "whipping boy" (for example, a spouse or co-worker). Or the target may be an entire group, as is often the case in acts of bigotry. An example, is when we blame recent immigrants for the state's high unemployment rate.

Protective blaming is common in this culture. One such self-maintenance strategy is to assume the initiative by strategically blaming oneself, to maintain personal balance. Self-blame, say Fossum and Mason, "keeps the blamer in charge of the interaction and thus reduces surprise."[9] This suggests that controlling is connected to blaming and reminds us that one *topos* may be related to another.

5. *Anger.* Rage is central in hard dimensions of this *topos.* Expressions of rage are about protecting the self through great anger, especially against others. Why would one resort to rage when such behavior is almost sure to be unacceptable and therefore self-defeating? It's because of the urgency of the narcissistic need, notes Mario Jacoby. It comes out of frustration

or rejection, from abject helplessness; it's the behavior of the angry child of any age unable to appreciate the values of social control. Rage is a strategy of those moments when the grandiose self, though needing to be all-powerful is powerless. It's when "the world is not as I want it to be,"[10] and I can't do anything about it. Specific motivation arises from threats to status, pride, dignity, and identity, and other sources of humiliation that bear on the self-concept. Revenge is a common goal of this hostility.

6. *Denial. Denial* is a self-saving strategy in which one refuses to acknowledge unacceptable feelings or ominous reality. When inventing from hard, dysfunctional *Denial*, we cleverly and detrimentally deceive ourselves, creating the inability to feel a feeling. Truly we do not *have* the feeling. Made imperceptible, a given threat becomes effectively nonexistent.

But such denying is not dishonest strategy, only ill-chosen. For example, a certain shameful event may be too much for us to face, so we wipe it from consciousness; effectively, it never happened. We may deny that we have loving feelings, or that we are susceptible to pain, or that we ache for soothing, or that we are miserable in self-deprivation.

Through *Denial*, we make a significant part of the self unavailable to others, removing it from the arena of immediate interaction. Therefore, when resorting to unfavorable *Denial* and withholding ourselves from others, we limit communicative potential and the range of pleasurable relationships.

In one rhetorical sense, to deny is to refuse to recognize an exigence (an occasion for something to be said). It's to choose not to take note of some painful condition or statement, even though a response would be normal and expected. Everyone has had that experience at one time or other, and everyone has had the opposite experience: when we choose to face the pain and open the communication. Levels of security change. **Yesterday's exigence may be today's nonevent**; what one denies today as having no meaning—when one's low confidence level wiped it out—one may later accept as an opportunity for confident communication. **In choice of communicative strategy, what a difference a day makes**! But more often than not, the receiver is the main variable: **What a difference the audi-**

ence makes! In either case, the issue is readiness to risk communication.

Certain uses of humor constitute *Denial*, often serving quite creatively and with ingenious rhetorical effect. A quick chuckle or ready joke may be effective in pushing a conversation away from a heavy, unwelcome topic. Yet the reference here is not to genuine cheerfulness or the pleasure of communicating with a light-hearted persona; it's to the dysfunctional practice of always "laughing it off." There are times to play the role of comedian and times to play it straight.

7. *Withdrawal.* Recall that *Withdrawal* is about protecting the self by "not being there," physically or mentally. This is not unusual, but here again I want to stress the harmful aspects. Hard behaviors range from actual physical departure to some form of depression or dysphoria, when the communicator becomes "noncommunicative," escaping from interpersonal involvement, forgoing social activity. It's to leave the scene, resign, flee, take cover—to put the self out of action, to hole up. One more assault on self-esteem may be more than the system is ready to take; and with too great an emotional load to handle, it virtually shuts itself down.

In certain cases, *Withdrawal* means holding back on revealing emotions or opinions, keeping inner feelings under wraps. Is this what being the so-called "quiet type" means? Perhaps, at least in particular instances. For some, withdrawing is a regular way of life, a pattern of getting by. As such, it's a questionable mode of self-maintenance.

8. *Prevarication.* In my excellent thesaurus, *Prevarication* is included under the general heading of "Uncommunicativeness." I'm pleased by that because it puts a focus on one of the important senses of the term. In this sense, it refers to such acts as equivocating, evading, and even "hemming and hawing." But *Prevarication* is also under "Falseness" in my thesaurus. In this sense, it refers to such acts as "stretching the truth," lying, and exaggerating.

Prevarication is about protecting the self through avoidance or resort to dishonesty or evasion. The truth may be too hurtful to admit; maintaining self-esteem may demand falsehood or circumvention. Among human strategies that can prove hard in communication are counterproductive overstatements and understatements, dodging of facts, vacillations, and falsification or fabrication of one sort or another, fakery and plagiarism, cheating, putting on a "false front," deceitfulness, *and* the common act of not disclosing feelings, beliefs, and other personal information (in this case, akin to *Withdrawal*).

We may have a deep need to seek special status; thus the self-aggrandizing lie or communicative "zigzag." One common act, "saving face," seems to be represented in most—if not all—cultures, hence the many forms of protective falsification designed to accomplish it. But when in hard form, a prevarication keeps communicators apart. That's the key to the difference between soft and hard forms of any strategy.

CLASSIC FICTIONAL CASES

Though most day-to-day reactions to felt narcissistic threat are ordinary and useful, extreme instances can result in tragedy. Literature is an excellent source of momentous and clearly relevant examples of personal calamity relating to narcissistic fallibility and dysfunctional acts of self-maintenance. The best plays and novels capture that. The matchless tragedies of William Shakespeare, for example, deal with prominent souls *burdened by the weight of self.* Each possesses a *tragic flaw,* as we call that "burden." In Shakespeare's stories, the tragic flaw is found in people occupying positions of greatness: Hamlet, the Prince of Denmark; the mighty King Lear; Othello, soldier of distinction; and Macbeth, another mighty king. Leading lives as persons of consequence, all these men stand out from other mortals; all find themselves forced to face a challenging circumstance and decision on exigence, while dealing with their onerous narcissistic burden. They are at odds with *themselves,* attempting to measure up to their self-perceptions. All are shamed by felt weakness, and they wage a monumental but unsuccessful battle in their responses to ultimatums of their personal ideologies and conditions of existence. All fall tragically.

Why are Shakespeare's narratives often judged the finest of literature? Is it not because they're convincing in their portrayals, faithfully treating as they do the struggle of humans with themselves—taking arms, as Hamlet envisioned, "against the slings and arrows of outrageous fortune"? Yes, but there's more than that to the playwright's genius, and to convey this I'll use the words of another Shakespearean character, the one who admitted, "The fault . . . is in ourselves." That's the point! We are imperfect, not certain of ourselves in all acts and at all moments. To be human is to know about human fallibility, and most of us accept that, in general terms at least. But it's the individual's *perception* of his or her fallibility—and the penalty assessed by the self for infraction—that produces the stories of unhappiness of the type I'm discussing here.

Shakespeare's great figures grapple heroically with their fallibilities but are unable *to come to terms with themselves.* Thus we have true tragedy. I believe that Shakespeare would understand this psychological interpretation of the struggle of his people. He would lend an ear to our discussion of self-deficit and be able to appreciate our view of the profound narcissistic horror known to Hamlet and the others. Creating believable and powerful human drama long before Sigmund Freud instructed us on analysis of the psyche, Shakespeare gave us models of people who were opposed to themselves—their own victims—and whose calamitous crashes took others with them. Let's select two of these for brief analysis and then add a few more cases from other sources.

Hamlet

Weighted down by an enormous obligation, the melancholy Hamlet broods over taking appropriate action to meet it. He has promised vengeance to the ghost of his slain father; that is, filial duty is firmly installed in his self-concept. But in the grip of paralyzing introspection—"conscience does make cowards of us all"—he cannot bring himself to act: to organize and exercise control over his life. As an example of his pressing need for redemption, consider the moment at which he comes to a stark realization of one set of alternatives: he can resign himself to circumstance and continue suffering—evading the big issue—or he can meet his "sea of troubles"—through suicide, the ultimate defensive act of withdrawal.

Hamlet faces a true dilemma, for while death will relieve him of his shame, neither path will end his obligation.

We must see Hamlet as an *individual apart*, saddled with paternal obligation—and pain, dedicated to correcting a wrong. He acknowledges that he was "born to set it right," to assume the heavy load *alone*. What a great and tyrannical force was the narcissism of Hamlet's self-concept! His is a story of expectations chiseled in under the mighty influence of parental—and cultural—authority. In narcissistic seclusion, he stands by himself unsupported, suffering incredible agony. On a lesser scale, this is the condition of many a person, attempting to cope with behaviors chosen in conformity to a dominating and frustrating perception of self. **The self-concept will rule**! What topic of literature is more relevant to real life? None, I believe.

Othello

Othello is an honored general, a steadfast and stalwart commander of the armed forces of Venice. He is a Moor, a black man, and husband of Desdemona, a white woman. Though successful in dealing with his father-in-law's objections to him as Desdemona's husband, Othello is unprepared to contend with the backhanded craft of evil Iago, an officer whom Othello had declined to grant a promotion. Aching from the slight, Iago will have his satisfaction against Othello. His plan of treachery is to plant seeds of self-doubt in Othello's mind that will create uncontrollable jealousy in the general and his downfall. With occasional subtle comments that suggest Desdemona's intimacy with Lieutenant Cassio, Iago succeeds in stirring up feelings of suspicion and mistrust in Othello. At first, Othello easily dismisses the hints. But eventually Iago penetrates the great man's seemingly secure self. The proud officer and loving husband—in every way a good man—succumbs to a lesser being's malice. In one terrifying instance, he who had been a complete gentleman, in jealous rage publicly strikes his wife. Finally, unable to endure the constant pain, Othello goes to Desdemona's bedchamber and smothers her. Immediately thereafter he learns of Iago's vile handiwork; absorbed by grief, he kills himself. In this act of merciful withdrawal, Othello took his self out of communication with others—and himself.

Neither in literature nor in real life do we find a better example of narcissistic evil than in the behavior of the terribly injured, morbidly defensive, and pathologically proud Iago. But the point to be underscored here is this: A stable and sound man fell when an assailant violated the core of his narcissistic sensitivity. The productive forces of self that had taken Othello to military glory eventually led to tragic self-defense and ruin. As with all—the eminent and the ordinary—the narcissism that made him strong also made him weak.

Modern psychiatry might call Othello's violent behavior regression, an infantile response to his plight, a move to return to the omnipotence of infancy. The acutely defensive Iago broke into the general's psyche, and once he gained entrance to the archaic but still-smoldering deposits of earliest personal history, he fanned the embers of rage that he knew were there. As an adult, Othello the competent soldier had handled fire, but when reduced to a primary level in perception of exigence, he could not handle the fire within himself.

Othello's story is everyone's, if we believe that all humans—even the strongest—are limited in what their narcissism can endure. **Though rarely as dramatic or disastrous, the story of injured narcissism and its impact on others' lives is common.**

Willy Loman

We'll now turn to an illustrative life of modern time. The subject is sixty-three-year-old Willy Loman, the main character in Arthur Miller's play, *Death of a Salesman.* First is the personal story about Willy himself and his loss of status, his decline from self-defined popularity as a traveling salesman who was known and embraced by all in his territory. Willy's dreams are of the past, of a better time. He recalls the days when doors were open to him: when he was welcomed and well-liked by all. The second theme is social and cultural, with the play taken as a comment on a materialistic culture—one of false values, the illusion of the American success ethic, phony advertising, excesses of a publicity-conscious culture, and all the rest.

The time comes when Willy no longer makes the grade as salesman. But he keeps to his romantic vision, refusing to give up the illusion. He, who in childhood had been abandoned by his father, is abandoned once more. He's a has-been, rejected by those he used to represent on the road. Gone are the days when Willy, the successful drummer with a smile and slick talk, knew himself as a real hit out there. What personal satisfaction is greater than to be confirmed in your favorite role? Central here is Willy's perception of personal majesty. But now the company refuses to let him travel for them anymore, nor will they let him retreat to an office job. He's not needed.

Sorely weakened, Willy must discover how to achieve self-balance. In misery from rejection and subconsciously realizing his own emptiness, he can do nothing but clothe himself in protective armor (Over the years, he had proved himself good at it.) He draws on *Denial* as a major strategy, as we see from his blindness to his own ordinariness and his sons' mediocrity and lack of accomplishment. *Anger*, another *topos* from which Willy invents, becomes increasingly central as he experiences the frustration of doors closing in his face. Still another Loman stance is *Prevarication*: the sham, evasion, and fabrication that pervade his thoughts and actions. But standing out is the *topos* of *Withdrawal*. His is a fantasy world, full of imagined greatness and ill-considered priorities and choices. In his unreal quest for safety and solace, he never reaches—has never reached—maturity. He remains an empty man ideologically, existing in moral retardation. His last act of *Withdrawal* is to take his own life, in unbearable disillusionment, finally knowing his lot. He gives up denying that he is more than "a dime a dozen."

Bernarda Alba and Her Family

One of my students, David Rojas Gaytán, studied the dysfunction of the family in Federico Garcia Lorca's play, *The House of Bernarda Alba*. His observations, some of which are included below, are pertinent to our discussion of self-maintenance in communication. Bernarda, the head of her household, despotically controls the activities of all members: her five daughters and the widowed maid. Her goal, which she pursues through repression, intimidation, coercive control, and violence, is to sustain a family reputation of propriety. She takes this goal as something required of her in their rural community in Spain, in a Mediterranean environment of oppressive cultural restraint. But her protective mission arises from more than cultural forces; she compounds and exacerbates conditions with energy produced by a peculiar narcissistic perversity. It is Bernarda's intense stultifying control that turns communicative dysfunction to tragedy.

With gun in hand, she prevents one daughter from escaping in the arms of her lover. She fires at the lover but misses, and he flees the morbid place. In despair, the daughter hangs herself, becoming free of the house of Bernarda Alba.

Though her daughters are of age, Bernarda will not treat them as adults. Nor is she inclined to extend any rights to them or communicate civilly with them. Handling them as subjects and suspects, always regulating their activities and never trusting, Bernarda closely monitors all her daughters' movements. She berates them often and unmercifully, naming them "weakling" and "worthless insect." Occasionally, she strikes them.

Strategies from the *topos* of *Denial* are also available in her maladaptive repertoire. For example, after the daughter's suicide, she declares triumphantly, "My daughter has died a virgin. Carry her to her room and dress her in white. No one will say a thing. She died a virgin." In this, we can see the resort to self-supportive *Prevarication* as well.

Collected shame of family and culture is the chief source of motivation in this story. She's fully occupied with a sense of deficiency. Bernarda's perceptions of community expectations dictate an unyielding imposition of a cruel standard of conduct. Moreover, against her rigidly constructed facade of social conformity, there is but token resistance by household members. Avoiding community judgment—keeping up appearances—becomes a joint, cooperative act. In their collusion is clear evidence of pervasive and crippling co-dependence. Members create their unfortunate symbiosis under the dismal leadership of a terrified, tyrannical matriarch. Communicatively indisposed from insufferable self-doubt, she enlists the others for ruin. They continue in isolation. Unable to assume roles of a healthfully dissenting audience (a "good audience," as it will be called in Chapter Six), they communicate incestuously (but impotently), with disastrous consequences.

Captain Ahab

The pen of Herman Melville has produced an illuminating drama of defense: the story of Captain Ahab in the novel *Moby Dick*. The resolute leader of whaling expeditions has lost a leg in an encounter with Moby Dick, the great white whale. After that disaster, Ahab resolves to kill the beast. Injured more than physically, the captain commits himself narcissistically never to yield to the will of any man or to God in carrying out his personal obligation to bring in Moby Dick. Taking to his purpose as one possessed, Ahab involves the entire crew of the *Pequod*, some unwillingly.

The sailors keep a sharp lookout for Moby Dick, following all leads on his whereabouts. Several times they make contact with their object and are thwarted in their goal by the whale's strength and maneuvers. Good sense would have them discontinue the hunt. But backing off is not a choice that Ahab will consider; such is the passion of his purpose. The word "self-respect" is hardly enough to name what is at risk for this psychologically maimed man. We may begin to appreciate the motivation that propels Ahab, if we can understand that the full force of his pathologically empowered self is devoted to attaining this one grand objective. In Heinz Kohut's interpretation, Ahab is in "the grip of interminable narcissistic rage," and he "would rather die than live with shame."[11]

Sighting the huge animal once more, crew members thrust a number of harpoons into its body. Enraged and refusing to relent (Note that Melville endows Moby Dick with human emotions and narcissism, not unlike those of Ahab himself.), the powerful beast splinters the whalers' small boats and then shatters the ship itself, ramming it at full speed. Ahab and all but one of the others perish.

Thus this man of single-minded dedication, driven in blind arrogance by an unremitting personal commandment, brings to destruction nearly all of a ship's crew. Again, as is often the case in real life as well as in good fiction, others are pulled down when such narcissistic giants fall. Hubris rarely follows the pattern of a lone tree falling silently in a distant, uninhabited forest.

THE GREAT HUMAN IRONY: OUR OWN WORST ENEMY

Beyond the tragedies of literature, we all know cases of people who seem to be their own victims, even while motivated to sustain themselves. **It's a fundamental irony of human existence that those whose need of communication is the most desperate are the least able to help create it.** While searching anxiously for resolution of their narcissistic travail, they act against themselves. This is what some mean when they say, "He's his own worst enemy" or "Everything she does with people is self-defeating."

If so highly motivated, why can't those in dire need find satisfaction with themselves? Why do they resist giving themselves the freedom necessary to communicate with pleasure? Because there are times in their lives—moments of great apprehension or hopelessness—when keeping the self together seems possible only through fiercely selected defenses: retreating, controlling, or accusing—even in relating to those who care. Off goes the intrapersonal emergency alarm, and the message "Save the self!" drowns out "Be a communicator!" When that happens, prospects fade for shared respect and civility in communication—not to mention real satisfaction.

But must we let ourselves be controlled by self-defeating maintenance motivations? Yes and no. Yes, whenever we define communication as armed interaction. No, when we're able to acknowledge our potential rhetorical power and remember that **we do have choices on how to maintain ourselves.** *How* is the primary issue. Communication doesn't have to be "hardball." Effective and constructive maintenance strategies are as numerous as the hard kind. And it's much happier for everyone when we play the game with the soft kind. **Everyone can score in communication.**

Try This. Find a video that has obvious unfavorable self-maintenance content. Here are some good bets, available at most video stores.

"Twelve Angry Men"

"That Championship Season"

"Ordinary People"

"Who's Afraid of Virginia Woolf?"

"Mystic Pizza"

"Grand Canyon"

You may know of additional titles that are just as promising. Study your chosen film, and prepare an analysis of maintenance behaviors that appear to be maladaptive, addressing one of the principal subjects of this chapter as listed here.

Shame and Self-Perception

Soft versus Hard Narcissism

Defenses of the Self: Universal and Necessary

Maladaptive Self-Maintenance

Alone—Afraid—Aidless—Angry

His/Her Own Worst Enemy

Chapter Four

The Communicator in Action

MAIN THEMES OF THE CHAPTER

- Self-maintenance strategies are good or bad depending on adaptive value.
- Favorable narcissism is adaptive, motivating functional self-maintenance communication.
- The Communicative Disposition serves as a practical model for evaluating self-maintenance in communication.
- The six keys to a Communicative Disposition are other-awareness, capacity for intimacy, situation awareness, inventional strength, sense of personal power, and acceptance of oneself as a communicative strategist.
- Self-maintenance strategies are inherent in common communication processes.
- The audience is the final determiner of rhetorical gain and loss in communication.
- Each of the eight self-maintenance *topoi* is a package of rhetorical options from which communicators invent enthymemes and roles; some work well, some don't.
- Communication is an uncertain enterprise.

NO SUCH COMMUNICATOR

Let's imagine a conversation something like this:

First Person: I have a friend who is never defensive in communication.

Second Person: Really? You mean that you know someone who never tries to control the interaction, is never competitive, never shows scorn, never blames, never gets angry, never ignores the facts, never retreats from an encounter, never exaggerates, and never . . . ?

First Person: Hey wait, he's only a good friend—not some kind of flawless *machine*!

Do you know any such flawless machine, a human being who's *never* defensive in communication? I don't. Defensiveness will enter everyone's communication, in one way or another. **Given our nature as human communicators, each of us is nondefensive only relatively.**

FUNCTIONAL SELF-MAINTENANCE COMMUNICATION

In the adventure of living and communicating, most individuals experience more strain than we can know. They handle it; they carry on. A case in point is Janet. Remember her from earlier chapters? She's the very motivated person in management with an oil company. As with all executives, much of her work is in communicating. She's a normal high achiever. Although she doesn't fully realize it, she carries her share of past hurt, but it's nothing she can't take care of. She's strong—certainly others see her that way, and she doesn't give up. She puts considerable effort into crafting the right messages in her daily professional activity because she has standards, and she doesn't want to "mess up." Not doing her job would disturb her self-concept, her personal ideology as a professional. She receives high praise from bosses and others in the company and wants that to continue.

Eventually, Janet may even find ways to function with less stress, reducing the self-imposed pressure from maintenance processes of control and perfection—*and* also continuing to produce ably (probably better than ever). Let's hope so. There are lots of her type, and they succeed, enjoying the gains that for them outweigh the emotional costs. Overall, their self-guarding strategies in communication are adaptive.

Remember, the mechanisms of both healthful and unhealthful maintenance maneuvers are the same. **It's the adaptive value that gives the healthful maneuvers their effectiveness.** While communicators invent strategies to achieve their purposes, not all strategies do the job; some serve well in relating to others, and some do not. Willard Gaylin puts it this way: "When they do not work—i.e., when you pay a bigger price for the defense than for that which is defended against—you have to begin to examine the behavior."[1] Gaylin's point introduces a main topic of this chapter: facilitative versus maladaptive self-maintenance strategies in communication. We'll get to that soon.

Communication as Productive Narcissism

At this point, it's clear that successful communicators, while they must take care of themselves, are always busy caring for their audiences. **Functional communication requires satisfaction of my needs and yours.** To communicate with you, I adapt my self-sustaining behaviors to your needs, as you do with me. We defer to each other; we make compromises. That's the way we communicate. Favorable narcissism is adaptive; it's useful in the communication process. It helps us get what we want and need, motivating effectiveness in communication. That's good. For example, pride—a product of narcissism that's connected directly to self-esteem—inspires some people to bring forth their best. It may be pride that motivates an employee to make special preparations for tomorrow's important telephone conversation with the regional manager in Montreal, or to revise carefully some promotional copy, or to criticize respectfully a colleague's continued poor performance. Coping with such exigencies requires design and care: judicious use of one's narcissism, we might say.

Take the following case. One afternoon, when inclined to blast the head off of co-worker Fred whose view on a company policy she strongly opposed (Fred often "got under her skin."), Donna immediately sensed how her attack would appear to Fred and onlookers. So, instead of lashing out at *him*, she raised a question about the *policy*, making that the issue and compromising on her desire to "let Fred have it." Clearly, her second thoughts, given priority over her initial impulse, were also from *self* interest. But they amounted to more than that. She turned her narcissism to constructive purpose: saving herself, while benefiting others. By changing to a softer, more civil position, she protected her reputation and self-esteem. Her restraint was defensive but commendable.

Donna was able to communicate by inventing a self-protective strategy. Making a critical choice, she revealed real communicative competence. Are such choices automatic for her? No, not for her or many others. But she's learning, and we see from her case that **self-sustaining strategies can be rhetorically valuable, when they help the communicator to maintain balance while fostering desirable social cohesion**. The pleasures and perils of interaction with others call for just such strategic adjustments, all of which figure prominently in one's Communicative Disposition.

SIX KEYS TO A COMMUNICATIVE DISPOSITION

Now, let's examine the six keys to a Communicative Disposition, including *variables* of each and *realities* of narcissistic self-maintenance. This examination will give us a standard for evaluating the usefulness of the self-maintenance components of messages. Next, we'll review the five basic processes of communication discussed in Chapter One—but this time introducing favorable narcissistic dimensions. Then we'll be ready to move to a full discussion of facilitation vs. maladaptation in communication.

A Communicative Disposition[2] is a standard to use in evaluating narcissism in communication. It's a practical model that takes into account and accepts our human nature, urging us to look at our narcissistic foibles and to learn from them. The word "disposition" refers to a person's tendencies in thought and action. Disposition is one's mind-set, temperament, and outlook. **Thus, to have a Communicative Disposition is to have behavioral, cognitive, and emotional tendencies that are advantageous in communication**. Also, a Communicative Disposition is an ever-developing asset. Always in a dynamic state of *becoming*, it's an indicator of one's potential for growth, of the way communication can be.

1. Other-Awareness

No personal attribute is more useful to a communicator than awareness of the feeling states, thoughts, and conditions that affect receivers while interacting. As senders of messages, we need to know about our audiences in order to make appropriate decisions regarding roles to assume, construction of enthymemes, and other identification strategies. Sensitivity to others' interests, gender traits, ideas, orientations, and religious and cultural influences is a key to mutual interactive success.

Variables

Among the variables in a communicator's level of awareness are attention, perception, and empathy.

Attention. To be attentive is to be open to others' current states and feelings and to be aware of issues and experiences bearing on their lives. Also, to be attentive is to be ready to account for specific verbal and nonverbal cues that may be significant parts of messages you receive.

Perception. A perceptive communicator is able to get reliable impressions on where the other person is "coming from"—to be discerning about backgrounds, feelings, and points of view related to the exchange. It's to sense responses to messages and note changes in the communicative climate.

Empathy. To be empathic is to feel with the other person, as he or she feels: to be able in some measure to experience an emotion or condition as the other person does and, for the moment, to assume that person's perspective.

Narcissistic Reality

Why do we pay attention to another? Real attention comes from *wanting* to get the message: from being motivated to listen and carefully observe the essential features of the sender's message, noting both verbal and nonverbal elements, including specific words, relevant bodily movements, and vocal characteristics. To pay attention to another is to show that you care, and it's basic to enjoyment of the rewards of interacting, of confirming and being confirmed. **A communicator pays real attention when he or she anticipates finding something satisfying in the interaction.** Thus, there's always a degree of self-interest influencing choice in listening. A person's self-investment in the communicative event is vital.

Our personal perspectives have a function also. I've heard it said of a woman named Amanda that "She sees only what *she* sees." Of course she does. But her particular way of observing—with an obvious dash of subjectivity—often proves advantageous in her communication with others. For while objectivity implies a logical perspective and detached point of view, Amanda's very subjectivity—her ability to *feel*—helps her sense and identify with *another person's* emotional state. Subjectivity and sensitivity are related. And remember, through others' revealed narcissism we can know their feelings. When a person who feels neglected withdraws, that disclosure of emotional imbalance sends a signal and therefore is potentially a positive act.

Subjectivity and empathy are connected, as well. To feel the pain of another requires bringing one's own experience of pain and sense of pain to the interaction. That's a narcissistic act, but with a useful self-maintenance function, it's a part of a Communicative Disposition.

2. Capacity for Intimacy

To discover and acknowledge closeness and kinship with another is a core function of communication. Most exchanges do not require a deeply intimate investment from a communicator. For instance, when a friend asks, "Can I use your car for five minutes?" you may immediately answer, "Sure, go ahead." But that quick three-word answer reflects a degree of intimacy, and certainly trust. In that casual interaction, the favorable view of the relationship allows for a brief and easy response to the question. Not much is felt; not much has to be said. That's because of the understanding and good will that have been built together in prior experiences. But if someone else had asked to borrow the car, your response might have been more guarded.

Variables

Among the variables related to capacity for intimacy are willingness to share and trust, safety, and need.

To Share and Trust. To share something of yourself willingly is to show generosity and give up a bit of personal privacy, to take a chance. It's to trust others with personal information or something else of value, even though there's the possibility of being hurt. Indeed, every time we get involved in a conversation and show personal facets of identity, we show trust. But that has to be. **We can't convey messages without some self-disclosure.**

Safety. Because self-disclosure is an essential part of communication, safety is a variable. Without feeling secure with that person, in that situation, and on that topic, the potential for intimacy and satisfactory communication is limited. **Only when feeling safe enough will we risk opening up to communicate.** And it's often true that the greater the interpersonal threat, the greater the importance we attach to self-maintenance.

Need. It's no surprise to read that nearly everyone has a real desire to make connection to others, to enjoy the blessings of relating. To be confirmed by a significant person is to realize one of life's foremost satisfactions. A need for intimacy is intrinsic to a Communicative Disposition.

Narcissistic Reality

Narcissistic interests enter into all manner of interactions, often usefully. For example, a willingness to share facets of self may stem from an interest in managing communication: to gain control by detailing facts of one's background. If the use of personal power benefits the participants, it may be accepted as a good act, even though it's from self-interest. Of course, interests of self-management function significantly in motivating communication.

In the same sense, insecurity can be viewed positively. Without some feeling of insecurity—for example, from needing another's caring response—your capacity for intimacy may be less than adequate, in that the motivation to share yourself is insufficient. And conversely, complete security (But it's never really complete.) can lead to inertia and passivity in communication. As a professor friend puts it, "Optimum insecurity is a prod to progress; it gets people moving." In the case of communication, optimum insecurity provokes effort to share oneself with another and thus receive benefits. **The need of one to meet uncertainty, doubts, or vague feelings of emptiness and disorder can instigate rewarding moments of communication.**

3. Situation Awareness

An effective communicator is able to "size up" a situation, to get a feeling for what it's about. Think of the questions that arise.

- "What kind of scene is this anyway?"
- "What's my role here?"
- "What do I say or not say to her?"
- "Is this a situation for offering advice, for giving him words of encouragement, or for correcting his error?"

Answering such questions may require more than a second or two. **Being aware of the nature of a situation and its requirements is a mark of communicative sophistication.** Consider the situational misjudgments behind statements like "Now I see what you meant about company 'rules' on office parties" and "Oh, didn't you know that we were expected to bring a money gift to the bar mitzvah?"

Variables

Attention and perception are among the chief variables in situation awareness.

Attention. Freedom from self-concern is an issue in attention. The communicator who is insufficiently free of absorption with personal needs or status is not ready to make adequate judgment of situational conditions.

Perception. To be perceptive is to note specific features of situations that may suggest modification of communicative behavior, e.g., through choice of appropriate role. It's to be "heads up" on opportunities, rules, and other situational constraints—for the sake of success in communication.

Narcissistic Reality

Observance of social conventions, e.g., situational rules, can be a real test of maturity. Yet good communication often requires just that. **Often there are times when social conformity has more communicative value than unmodified individuality.**

But one may say, "I've grown away from following rules; I'm my own person now, doing it my way." In general terms, there may be nothing wrong with that kind of individuality, except when success in communication depends on accommodating individual audience needs and finding *common* satisfaction.

Success in communication often hinges on subordinating narcissistic gratification and showing respect for customs, conventions, cultural factors, or other situational constraints. Of course! Effectiveness and mutual satisfaction require our observing variety among situations and perceiving specific differences. Thus situational awareness is a significant part of a Communicative Disposition.

4. Inventional Strength

Communicators are inventors whose chief function is to invent content and strategy in their interactions. To invent is to decide on issues and put a message together: a message of enthymemes, stories, backup evidence, feelings, reasoning, and beliefs. In making these decisions on messages, the communicator is influenced by personal ideological structures and narcissistic factors. Reflections of the self are very important elements of message content, for they affect reception. For example, a sender's persona and roles figure prominently in the receiver's response, as we'll see later.

Some of us who study communication and human development try to trace origins of communicators' patterns of invention back to ideological foundations, particularly to family and the cultural influences of infancy. In so doing, we discover certain tendencies and occasionally a potent hypothesis, e.g.: **Out of both advantage and adversity come predispositions of the self that influence inventional strategy.** All kinds of early experience affect future choices in communicating. Have you heard this expression of Alexander Pope, "Just as the twig is bent, the tree's inclined"?

Variables

Among the chief variables in invention are exploratory mentality, objectivity, safety, and judgment.

Exploratory mentality. This variable relates to a communicator's level of will and energy in investigation, curiosity, inquisitiveness, and imagination.

Objectivity. As the state of relative freedom from self-interest, this inventional variable relates to power in independent thinking and degrees of impersonal decision-making.

Safety. Here it is again, often the weightiest and most prevalent variable of all. Personal safety needs guide us in deciding on message content. But consider the other side of the topic: courage in communication. As it applies to invention, courage refers to an individual's risking personal reputation or popularity in constructing a message. When communicators "go against the grain" of audiences' values and beliefs, they risk rejection of their messages and disconfirmation. Recall John F. Kennedy's book, *Profiles in Courage,* about human beings who dared to speak out—bravely inventing messages that were threats to others.

Judgment. This final variable is related to perception, but more specifically it refers to discrimination among materials that are available as content for a message: Some material is appropriate and promising in communication; some is not. It's a matter of rhetorical judgment.

Narcissistic Reality

In growth, we open ourselves to mental exploration: We discover and store information, ideas, explanations, and positions on issues. When dissatisfied or uneasy with existing states or conditions—social and personal—we sense exigencies (conditions that prompt communicative activity). In response, we invent messages for others. **Thus does an unacceptable condition, troublesome or perhaps menacing, inspire invention of message content and communication.** Rhetorical energy and a creative and imaginative spirit for discovery of material are important in communication.

Again, we do know that insecurity can instigate courageous communicative activity: e.g., when a person, fearful but not disabled by fear, is motivated by personal need to take action and perform well. In some such cases, the spur to taking a chance is tied to a questioning of self-worth. The courage of Winston Churchill, great leader of World War II, is an example. It's been suggested that his heroic deeds were integral to his self-maintenance strategies, that they arose from relevant narcissistic sources (from a need to prove himself).[3]

Good judgment may reflect a person's independent attitude and unique powers of reflection. Even though related to narcissistic need, such a rational perspective is valuable in constructing messages in given situations, especially when dispassion and detachment seem to be fitting.

Why does judgment belong in this discussion of narcissism in communication? Because in communication, judgment is not entirely separable from emotion and self-protective activity. But can invention, affected by the power of narcissism, yield productive enthymemes (fruitful lines of thinking)? Can good communication result? Yes to both questions. Take the case of a normal self-occupied person, who in conversation or public speech hazards a radical or avant-garde idea and stirs audience imagination. Even if the communicator's individualistic pattern of logic and perhaps unorthodox proposal are unconvincing at the outset, they may open up an inquiry and useful debate. In communication, there are times to appreciate another's peculiar narcissism in ideology, even when it arises from unique needs of self.

Here is another illustration. Consider those university professors whose narcissism spurs the research that yields material for their scholarly writing and lecturing. Their personal judgments and self-concepts are bound up with their findings. Though Historian X carefully checks his evidence and brings to bear his commendable powers of reasoning, you can be sure that his style of writing and speaking, reflecting the self that he brings to tasks of communication, will influence his audiences. For the same reason (and others), you can be sure that his conclusions will be questioned by other historians. Partly that's because the "truth" of any historical event is impossible to determine and any one historian's interpretation will never be agreed upon by all others. But it's also a result of the way Historian X grew up. And to meet his biases and subjectivity, his teachers saw to it that he was academically well-trained, yet he will always see things as affected by *earlier* training as well: the socialization provided by long experience with his father, mother, and all those others—not to mention vast cultural, religious, political, and educational experience.

His particular background, with all the early advantage as well as adversity, sparks his work, enriches him professionally, and contributes to his reputation as a scholar. And, of course, it contributes to his personal narcissistic nature, helping in self-maintenance. But while supplying vigor, his narcissism is also one of the forces that prevents him from being perfect. He's very human and imperfect, yet he writes good history. Why? Because success is attributable to how the self feels as well as how the mind thinks. To account for the enthymemes of historians (and the rest of us), we must know of human narcissism, particularly as it relates to strategies for maintaining the self in communication.

5. Sense of Personal Power

Social strength and communicative effectiveness are inextricably linked; the consequence of that connection is a gratifying sense of personal power. To feel influential among others is one of the most satisfying human experiences. Thus we recognize the importance of personal potency: as shown, for example, in confidence, good humor, and interpersonal ease.

Variables

Among the principal variables here are self-knowledge, safety, and self-acceptance.

Self-Knowledge. "Know thyself," said the ancient oracle. Put that thought together with Francis Bacon's "Knowledge is power," and we can assert something profound: to know oneself is to be powerful. Certainly that's true in relating to others; self-knowledge is one of the most valuable kinds of wisdom available. The person who is well-acquainted with personal sources of strengths and weaknesses, traits, goals, and various attributes has a base for functioning self-assuredly with others. **With self-understanding, we have a sound foundation for development of good feelings about ourselves and our communicative strengths.**

Safety and Self-Acceptance. Two other variables, safety and self-acceptance, can be taken together here. Indeed, they can't be separated from self-knowledge. A feeling of comfort and well-being in interpersonal interaction—derived in part from knowing oneself—provides the confidence necessary to communicate satisfyingly. From that, come self-respect and a sense of personal worth, dignity, and power.

Narcissistic Reality

It's a hopeful sign when a person who's ill at ease with himself or herself finds that lack unacceptable and takes corrective steps. Awareness and action, inspired by dissatisfaction and hope for personal growth, can result in good choices in communications. Thus does felt deficiency motivate for effectiveness. The same kind of positive response is possible when the motivation is insecurity or a feeling of diminished self-respect. Needing to meet conditions as they exist, we act from self-interest. And if the action also contributes to communicative goals of the others involved, it's good. **Vigor in self-maintenance comes from awareness of shortcomings, and it can serve important interpersonal purposes.**

6. Acceptance of Oneself as Communicative Strategist

This final key to a Communicative Disposition may seem to overlap with others above. But here I'm stressing *acceptance* of the role of strategist. We *are* strategists.[4] This is not a reference to manipulation, not in the negative sense. What I mean is that we exercise choice regarding what to say and how to say it; we make decisions about what will work with others. We must! And when effective, we're able to influence others to respond. Remember that we have *options* in our message-sending, and only the foolish or incapacitated will operate against their own self-interest. One significant indicator of social growth is acceptance of our role as communicative strategists.

Variables

There are two significant variables in acceptance of the role of strategist: cognizance and maturity.

Cognizance. Cognizance here means awareness of a reality in human behavior: **Whether we consider it nice or not (which it sometimes isn't), people relate to each other strategically.** Furthermore, at times they'll say things to one person that are different from those said to a second person—and be moral persons nonetheless. Effectiveness and consideration for others call for adaptability, in both content and strategy. In this regard let me tell you about a dear friend of mine, probably the most uncalculating, straightforward, sincere, moral person I know. If you asked her whether she adapts to different audiences, she'd very likely say no. And yet, by listening to her talk on the telephone, I can almost always tell which of five or six family members she's addressing. Without conscious intent, she tailors her remarks, using certain thought patterns for one person and other patterns for another. Her topics change with receiver, as do vocal intonations, kinds of laughter or chuckles, and so forth. She's a rhetorical strategist. And so are the rest of us—or at least we'd better be!

Maturity. In our social sophistication, we learn that humans must be pliant in communication. To ignore the virtue of adaptability is to hold that people move from communication to communication innocently: without purpose, interest in outcome, or a sense of responsibility for their actions; without need to influence events, oblivious to receivers' characteristics. Are we that innocent (and foolish)? No, we are not. We are rhetorical creatures, communicative and practical people with goals of our own. **Much of our success in communication comes from our power to adapt in pursuing our goals.**

Narcissistic Reality

To accept and welcome the basic role of communicative choice-maker is to accept a very large part of our selves—not to mention the vital function of that big role. To be sure, we all lost our rhetorical innocence by age two, probably earlier. After all, we started learning how to be effective with others before we were ten months of age, when we began to act with intention. Given our uncertain status in infancy, in that bewildering environment, we needed to invent means of being effective. From good and bad influences of socialization, sometimes by hook or crook, we did what was required to take care of ourselves, and we've been doing it constantly ever since. Over time, we refined our maintenance strategies and established them as fixtures in our communicative repertoires. They work, and we keep using them. Some don't work, but we may keep using them anyway, a subject that we'll look into when discussing maladaptive self-support.

Making Our Way

One's Communicative Disposition is built in part from favorable narcissism, a sense of self that helps with success in communication. As we found in Chapter Two, foundations of character and behavior are set down in infancy, and a vital part of the infant's growth is acquisition of a kind of strength that outfits him or her to become an effective communicator. Like all positive attributes, a Communicative Disposition results in large measure from optimal frustration and positive responses to the distresses of infancy.[5] The shapes and expressions of the self-maintenance strategies that develop are a significant part of each individual's personal entity called *self*.

Elements of a person's patterns of self-care can intrude upon communication and be major distractions, or they can contribute importantly to a Communicative Disposition. A prime contribution lies in the critical area of motivation. **Knowing that communication is related to just about every one of life's involvements, we ought to value no resource more than a Communicative Disposition and understand its connection to maintaining the self.**

In laying out these six keys in a broad fashion, I recognize that specific features of communicative effectiveness will vary from person to person. In fact, we might go so far as to say that one person's liability can be another's strength; her social insecurity may be a help, while his may be a hindrance. Certain forms of protective activity can turn out to be creative and useful, while others will be disabling. In discussing human behavior, we must always be mindful of purposes, individual exceptions, and situational variations.

Further, complete satisfaction is never achieved in communication. It's just not in the cards. **We're only relatively successful in communication**. There's no way to be completely attuned with another. Some of my favorite enthymemes will not work fully for you. Regardless of our varying choices in enthymemes, all you or I can expect is *partial* return—or some *degree* of success. Think about that. What does 100% success mean to us anyway? Who is the communicator whose success record is at the top—or anywhere near it—on *any* scale of measurement? Such a person cannot be found; in the interest of accuracy and fairness to ourselves and all others, we've got to accept our imperfectly interactive selves and make our way from there.

FACILITATIVE SELF-MAINTENANCE IN COMMUNICATION

Before going on, we need a reminder of the theory on relating to audiences. A brief review will be sufficient here, since we covered most of it in Chapter One. To show benefits of maintenance strategies, I'll include a useful narcissistic dimension in explaining each element.

Sending and Receiving

The work of senders and receivers is to encode and decode messages: saying things, reading feedback, and adapting.

But how can you tell when a communicative transaction is going right? A good sign is when the sender and receiver, intent on coming to an understanding as talkers and listeners, are able to overcome "noise" in the circuits and reach mutual satisfaction. "Noise," remember, is any intruding distraction—physical, psychological, religious, cultural, political, and so forth.

As communicators, we have a coping self that enables us to

meet conditions as we find them. This is a "public self," what others see in action: the *persona,* the sending and receiving part that's out there, appearing and being effective in various situations. And in any exchange, people disclose basic marks of their sending and receiving personas, including acquired self-maintenance strategies.

Sending and Receiving: A Useful Narcissistic Dimension

A prime reason for the effectiveness of senders and receivers is that they *want* to communicate. Why? Because they don't want to be apart from each other. To be apart is to be alone and to be alone is to be without a source of assurance and confirmation. Thus, an all-important functional dimension lies in the *need* for rhetorical identification: People are motivated to send and receive messages because they need to be with others—to be secure with others. Probably you can think of specific exceptions. But go this far: We suffer some measure of insecurity when kept apart from responding others. **In communication, we strive to repair the breach.** Accepting that, you know much about who we are as senders and receivers in communication: creatures seeking the comfort of acknowledgment and affirmation.

Exigence

An exigence is what kicks off communication, prompting the sending and receiving. A person decides that a statement or condition is *exigent.* That is, it must be answered; something must be said. So that person decides to be a sender, creating a specific message designed to meet that felt requirement. Now, what I as a sender may perceive as an exigence, you may not. Let's say that I feel it necessary to call Diane to tell her that she embarrassed me last night. But you may say, "Why waste your time telephoning her about that?" **Different exigencies for different folks.**

Perceiving an Exigence: A Useful Narcissistic Dimension

"Why waste time telephoning Diane?" you ask. "Listen," I respond emotionally, "If you want to know why, I'll tell you; it's because she has to know how I feel, for the sake of the relationship." I'm defending myself, as you can see, but in coming to that defensive stand, I may be seeing things right, seeing that corrective communication is indeed needed. This is how defensiveness can be useful and my move constructive. Can you think of a recent experience of your constructive defending from such an exigence?

Roles

Elements of everyone's identity show up in roles assumed for self-maintenance. Since people are constantly taking on roles in their communicating together, one way to grasp others' meaning is to understand their roles. **We are as seen in our invention of communicative roles**. The role data perceived by a receiver will influence the outcome of an interaction. Thus, identity has a necessary place in communication, a perspective that will help us to understand narcissistic phenomena and appreciate the function of roles.

It's likely that just about every message we formulate in response to an exigence can be analyzed for the role or roles that convey it. "What's Rob's purpose?" asks Leroy. "He's sounding a lot like a *financial adviser* to me," replies Anne; "Maybe he wants to recommend an investment." In naming Rob's role as financial adviser, Anne grasped what she heard to be his message.

If it's your job to orient new employees where you work, you may find yourself doing a lot of coaching. In fact, you may be the *coach* in numerous other scenes as well: for example, when you help a friend who isn't sure how to approach someone he'd like to meet.

Assuming Roles: A Useful Narcissistic Dimension

Wanting to coach your friend, you say, "Look, I know something about approaching a person. Let me give you a couple of tips that I've found helpful." Obviously, you the coach don't operate without personal motivation in this instance. Agreed? You have expertise to offer. And more than wanting to be of assistance, you *need* to get some kind of credit, if only a feeling of worth as a helper. Carrying out the role—whether called "coach" or "helper"—will provide satisfaction for you. To feel good is to have increased self-esteem. You'll feel stronger for having served your friend. People like to assume roles that are satisfying and self-justifying. This is one way that narcissistic needs are useful in communication.

The Enthymeme

Using Aristotle's enthymeme, we can get an inside view of the transactional process of communication, realizing how people make it happen together. We all carry around bundles of premises—premises of our ideological storehouse, as marked by our self-concept. They are called lessons or principles or values, and we use them to decide things and build messages to send to others. They supply premises of enthymemes that we operate by in our communicating. **People with whom you communicate see the operating premises of your enthymemes as reflections of your personal outlook and ideology.** Use this idea when observing two people in conversation, a man and a woman perhaps. Look closely for her major premise as she attempts to convince him to join the physical fitness club. What is her premise? Is it one that seems to highlight values of having an attractive body? Good health? Long life? When you locate that operating premise, you'll know what particular interests and values dominate her message. Indicators are always there, though they may not be stated explicitly.

Also, you can find at least one major premise of an enthymeme behind each assumed role. It's what our persona, our public communicating self, stands for, feels, or believes in, as seen in interactions with others. When I can understand your premise or you can understand mine, we're able to communicate from that base. This model of the enthymeme helps us to appreciate communication as a cooperative process. For example, communicators who discover shared values about treatment of animals can proceed from there, talking together about a specific case.

Building Enthymemes: A Useful Narcissistic Dimension

In the interest of coming to agreement with one another, communicators may be inclined to brush aside real points of disagreement. It may be that they want to show good intentions. That's fine, but not for every occasion. A hasty sharing of premises is not always desirable. Conflict—as functional self-support—can be useful in furthering a genuine exploration of issues. When our premises are in conflict, I should be able to find civil ways to defend mine, and I should expect the same from you. Only rarely would it be advisable for us to gloss over differences. Arguments have value: as, when for the good of the relationship, I insist that my position be heard.

Indeed, such an act of self-interest may be the only way to reach mutual interest. Such clearing of the ground with conflict can eventually lead to the cooperative building of a firmer enthymeme and a more solid base of understanding. Also, confidently standing up for oneself may enhance credibility and add to self-esteem. But, as we'll see in the last chapter, the quality of communication depends on why and how we do it.

Identification

The ultimate in communication is identification or attunement. For to identify with others is to reach and affect them, finding kinship in background, purpose, philosophic outlook, or specific areas of interest. The result of the process of identification is cohesion with one's audience.

Identifying: A Useful Narcissistic Dimension

As is clear at this point, even a message of self-interest may be attractive to a receiver and effective. **Strategic efforts of the self-involved, self-maintaining communicator can serve to bring about identification of sender and receiver**. But only if the communicators are rhetorically observant. Take defending, as an example. Psychologist Guy E. Swanson discovered that "a successful defense will be one that a participant . . . will find consistent with standards to which all parties can refer. The defense cannot be arbitrary."[6] Since identification of sender and receiver is the issue, standards of mutual acceptability must be discovered.

But should identification be the goal of *all* communication? No. While it seems almost sacrilegious to suggest benefits of resisting identification, some exigencies may call for just that, to protect oneself. If being responsive to someone's message would not be good for you, your sense of self-respect may insist on your choosing to keep your distance—not offering a cooperative persona. **Your capacity to resist a linking of your self with another self may be critical.** For instance, when a person wants to talk you into something that would conflict sharply with your ideas on fairness or sense of dignity, you may anticipate not being able to live with yourself if you were to agree. Though a "no" message tends to disconnect the selves of communicators, it's the right message at times. Such rejection of the other's perception of an exigence—showing no interest in communicating cooperatively on that topic as set up by another—may be a better course of action.

Another example of healthful resistance to an invitation to identify is seen in the case of a father lecturing an adult daughter as if she were a child, perhaps in giving her unwanted advice on spending her money. How should a mature, self-esteeming daughter handle a parent's talking down to her? Of course, her words will be her own, but the quality of her response should be something like this: "Father, I'm a big girl now, and only my adult persona is available to communicate with you."

One more example of questionable identification is so-called "identification with the aggressor." In this instance, one seeks the security of identification with a powerful person or group. We see it in gang membership and adherence to antisocial models. True, such identification as a self-supportive strategy may be tempting and it may suggest obvious advantages, especially in the short term. But one drawback is that it constitutes a withdrawal from communication with diverse others, particularly those who could contribute to one's good growth.

COMMUNICATIVE RANGES: FROM EFFECTIVENESS TO DYSFUNCTION

With the framework of a Communicative Disposition and relevant communication theory as background data, let's go now to the field of action: to making choices—good and bad—to maintain the self in communication. As we know, situations vary from promising to doubtful to disastrous; some purposes are worthy; some are misguided. Some strategies work to influence the outcome favorably; some backfire. Those are facts of life. **Communication is uncertain. That's why we're careful—ready with safeguards—as we put our vulnerable selves into the presence of other selves.**

There are also the paradoxes. For instance, a certain strategy, while seeming questionable or even silly, may serve adequately in achieving attunement with others. Even if you don't believe in the existence of rhetorical "mystery," at least you'll have to admit that workings of some interpersonal phenomena are well-nigh unexplainable. Most phantom forces in communication are due to peculiarities of time, place, situation, and the people involved. Given the complexity of elements, we can never have a full answer to why any interaction happened as it did.

But we do know that we act with practical purpose, using what we have available to reach others with our role-playing and enthymemes. It's rhetorical value by which we judge the usefulness of self-maintenance strategies, and predicting audience response is a constant aim in communication.

The *Topoi*

Recall that *topoi* are groups of strategies from which people invent specific communicative approaches in given situations. As conceptions for action, they are basic to choice-making in communication: when people with aims and messages act purposefully upon others and are acted upon by others. The *topoi* offer options in communication, in accord with immediate purpose, audience makeup, and dictates of personal ideology, including self-concept. The strategic groups are *Control,*

Achievement, Opposition, Attribution, Anger, Denial, Withdrawal, and *Prevarication.*

One way to illustrate strategies in communication is to contrast facilitative and maladaptive role choices, showing self-maintenance ranges. I'll do that throughout this explanation of the eight *topoi,* occasionally explaining by referring to processes of communication: to sending and receiving messages, perception of exigencies, assumption of roles, construction of enthymemes, and creation of identification.

1. *Control*

Behavioral Range: **from ordinary effort to be effective in communication to intense regulating**

In communication, it's smart to do some controlling: for example, in public speaking, we need to organize the speech appropriately with an introduction, main purpose, body, and conclusion. Look closely at successful people in their work. Note that they're in control—in the best meaning of the word. In setting up an important appointment, they'll make plans on when and where to conduct it. One of Janet's useful attributes is her gift for beneficial regulation; she values order. It makes sense for communicators to seek strategies that will give them some power over events and be effective. One can observe the effects of *Control* in all communication, from the most formal public address to friendly conversation. It takes a certain amount of management to accomplish any task, including communication.

But inflexibly attempting to dominate an interaction or imposing rigid controls is extreme; inventing communicative strategies for total regulation is of questionable value.

Enthymematic Patterns

For *Control,* here are representative major premises of sample enthymemes; some definitely show promise of success in communication, while the fate of others may depend on conditions.

- In preparation for oral presentations, it's smart to make an outline, written or mental.

- A very clear purpose is needed for oral presentations.
- Being in control of an interview helps to avoid embarrassing surprises.
- Knowing others' names and backgrounds helps to avoid shame and problems in communication.
- Those who count on co-workers to do it right, ask for disaster.
- Before presenting your idea to the board, line up the support of members.
- A leaderless group will accomplish nothing.

Facilitative Roles

Many functional roles are available from the *topos* of *Control*, and communicators invent them as exigencies arise. Knowledge of conditions and the people involved will suggest which roles might be appropriate at a given moment. Needless to say, in many situations role choices are made quickly—often almost automatically, or so it seems. Among standard roles of facilitative *Control* in communication are *supervisor, leader, mediator, chairperson, guide, ambassador, teacher, police officer, governor, planner,* and *parent.* Evidence of assumed roles may be seen in the communicator's enthymemes. Consider the example of a friend who says, "You know, if I were you, I wouldn't loan $500 to a person who's already deep in debt." That's an enthymeme, a line of reasoning based on the unstated major premise that a person in debt cannot be relied on to pay back loans faithfully. Also, a role is reflected in the enthymeme. What is it? Of course, there can be different answers for that question. You may see the role as *guide*, or possibly *adviser.* What about *cautioner*? Let's take the role of *cautioner*, and to show meaning and substance, give the role a real title. What about "Safety Director" or "Father Figure"? What are some other fitting titles? Giving names to roles will increase understanding of communicative interaction.

Maladaptive Roles

The discussion so far has shown that effective sending and

receiving in communication can be viewed in terms of enthymemes and roles of self-maintenance. Now, the same theory can be applied to ill-advised enthymemes and maladaptive roles in communication. Below are examples of roles from the *topos* of *Control* that seem to have a negative force. Each has a *hard* look.

Big Regulator	Lone Pillar
Strong and Silent	Despotic Invalid
Top Boss	Slave Driver
Dictator	Victim
Individualist	Manipulator

Perhaps you can add names to the list.

You can imagine the kinds of maladaptive enthymemes that these role-players invent and try to impose on others. When recently have you observed one of these roles tried in communicative practice? Name an instance. What was the situation? Who said what to whom? What did the respective participants seek to accomplish? (Each of them had a purpose, at least one, and each was motivated toward self-maintenance, to care for the self.) What was the outcome?

All of the ten role choices listed above suggest real communicative limitations. They give indication of drawbacks, revealing postures or attitudes that don't seem to give senders and receivers much chance of identifying with one another. The list radiates inclinations like rigidity, solitariness, imperiousness, manipulativeness, self-pity, and superiority—all potentially adverse regulative influences. None seems to be a condition of strength in furthering a meeting of minds with others.

Now why would anyone who is dedicated to self-maintenance—and wants to be effective—take on one of these roles? Because from narcissistic uncertainty, the sender has become convinced that success depends on tight regulation of all elements, including audience behavior. **To be a hard controller in communication is to be without a proper appreciation of**

the sender-receiver relationship. Genuine audience respect and mutual satisfaction will not come out of that.

Behind each hard strategy, as noted above, is a feeling of insecurity. The more unsure communicators are about their personal status, the greater their self-maintenance need. The depth of their fear explains their desperate adoption of a doomed role, and that forecasts problems in communication. Preoccupation with personal status detracts from listening and responding effectively. All too frequent results are unsteady relationships, an absence of real intimacy and love, and alienation from co-workers and others. To loosen up or "mellow out" with audiences—necessarily making the self vulnerable—is to lose power, or so the players of hard controlling roles feel.

Here's one more disadvantage to hard forms of the *topos* of *Control.* Ordinarily, only subservient or immature receivers will identify with determined controllers. **Self-esteeming persons are unlikely to "buy into" arbitrary or exploitative enthymemes.** Communicative limitations suggested by maladaptation in *Control* are obvious; its strategies can be very destructive. Often what is called "poor communication" is actually self-maintenance communication that backfires. An ill-conceived choice in *Control* may be the problem.

2. *Achievement*

Behavioral Range: **from ordinary effort toward adequacy in accomplishment to incessant striving for perfection**

When inclined to sustain the self through accomplishment, we communicate either at a balanced and reasonable level or at an exacting and unrealistic level, e.g., in vehement preoccupation. Is his competitiveness healthful or overly intense, you might ask about another? Does she always need to be the winner and the supreme best every time? Is she unchallengeable? And so forth. Attitudes on the advantageous end of the scale are obvious: They contribute to solid accomplishments.

Achievers are active people. Conscientious achievers are highly motivated, able to get the communicative work done, and sometimes creatively. Janet, our familiar case, exemplifies this narcissistic predisposition. To achieve as a communicator is to act with purpose and to be mindful of the need to adapt to others—to meet their peculiarities, backgrounds, and immediate feelings or attitudes. Communicating effectively is one of the accomplishments of such achievers.

We all know people who have an ideology of *Achievement* at the heart of their self-concepts, and thus at the heart of their lives. They do accomplish. But there's a downside: Inability to live up to their self-structured ideal can lead to hindersome shame. In the extreme, they function well only as achievers, and without constant activity to accomplish and meet goals, they would be deprived of identity and lost. Literally, their roles of *Achievement* sustain them through thick and thin. This is how they carry on from day to day, in single-minded dedication to accomplishment.

Enthymematic Patterns

For *Achievement*, here are some representative major premises of sample enthymemes; some will prove useful under good conditions and others unreliable:

- If a job's worth doing, it's worth doing faultlessly.
- To accomplish is to gain self-respect.
- Time-wasting is a vice (or time is money).
- Show no faults, have no shame.
- Competition is personally rewarding.
- Being acknowledged as kind is gratifying.
- To be seen as a superb communicator is good.

Facilitative Roles

Communicative strategies drawn from the *topos* of *Achievement* reflect the persona of the ambitious, performance-oriented, hard-working individual. This individual holds a positive view of the work ethic and competition. He or she sets goals and is motivated to do a good job—in a timely, responsible manner. Tom, the ready student, may be an example.

Some of the strategic roles reflected in facilitative messages of the achiever are *doer, builder, performer, loyalist, scorer, supporter,* and *originator.* Adding texture to certain of these general roles, we might come up with names like "Prime Mover,"

"Ace," "Winner," and "Star." Another one, sometimes with a less than desirable connotation, is "Workaholic." In her own way, Janet, the company manager, assumes roles like some of these.

Maladaptive Roles

In the extreme, behavior in *Achievement* is commonly called "perfectionism." Persons so inclined may be considered obsessive or driven. Their self-maintenance strategies can be self-defeating.

An example is the student who broke down in my office after learning that she had received an A- on her term paper. "I cannot accept that put-down," she pleaded from the depth of her soul. Then she burst into tears. In our discussion of the problem, she told of difficulties in relationships, particularly in regard to her total inability to understand people who had a casual or indifferent attitude toward duties and accomplishment. She said that some people considered her "overly grim" and "preoccupied with work." Always conscious of the quality of her behavior—always "under the gun" of her self-concept as achiever, and unyielding in her resolve to perform admirably, she could not free herself for enjoyable give-and-take with others. She was not disposed to risk the less rigid kind of behavior needed to communicate well with others.

Below are examples of roles carrying *hard* self-sustaining content from the *topos* of *Achievement.* They show detrimental ideology and counterproductive potential for many communicative situations.

Holier-than-Thou	The Fairest of Them All
King of the Mountain	Elitist
Polly Perfect	Best Man
Martyr	Company Slave
Performing Bear	Grindstone

Perhaps you can add to the list of maladaptive roles. Have you recently observed any one of these in communicative practice? If so, what were the situations? Who said what to whom? What did the respective participants seek to accomplish? How did goals of self-maintenance affect communication? What was the outcome?

One of the communicative limitations suggested by the above list of ten unfavorable roles in the *topos* of *Achievement* is the obvious separation from audience: with the role player "miles apart" from others and disinclined to take steps to reduce the distance. Along with the factor of distance may be an air of superiority, suggesting insecurity as a major influence on the person's behavior. These and other conditions of self-absorption constitute one of the toughest obstacles to effective communication that you'll find. To communicate, participants must invest in each other, giving up excessive self-absorption. Weak, perfunctory expressions or token gestures don't promise much return. What's needed is an interactive spirit and rhetorical generosity, a real giving of self. When narcissistically isolated, we cannot cooperate with audiences in building enthymemes and bringing about identification.

To assume perfection is to have no peers, no basis for discovery of *kindred* spirit. Meaningful exchanges and lasting relationships cannot be formed from appearances alone or from one-sided postures of rightness or propriety. Communication is built from a willing sharing of personal substance, the common stuff of self that is possessed by caring people.

3. *Opposition*

Behavioral Range: **from useful counteraction to contemptuous challenge**

If or when inclined to defend through *Opposition*, we assume the attitude of dissenter or objector. We may be possessed of antagonism or disdain toward the other person or position. Our messages range from rational disagreement or confrontation to bitter condemnation. Resistance and rebuttal, antipathy, dislike, and sundry innocuous or uncomplimentary oppositional messages are frequently expressed in ordinary interaction. Of course, the *topos* of *Opposition* has its uses in communication: to meet those occasions calling for a counteractive message, for debate or protest. There may be times when an act of opposing may be the only way to awaken another from indifference or apathy. Then, there's the useful role of "Loyal Opposition." Valuable in a community is the person willing to represent alternate views. As a teaching friend used to say, "The good professor is the one who presents the other side."

Enthymematic Patterns

From the *topos* of *Opposition*, here are some representative major premises of sample enthymemes: some good, others questionable.

- To be adversarial is to be honest.
- Others must know when you disagree.
- A show of contemptuousness will keep contemptuous people away.
- One way to get respect is through dissent.
- Communicating defiantly reduces shame.
- Show disgust when harassed, or they'll keep doing it.
- Few are the proposals that won't benefit from criticism.
- Make a challenge, to bring out all issues.
- If you want to save face, don't go along with anybody.

Facilitative Roles

I think communicators choose strategies from the *topos* of *Opposition* more than one would expect, and many expedient roles are available. Among roles of facilitative *Opposition* are *plain-speaker, judge, chastiser, blunt instrument, confronter, refuser,* and *blocker.* To add glitter to roles of Opposition, we have such as these: "Devil's Advocate," "Ready Refuter," "Frank and Ernest," "Candid One," "Scale Balancer" and "Reliable Objector." Perhaps Janet should cultivate one of these roles and break out now and again with *plain-speaker* or "Candid One."

Maladaptive Roles

While dissent or disapproval may be just what's needed in

given communicative interactions, one can go too far. Behaviors like stiffness, recalcitrance, arrogance, scorn, and impudence are less often useful. When chosen roles drive wedges between senders and receivers, it's practically impossible to promote cooperation in structuring enthymemes and bring about attunement. Remember Dennis, the man who couldn't get along with people and who was fired from the third job he'd held in a year? He seemed bent on choosing misguided roles of opposition.

Maladaptive roles are those that put noise into the circuits of communication. Reflecting negative perceptions of self and others, they work against positive purposes in most interpersonal interaction. Some of the roles played from the *topos* of *Opposition* which may prove to be maladaptive are

Obstructor	No-sayer
Just B. Different	Deaf Ear
Wrangler	Repudiator
Ms. Negativity	Lampooner
Noncooperator	Combatant

Perhaps you can add to the list of maladaptive roles. Have you recently observed any one of these in communicative practice? If so, what was the situation? Who said what to whom? What did the respective participants seek to accomplish? What was the outcome?

Again, we are discussing obvious maladaptation and communicative noise. With their obtrusive content, the roles listed above often serve to exacerbate the conditions that divide people. Incorporating problematic self-maintenance strategy, they introduce disturbance and disruption into an interaction.

Before moving on, I should mention certain borderline strategies: for instance, *Opposition* through chutzpa, cheek, brassiness, and gall. These are perceived by some receivers as effrontery or insolence, but in some situations, they serve good purposes: for example, when a brash expression of honest opposition—perhaps combined with humor—will do some good. Of course, circumstances and exigencies vary. **Rhetorical good sense is the key to success in communication.**

4. *Attribution*

Behavioral Range: **from determining origins of conditions to emphatic blaming**

Attribution for self-maintenance takes us to goals of tracing responsibility, making judgments on cause or error, fixing culpability, "getting to the bottom of things," and crediting and discrediting performance. There are occasions that call for strategies to get at the root of circumstances, and narcissistic energy can contribute to this end. A strategy from *Attribution* in any given instance may be focused on others or oneself. The communication may be marked by goodwill or unmistakable enmity. As with all of the *topoi*, the communicator's act has a protective dimension, a fact that may not be immediately evident.

Enthymematic Patterns

For the *topos* of *Attribution*, here are some representative major premises of sample enthymemes.

- Determination of efficiency is basic to effective functioning in any organization.
- No one should escape accountability.
- It's important to know the causes of things.
- When fault is fixed, others are protected from shame.
- No one is free of responsibility in this life.
- If you make a mistake, accept the fact.
- Self-delusion about beginnings of conditions is not healthful.
- A sincere apology helps everyone.

Facilitative Roles

A number of functional roles may be invented from the *topos* of *Attribution.* A communicator may find an exigence for *Attribution* (an occasion for speaking up) when a friend attempts to blame her brother for her own mistake, a child refuses to admit participation in a bit of mischief, a person believes that justice or fairness will be served by censuring another's action, a subordinate misunderstands guidelines on the sharing of duties in the department, or when he himself makes an error. To improve the workplace, an administrator or group may need to determine responsibility for a slowdown in output. Some of the values motivating choices in *Attribution* are justice, honesty, profit, progress, and fair play.

Think back to the self-maintaining response of Tom, the college student who didn't have the answer to the professor's question. He acknowledged his lapse with self-respect and took responsibility gracefully. His role as willing self-corrector was functional.

I used to wonder why "locals" in places where it snows a lot are so quick to refer to newcomers or out-of-towners as bad winter drivers: "Look at 'em, bangin' into trees and cars; people from down in the valley aren't used to driving on our ice up here." I've heard that kind of statement many times, often made without any knowledge of the driver's experience—or residence. There are people who *have to say it.* But why blame non-locals? And why free locals from blame? Why do we judge nonmembers to be incompetent? One explanation is that such condemnation is a ritual to provide social cohesion: It's acknowledgment of "who we are together up here in the mountains": identification of "us locals" as sensible and hardy folk who are to be distinguished from the uninitiated. It's defensive, and it gives community members a mark of common identity.

Attribution roles that could be facilitative are *ascriber, accountant, apologizer, parent, reformer, certifier, justice-seeker,* and *credit decider.* In the ancient Roman republic, a prominent person was chosen to be the Censor, one of whose jobs was to keep watch on the behavior of citizens. The most famous was the elder Cato who became known as Cato the Censor. *Attribution* was one of his chief *topoi*; he drew from it many times and often was challenged in court because of his attributions. Our society too has watchkeepers. You've heard about "Whistleblowers." Other watchful communicators could be given names like "Monitor," "Pinpointer," "The Tracer," "Faultfinder"—and "Roman Censor." In this culture, I'm sure that not all of those are facilitative—not all the time. But *Attribution* can be of value in given scenes of interpersonal activity—for example, when for the sake of a relationship or other good cause, people need to be reminded of the effect of their participation. **Attribution qualifies for use in self-maintenance.**

Maladaptive Roles

Why is it easier to discuss the negative side of this *topos*? It may be because blaming is often considered entirely avoidable. But whatever the maintenance value of *Attribution*, communicators must to be very careful in handling it. The reasons are obvious. Remember, too, that *Attribution* is not always an interpersonal activity. The interaction may be in*tra*personal, with self-blame the strategy. Dennis, one of our recurring examples, was very hard on himself. Although he excoriated others, including his co-workers and girlfriend, he himself was often his target. He knew the role of "Self-blamer."

The point to remember here is that hard narcissism does motivate maladaptive blaming. The following list of strategically assumed roles illustrates that.

Prosecuting Attorney	Persecutor
Stonecaster	Castigator
Nitpicker	Exposer
Scapegoater	Damn Me
Guilt Builder	Finger Pointer

Perhaps you can add to this list of maladaptive roles. Have you recently observed any one of them? If so, what was the situation? Who said what to whom? What did the respective participants seek to accomplish? What was the outcome?

Those with an interest in "winning friends and influencing people" are prudent in choosing the *topos* of *Attribution* from which self-maintaining invention often backfires. Some communicators who invent from this source are clearly more occupied by feelings of personal deficiency than by the art of making connections with receivers and working up enthymemes with them. That is, they're unhappy with themselves for some reason, and their communications suffer consequently. But doesn't feedback tell the blamer when it's bad strategy? Sometimes not. Though signs are unmistakable to others, the person dominated by hard narcissism can't always read them accurately. Beset with putting others down—or with self-recrimination—the castigator won't get the message.

5. *Anger*

Behavioral Range: **from ordinary indignation to rage**

Strategies drawn from the *topos* of *Anger* can be useful in communication, to the extent that they further sender's and receiver's goals and don't abuse or alienate anyone. It's true that there are occasions when momentary alienation may be a communicator's goal, perhaps with the purpose of getting attention. **There are situations that call for "shock communication," when milder messages can't break through another's narcissistic barrier**. Too, *Anger* provides a contrast in message content, helping the receiver to know the depth of a sender's feelings. While there are exigencies that justify indignation and the like, the basic question is, as always: What's the probable audience response? A message that's appropriate for one receiver might not be for another.

Enthymematic Patterns

Among the major premises from *Anger* are the following:

- If they don't get the message, shake 'em up.
- The key to communicative success with anger is responsible use.
- If *Anger* worked for me in my first marriage, it'll work in this one.
- Sometimes the only way you can get a person to understand is to get angry.

- Strong medicine may be required to treat chronic apathy.
- If you show your rage, you won't be exposed to shame.
- Rather than store wrath, let it out.
- If I let him know I'm really "ticked off," we'll get along better.
- I communicate better when I show my honest anger.

Facilitative Roles

A number of facilitative roles are available from this *topos.* As you might imagine, most are found near the softer end of the continuum. Among them are *arouser, disturber, truth-spieler, prompter, focuser, protestor, expresser,* and *penetrator.* Some apt titles are "Trumpeter," "Bell-Ringer," "Jolter," "Announcer," and "I.M. Indignant."

Without open disagreement, people in relationships may not have the opportunity to resolve their problem.[7] And without occasional and sensible use of *Anger,* one may be taken for a person who can be walked on. Another example comes from civil rights protests in which discontented leaders have adopted strategies of *Anger* to expose "the establishment" as a force of alienation, thereby exciting sympathetic groups and building cohesion with them. People rely on expressions of *Anger,* even rage, to balance the scales in situations when wrong has been triumphing over right. In this regard, an angry word is sometimes a cry for help or confirmation.

Moreover, *Anger* may assist intrapersonally to reduce one's dissonance or provide mental balance. Interestingly, Stella Adler, the famous teacher of method acting, used *Anger* as a pedagogical strategy, motivating her students to realize the depth of their potential for emotional experience. Her exercise helped them to break through their restraints on expression.

One of the best justifications I've read for inventing from Anger is in John and Kris Amodeo's writing. They distinguish between "clean" anger (soft *Anger*) and destructive anger (hard). The latter is hurtful, while clean anger is healthful. Everyone has angry feelings, and rather than keep them bottled up, a person should find ways to let them out for the sake of relationships. *Anger* can be used responsibly and without a mean spirit. Also, an expression of clean anger can sometimes lead one to important insights about oneself: for example, regarding what lies below surface thoughts, which is often very different from the feelings expressed and certainly deeper.[8] My hope for our Janet is that the touch of ire that we've seen in her will help her to know herself better as she continues to grow.

Maladaptive Roles

We resort to *Anger* as a self-maintaining measure, but while some expressions of *Anger* can be channeled and handled constructively, wrath and rage are often "noisy" and self-defeating in communication. Patterns of Dennis' wrath worked against him, as we've seen. Here are some of the ill-advised roles that communicators assume from this *topos.*

Mad Dog	Torpedo
Explosive Lady	Tigress
Hothead	Erupter
Hell-Raiser	Ugly Aggressor
Temper Tot	Killer

Perhaps you can add to the list of maladaptive roles. Have you recently observed an instance of the above? If so, what was the situation? Who said what to whom? What did the participants seek to accomplish? What was the outcome?

No communicative *topos* would seem to be less promising than intense *Anger.* But in certain circumstances a flash of verbal heat will serve as a necessary step toward unity of sender and receiver. It's risky, for it may thwart forces for identification and demolish bases for empathy and understanding. **Rage often breaks out just when clear thinking and compassion are needed most**. When an emotionally fortified self-maintenance strategy dominates, we are least likely to use our intelligence, for when under the rule of rage, communicative capacities are taxed to the utmost and may be inoperative in any ordinary and productive sense. Thus we lose any semblance of a Communicative Disposition. Besides devastating others, a hostile person's outburst may influence a receiver to respond in kind. The result of that is continued noise. Noise, noise, painful noise!

6. *Denial*

Behavioral Range: **from inattention to delusion**

In communication we have a choice of stimuli to which to respond, and subconsciously we may tune out those that we can't handle. *Denial*—tuning out—can be a useful maintenance *topos* but also quite hazardous. When in a threatening communicative environment, one strategy is to not perceive a message: to deny it as an exigence (have nothing to say). Messages or facts dealt with in this way, in the strategic interest of maintaining well-being, do not register as effective events.

Denial has a number of strategic forms. One involves a communicator's subordination of self—or so it seems—for the apparent purpose of according status to the other. An example is the strategy of "Little Me" talking submissively to "Powerful Big You." The purpose of "Little Me" is clear: to be effective by denying personal power.

Interesting uses of *Denial* are found everywhere in the general culture and subcultures. You may have heard it said that "he shut his eyes to" a certain fact or statement. Or she "played ostrich, with her head buried in the sand." Then there's the saying that "deep in his mind, he set the matter aside" or "she let it go in one ear and out the other." Though occurring below the conscious level, these instances suggest purposeful inattention. But, of course, to deny *is* to respond; to say nothing is to communicate a message.

A related strategy, but slightly different, is denial of emotional injury. We hear statements like, "He swallowed the insult," which means that he chose not to show pain, not answering the perpetrator. He denied the exigence, unwilling to risk getting involved with his feelings.

Have you ever noticed how humor—or "laughing it off"—may serve as a strategy of *Denial*?

In his discussion of denying sadness and fear, Alexander Lowen tells of its defensive and strategic character: It "enables the person to project an image of independence, courage, and strength. This image hides the person's vulnerability from himself and others."[9] Denial in communication is about protecting the self through refusal to acknowledge unacceptable feelings or threatening reality. Making an undesirable fact or situation "non-existent" can be advantageous self-deception.

Enthymematic Patterns

Among the denier's major premises of enthymemes are the following:

- What you don't know can't hurt you.
- If you look the other way, you won't get involved.
- Ignore something, and it'll go away.
- No knowledge, no shame.
- Nonperception may be the best perception.
- If it goes against your self-concept, gloss over it.
- It can't be a truth, if you don't act on it.

You've heard the expression "Just do it!" But have you considered that sometimes it means "So what if it hurts a little; stop dwelling on it and put your mind to better use." In other words, "Deny that minor pain and move on." At times, that may result in good communication.

Facilitative Roles

Some of the expressions and positions listed above may facilitate communication. What appropriate role names shall we attach to them? For one, there's "See No Evil." What about "Ignore-It-All" and "Swallow"? Any of these defensive modes may carry the day, given the choice between subconscious *Denial* of an overwhelming condition or meeting it head-on.

If a very shameful event is too painful to face, one may cope by wiping it from consciousness. Nick is in prison for car theft, but his mother tells others that he's "out of town on business."

She believes it. This mother isn't lying; she's denying. Inventing from *Denial*, Cynthia tells herself that her father is not dead; she must see it that way, for now. Similarly, to ease the pain of dismissal, Al wants to believe that he *quit* that job, but in truth, he was fired. With their defensive strategies of *Denial*, Cynthia and Al get over their rough and destabilizing moments. I know a man in his fifties who believes (incorrectly) that in high school he was not cut from the basketball squad, that he played on the varsity. He needs that perception, and I have no good reason to force my version of history upon him.

Folktales give interesting examples of *Denial*. Remember the emperor with the "new clothes" and his narcissistic use of *Denial*? He refused to know his nakedness.[10]

Maladaptive Roles

When a woman falls into denying her feelings, her susceptibility to pain, her longing for soothing and caressing, her sadness over deprivation, or her own lovingness, she may find herself hampered in communication. Others won't be able to sense where she stands or appreciate the fullness of her emotional self. When she's unable to "tell of herself," others can't know her. **Resort to Denial limits a presentation of the self to others**. It also prevents a person from experiencing both the sweet and the sour in life's daily fare. Staying out of touch may provide some comfort, but it also isolates us from what's really going on. *Denial* is a strategy with drawbacks.

Some of the problematic roles that people play from this *topos* are the following:

Tough-It-Out-Tessie	Cheerful Facade
Mr. Thick Skin	Cry-No-More-Baby
Cold Turkey	Iceman
Unreal One	I-Can-Take-It
Empty Edgar	No-See

Perhaps you can add to the list. Have you observed any one of these? If so, in what kinds of situations? Who said what to whom? What did the participants seek to accomplish? What were the outcomes?

Though invented for self-maintenance, a strategy of *Denial* can boomerang. Unfeeling or psychologically blinded communicators have problems, for they reduce their power to make profitable interpersonal investments and to conduct open relations with themselves. In their fear, those who deny—by regularly suppressing or obliterating essential parts of themselves—can't expect a good share of the rewards that ordinarily result from interactions with others. **When an act of denial is serious, one consequence is coldness, and when that sets in, relationships freeze up**. Ice thwarts growth and sometimes kills spirits. In communication, the felt vulnerability of deniers is keen. An ideology calling for self-isolation will produce frost in communication which is sure to yield enthymemes with limited vitality and appeal.

We can conceive of denying as the substitution of one self-maintenance strategy for another, the invention of an approach that's less real but appears more promising. Audiences, however, may be distracted by the new face, finding the substitute unreal or less than whole.

7. *Withdrawal*

Behavioral Range: **from mental to physical removal of self**

We have many opportunities to withdraw from others, and to accomplish that strategic options are available. We can seek to maintain ourselves by deciding not to enter social situations. Or we can enter, but anticipating hurt and dreading shame, choose to depart mentally or restrict our participation to certain topics or persons. We can also be generally noncommittal: guarding expression of thoughts and feelings, and remaining aloof. There are innumerable ways to retreat, to hold back, to limit involvement, and to maintain a safe communicative distance.

Nonverbally, we have access to varieties of physical and vocal strategies from the *topos* of *Withdrawal*: for example, turning the body away from someone, averting the eyes, folding the arms tightly, avoiding touching or other physical contact, sitting away from someone, lowering the head, and speaking inaudibly.

We know how to disconnect when we feel threatened and uncomfortable in an interaction. The most direct method is to leave the scene. But if going out the front door—figuratively or literally—is too obvious, one can go to the kitchen for a drink of water and from there escape out the back door. I know of a business manager who, while generally successful in his work, is unsure of himself when "difficult" employees come to his office with complaints. One of his escape tactics is to arrange for his assistant to listen in on his conversations with "Mr. Hardnose," and when the pressure seems to be getting too great, the assistant will poke his head in and say, "Hey, Jason, they need you down the hall." Jason will turn to the person in his office and say something like, "Sorry, gotta go; hope this can wait 'til next week." Jason is an escape artist.

Enthymematic Patterns

Here are a few major premises of enthymemes of *Withdrawal*, some of which are problematic:

- It makes good sense to put off some interactions.
- If shame is imminent, give attention to other things.
- When you don't look at her face, you'll feel less threatened.
- Knowing when to back off is an art.
- Not being there is the best way to dodge the bullets.
- If you can't stand the heat, get out of the kitchen.
- When playing rough interpersonal games, have an exit strategy.
- If you feel threatened interpersonally, send a surrogate.
- When the words hit close to home, I stop listening.

Facilitative Roles

The *topos* of *Withdrawal* offers numerous roles to use in communication, both functional and dysfunctional. Is Jason's

"Houdini" act functional? He's gotten away with it for many years, and it is rather funny. Too, I think that others are onto his ways and may accept his peculiarity. His general likableness and appealing sense of humor tend to balance things out.

At times, it's the better part of valor to postpone an interaction.

Even minor depression or dysphoria, a form of unhappy *Withdrawal*, has its uses. In dampening one's behavior—or others'—it can curb violence, and it may allow one's rhetorically disabled self to get off to the side for the moment to "pick up the pieces." Such a recouping defensive act can have value.

Names for other roles invented from the *topos* of *Withdrawal* are "Topic Changer," "Vanisher," "Veiled One," "Isolationist," "Insulator," "Departed Spirit," and "Tight Talker."

Maladaptive Roles

In analyzing *topoi*, we often observe a fine line between adaptive and maladaptive roles. As we assess the value of various self-maintenance roles, we must keep in mind a number of factors: for example, the nature of the exigence that influences role selection, the audience with whom the role is assumed, and the purpose for which it's assumed. A role that's appropriate for one situation may be wrong for another.

There's also the question of audience outlook. If the other person or persons understand and accept the role choice, the strategy may lead to a positive effect; if they are not responsive to the role choice, good results are less likely. Nonetheless, I think that the following roles have mostly negative implications, particularly if they cause climates of fear or mistrust or if communicators adopt them regularly.

Mr. Hide	Under the Covers
On Hold	Long Gone
Not Home	Silent Speaker
Resign	The Phantom
Out of Sight Man	Ms. Unreachable

Perhaps you can add to the list of maladaptive roles. Have

you observed any one of these in communicative practice? If so, what were the situations? Who said what to whom? What did the respective participants seek to accomplish? What were the outcomes?

Clearly, one who chooses to withdraw, removing the self from the scene—whether in mind or body—puts the self out of communication. It's self-imposed excommunication. But that's what the withdrawing person wants when communication seems to offer only continued self-diminishment—the experience of shame.

Narcissistic needs of the withdrawing person affect others, sometimes disadvantageously. This suggests the likelihood of extended dysfunction in communication, when audiences are poorly served. **Regardless of how one looks at Withdrawal, many roles of that topos are of limited value in providing reliable bases for identification.**

8. *Prevarication*

Behavioral Range: **from rationalization to falsifying**

Prevarication, whether mere evasion or lying, is a prevalent form of communicative behavior. Almost all of us find it expedient at some time or other to exaggerate claims, to equivocate, or to fib. Colloquially, we refer to someone's "storytelling," "stretching the truth," "beating around the bush," or "laying it on thick." Given our narcissistic vulnerability, these are acts to safeguard the self: to bolster our stature, aggrandize ourselves and accomplishments, and save face.

Sometimes our purpose motivates invention of indirect *Prevarication.* For instance, we resort to euphemisms, verbal disguises, and passive voice to protect against disconfirmation. Look at this sentence: "I must say that at this moment I am not entirely unopposed to your plan." Isn't that a silly statement? Yet it may help to prevent the door being slammed in a communicator's face. We make these selections, knowing that we can't build enthymemes with others when our major premises threaten them. Thus we proceed defensively, taking great care to keep the other from clamming up or fighting back.

One strategy of *Prevarication*—somewhat related to *With-*

drawal—is to assume an illusory self: for example, an overly accommodative persona which isn't representative of our true feelings. It can be a self that shows cheerfulness when we actually feel down. Replaced by an imposter, the "real" self hides out (That's the *Withdrawal* part.)

Clearly, we need to learn about supportive *Prevarication* and understand its uses. In doing so, we'll find that we can't call all of it all bad. To do that would be to judge all humanity as bad. Instead, let's be guided by this familiar premise on our communicating: **Always aiming to maintain the self and be effective, we have reasons for our choices**. And for our purposes, our reasons are good. So we believe, in choosing strategies of *Prevarication.*

Enthymematic Patterns

Here are a few major premises of sample enthymemes of *Prevarication:*

- A little lie can be a great shame preventer.
- If the self-concept requires the support of bragging, so be it.
- Without some rationalizing, one's self-esteem is difficult to maintain.
- At times, it's better to avoid the issue rather than confront it.
- An indirect message may spare pain for all parties in conversation.
- When emotions are high, sidestep that tender topic.
- A little white lie helps in civility.

Facilitative Roles

Remembering, as we must, that audiences and situations vary, what are typical roles of *Prevarication* that may have value in given communicative moments? I've observed quite a few. The role of *pussyfooter* can be used to buy time until one feels safe to communicate forthrightly. *Avoider* helps prevent an unnecessary clash. *Liar* (Too harsh a term? Is *fibber* better?)

spares another person a loss in self-esteem. All of us have had occasion to be the *excuser.*

Let's give the name "Pseudo-Socializer" to the one who assumes the guise of sociability to get through a hard moment of personal pain when in grief or melancholy. Though such a persona is more functional than noble, it's to be found in nearly everyone's store of roles. Consider also the possible communicative contributions of "White-washer," "Fabricator," "Pretender," "Kindly Kidder," "Soft-pedaler," "Neutral Party," and "Rationalizer."

Should we endorse these personas and their respective machinations? Or should we denounce them? Neither. Instead, I suggest that we take each one on a case-by-case basis, factor in all relevant data, and decide if utility squares with ethical values. As adviser and teacher, that's the way that I approach the usage question. Remember that all role presentations involve risk; all will cost something. If the adoption of a given role promises the sender and receiver worthy rewards that are equal to or greater than those possible from a different role, then the choice of role may be justified. Otherwise a substitute should be invented, possibly from a different *topos.* Whether applied to a brief interpersonal moment or to a long-standing relationship, such an approach to invention seems both realistic and wise.

Maladaptive Roles

The following role colorations suggest maladaptation.

Double-Dealer	False Colors
Plain Baloney	Pure Bull
Fact Cooker	Habitual Liar
Deceptive Sender	Bamboozler
Slippery Eel	Shortchanger

Perhaps you can add to the list. Have you observed any one of the above? If so, what were the situations? Who said what to whom? What did the respective participants seek to accomplish? What were the outcomes?

When the truth is too hurtful to admit or self-esteem is in the balance, communicators may reach into the *Prevarication* bag for a role to carry the moment. The choice, usually made without conscious thought, comes from a real need to save the self or others from humiliation and shame. This is universal motivation among humankind. If there are exceptions among us, regardless of culture or gender, I haven't observed them.

The stakes are high in communication. Though the narcissistic pain be unbearable or the narcissistic reward irresistible, the adoption of roles of *Prevarication* can be self-defeating. Such role choice can cost more than directness or honesty. The most critical possible loss is in *ethos*, that all-important element of communication that we ordinarily call credibility. In bringing about communicative identification, positive *ethos* is essential. **If our audiences are repelled by the persona we present or if they can't find something in us with which to connect, they turn from us or against us.** *Ethos* is the *very last* relational asset to squander.

CHOICE OF ACTION

To maintain the self in communicative interaction and achieve attunement, a person will draw upon any number of the *topoi* in the invention of strategies. I observe eight principal categories: *Control, Achievement, Opposition, Attribution, Anger, Denial, Withdrawal,* and *Prevarication.* Among other factors, our invention of strategy in communication depends on our assessment of rhetorical need, along with personal preference and ideology, including ethical standards. Strategies of rage, blame, evasion, and so forth, can be either adequate or inadequate, whether judged in a rhetorical or narcissistic sense. Any self-supportive strategy is a choice of action made to keep the self together and to reach others. Of course, it may or may not work to accomplish either end. Sometimes our messages are effective and we're confirmed as we want to be; sometimes neither happens. Yes, **communication is an uncertain enterprise, always an adventure and occasionally treacherous**.

The two final chapters are devoted to specific recommendations on functioning successfully in a world of people maintaining their selves. We are of that world.

Try This. Find a way to place yourself inconspicuously near the customer service desk of a large department store. Listen to the interactions as customers register complaints; for instance, when they return merchandise with which they're dissatisfied.

A. Prepare an analysis of two separate observations, addressing the following topics:

- The customer's purpose, as you heard it
- The store employee's purpose
- The customer's chief self-maintenance strategies, including defensiveness. Make use of relevant categories of *topoi.* Give names to roles assumed, e.g., "Mr. Indignant."
- The employee's chief self-maintenance strategies, including types of defending. Make use of relevant categories of *topoi.* Give names to roles assumed, e.g., "Mr. Patience Plus" or "Ms. Placater."

B. Classify the self-maintenance strategies as facilitative or maladaptive; then discuss the interaction from those two perspectives.

C. Prepare a concluding statement.

GUIDEBOOK

Chapter Five

Preparing Yourself to Communicate Better

CHOICES

The two final chapters are a guidebook to maintaining the self in communication, telling how you can apply the theory of the first four chapters to improve your own communicating. Chapter Five centers on *preparing* to make good use of self-maintenance strategies, while Chapter Six centers on *doing* it. I intend these chapters to serve two practical purposes: first, as a useful manual for your self-improvement and second, with your involvement in the material, as a working summary of the concept of self-maintenance in communication.

In this chapter, you'll find three clusters of thought on things you need to know: (a) about others in communication, (b) about your maintenance choices, and (c) about your future as a communicator. In each cluster, I've included a number of ideas and guidelines for you to consider and act on. My intent is to make the options clear and then leave the rest to you. If a given suggestion seems promising to you, you can take it and find your benefits.

As we open this guidebook, I'd like you to acknowledge that you have the potential for better communication. Know also, that success will take direct effort. As you consider the material in this chapter and think about strategic options—yours and others'—you'll realize that any plan to sharpen your vision and skills will place demands on you. Underlying the growth process is a truth: **You face tough alternatives in communication.** Included in the process is the recognition of others in your life and who you are as you relate to them. Then you have the matter of self-acceptance, often a major challenge in coming to maturity as a communicator. In all phases of communication, from learning and improving to inventing the content of a message, your basic function is that of a choice-maker.

You may ask, "After all these years of communicating, can I make it better, really?" The answer is yes, and it relates to choices again; **From good choices will come the opportunity for better times with yourself and others: real trust, reciprocal confirmation, and greater satisfaction and effectiveness.** In all my professional work in communication, I've never known anyone who didn't want more of that. It's worth trying—even worth a commitment.

CLUSTER A: ABOUT THE OTHERS

The following suggestions are based on principles of communication, most of which are long-established.

1. *MAKE HUMAN NATURE IN COMMUNICATION A FIRST AND CONTINUING STUDY.* Paraphrasing a line from the poet Alexander Pope, we can say that the proper study of human communication is humans. Lessons of human nature and the human condition have direct application to all aspects of communication. Basic issues are clear.

What marks human communicative behavior? What motivates people to say things? What do we *need* to say? What do we *fear* to say? How have life experiences come to affect our sending and receiving of messages? How do cultural variables and special interests affect the creation of identification among people? In what ways might the premises of our enthymemes not be shared by others? For what reasons might someone not confirm your roles or you not confirm another's? Why is it so gratifying to people when they agree on an exigence? What are your answers to these questions?

What kinds of narcissistic injuries are felt by people? Since all of us bring to scenes of communication our felt deficiencies (consequences of normal experiences of growth), you need to know something about these feelings, both yours and others'. What are typical examples of these deficiencies? What are the ranges of intensity? In particular, what are typical sources and expressions of shame among people? How does a sense of shame affect them? Specifically, how does felt inadequacy and shame affect levels of personal safety and well-being? Keep looking for answers to these questions.

How do personal ideologies and specific features of self-concept affect the invention, reception, and processing of messages? Others bring *to you* a host of premises on who they are and how they want to be *with you,* e.g., *as you are in your assumed roles.* And, of course, you bring the same to them. Facets of the self-concept are tied inextricably to the totality of our individual ideologies: our convictions, values, and ideals. Remember that regardless of the topic of an exchange, whether it's about capital punishment or eating healthfully, our respective concepts and ideologies will function as keepers of the information gate or at the very least as message filters. **Structures of the self-as-is and the self-as-idealized work constantly to influence all sending, receiving, and feeding back.**

Of particular significance in idealizations are thoughts and feelings on justice. What are gradations of beliefs on fairness, right and wrong, and deservedness? For instance, on whether someone should be promoted, or whether another is a genuine hero, or whether another merits the next available liver transplant. No ideological theme is more compelling than one's sense of justice. It's tied to the self-concept and is a very personal matter.

How do others maintain themselves in communication? Ideological orientations provide material for communicators' self-maintenance. In interactions, people seek to guard their stock of values and principles related to the self-concept; they seek to protect and justify what they stand for. Consequently, they'll seek ways to be "right." By "be right," I mean put themselves in the "best light," with messages that cover their narcissistic injury and ordinary felt inadequacy. In a word, they want to be seen as *shameless in others' eyes.* And the step from shame to defending is short. They're always ready to care for themselves—or they want to be ready. The same applies to you; **both you and your audiences want to protect values and principles—to be as you "ought to be"—to be shameless with each other!**

There are other questions to ask yourself.

- How effective are people with their self-maintenance strategies?
- In general terms, what kinds of strategies seem to facilitate communication and what kinds get in the way?
- How do people show communicative dysfunction?
- What will bolster a person's self-esteem and help in getting over a difficult and potentially shameful moment?

Try This. Take a few minutes to reflect seriously on each of these questions. Then write them on a note card, and take the card with you on the bus or airplane, or to the department store or any other gathering of people. As you look around, observe these people as interesting *communicators*, people who send and receive messages. Single one person out, and silently apply the questions to that person. Then go to others. As you observe interactions, what is the *human* nature of people in communication? What are some typical principles and values from which people operate? Every one of us has a packet of defenses and other self-maintenance methods, ready for use. **The more you learn about personal ideologies, narcissistic needs, and strategies, the better communicator you'll be with them.** Too, you can use the media as tools for learning about people in communication. For instance, watch their interactions on television. If you're selective, you'll find no better source of immediate information on the communicative strengths and shortcomings of people in various situations. It may be worth your while to conduct an informal study of revealed needs and self-supportive strategies: e.g., of politicians, reporters, talk show participants, interviewers and interviewees, and others who interact on camera and relate to us the viewers.

As you observe an individual in action, try to determine how his or her self-concept and general ideology influence invention of messages. Why did she speak up when he said that? Why didn't she remain quiet and not find an exigence in his comment? What roles did she assume and with what effect?

Why does she take on that role with him and a different role with another person?

Ask similar questions about their chosen enthymemes: Why did he refuse to join with her to complete that enthymeme—why didn't he "buy into" it and relate to her as she wished?

Look for signs of success and failure in identification, for moments of obvious confirmation and disconfirmation.

Note the narcissistic content of participants' messages in response to persistent questioning or challenges, i.e., when they're put on the spot by an interviewer or opponent. How do they maintain their status? How do they protect themselves from shame? What will provoke an individual to take a point too seriously? In earlier days of television, a man reacted to a comment by throwing a glass of water in another person's face. Very likely, most of the cues of rhetorical stress that you observe will be more subtle. But they're there, nonetheless.

Also, study messages sent by groups, whether as reported on television or in newspapers and magazines. Do you find that self-sustaining postures assumed by groups are a lot like those of individuals? To explore this, note group reactions when members are criticized or under threat for any reason. What strategic patterns of self-protection or justification are revealed in messages of teachers' unions as they plan requests for salary increases? Can you make any kind of generalization relating to the self-concept or personal ideology of school teachers as a group? In their public messages, do you observe any evidence of uneasiness related to self-concept or general ideology? Ask the same questions of associations of physicians when they're threatened by proposals to control their fees? Or what of labor unions anticipating federal legislation to outlaw striking? What specific groups on the local or national scene show obvious narcissistic sensitivity, e.g., as related to justice or their concept of rights and privileges? What group messages give indication of their vulnerability and sensitivity? As you may have sensed, these questions refer to group uses of self-maintenance strategies in communicating.

2. *AS YOU STUDY HUMAN COMMUNICATIVE BEHAVIOR, REMIND YOURSELF THAT IN COMMUNICATION YOU'RE NEVER ALONE.* At times, you may feel alone, but you can't be, except when talk-

ing to yourself with no one around. Communicators are interdependent; it's impossible to understand yourself as a communicator without taking into account others' levels of comfort and safety in relating to you: how they feel with you and how you feel with them. Nor is it possible to improve your communication if you ignore that interdependence. For one thing, when you and they feel relatively unthreatened *together*, you'll have a good chance of exchanging satisfying messages and experiencing mutual success.

Others need you, as much as you need them. **Problems arise when we deny needs of interdependence, when one or the other of us succumbs to extremes of individualism or other unfavorable narcissism.** We can't succeed in communication as solitary agents acting unilaterally—though we sometimes think we can. Our need of each other starts at birth and never ends. We become who we are from our extended interplay with others: from the mirrorings and attunements of early years to the identifying and confirming that continue throughout life. Without others, we would neither be who we are nor be able to continue as whole beings. Does this suggest communicative responsibilities and opportunities? It certainly suggests options and choices.

Thus, what we do in communicating is transactional, a dynamic and ongoing process of give and take. As you recall, senders and receivers participate *simultaneously*. **You're never a mere receiver or mere sender; you're both at the same time.** Notice that while you're saying something, she's saying things with her eyes and face, and because she affects you with those behaviors, you adjust your words and actions. As a receiver she's never in the position of waiting for you to stop before she can have her say. In fact, you're both "talking" all the time, even in silence. Adjustments in communication are constant.

3. *TO REINFORCE YOUR KNOWLEDGE OF HUMAN NATURE AND COMMUNICATION, EXTEND YOUR FIELD OF INTERPERSONAL CONTACT.* James Farrell said it well: "As experience widens, one begins to see how much upon a level all human beings are." And without practical experience, that rhetorical lesson may be lost.

One specific reason for expanding socially is to discover fresh sources of information about others and thus increase the potential for your own confirmation. Your sense of security and communicative potential depend on confidence in relationships. Barbra Streisand had words on that. Remember her song about people needing people? "They're the luckiest people," she sang. Underlying that lyrical sentiment is a real truth.

A few years ago a student of mine named Mike gave the class a wise thought on seeking interpersonal experience. He said, "Because it is unfamiliar ground that makes me feel insecure, it has become my goal to make more ground familiar." What a superb suggestion on extending interpersonal contacts; it's a real key to taking charge of your communicative development.

Following Mike's example, what piece of wisdom would you offer others on expanding their interpersonal worlds? Phrase it as a maxim or principle of interpersonal experimentation. Here's one: "In every new encounter there's a chance to learn something about communicating."

Practice communicating. Actively seek out opportunities to engage people, and by so doing to learn about their behavioral goals and strategies. Opportunities are everywhere. Initiate a conversation in the cafeteria, speak up in a group meeting, and say "yes" when asked to make an oral report or announcement. **Make each experience in communication a lesson about human nature.**

Keep a record of experiences. One way to get more out of your experiences is to keep a journal of specific communicative occasions and the people involved.

Try This. Select an event and write about it in a log. Among the topics to include are the following:

a. Description: for example, party conversation

b. Analysis of selected interactions: topics, messages exchanged and with whom; for instance, whether with a child or adult, with an authority figure or peer, with a stranger or acquaintance, and so forth

c. Descriptions and analyses of others' primary reactions, whether from insecurity or comfort: how it felt for them to communicate with you, what seemed to stimulate them, what seemed to be of little interest to them, and so forth

d. Lessons: what you learned from the event, e.g., about human fears, principal communicative strategies, goals, and favorite topics; about signs of maturity in communicators and signs of preoccupation with themselves, and so forth

e. Recommendation on how you might try to learn more about human nature on future occasions

CLUSTER B: YOUR SELF-MAINTENANCE ACTIVITY

While the focus in this section will remain on you, keep in mind that your audience is still in the picture—or should be. After all, it's because of your audiences—and with them—that you look after yourself as you do. **Communication is being together.**

1. *AS YOU STUDY THE DYNAMICS OF HUMAN PROTECTION, AND MAKE PREPARATIONS FOR FUTURE INTERACTIONS, YOU MUST REALIZE THAT FULL SECURITY IS UNATTAINABLE.* While continuing to seek safety and maintain the self, understand that a risk-free social environment can't be achieved. Full security is an illusion (which in your best moments you know and accept). If complete safety were possible to attain, we wouldn't be the self-protective creatures that we are. Psychoanalytic theory points out, that one great human goal is omnipotence, a regressive yearning to return to the bliss and security of the time in the womb and earliest infancy, before our innocence was lost. But soon all is changed, and we come to experience disarrangements, ambiguity, loneliness, and danger to self. We find out that unpredictable and paradoxical others must be dealt with and accommodated. That's the challenge, and sometimes the agony, of communication. It first occurs very early in our lives—and it continues.

But wouldn't it be great to return to those halcyon days and have it all to yourself again, to be the center of the universe? Here are some of the beautiful conditions you may have experienced, if only briefly:

- Serenity
- Perfection
- Assurance
- Superiority

- Power
- Clarity and Simplicity
- Freedom from responsibility

What heavenly words! What images would you add to the list? What if you were able to be truly safe; truly in charge; truly sure of yourself; and truly without fear? These conditions appeal because you grieve over your losses and now are unsure. You no longer have a sense of certainty, and you sometimes feel uneasy and frightened. You're on your own to look after yourself, forced to handle the surprises and bumps along the interpersonal road.

Contrast those words with another set. As an adult, you are

- far from perfect,
- anxious to be in control (but not),
- rarely assured on anything,
- superior to no other human,
- limited in power,
- faced with frequent doubt and complexity, and
- never free of responsibilities.

There are no absolutes for you now. That's the way it is, and you're not fully at ease. You're alone among many and in a risky existence; and when at your mature best, you know there are no assurances. There are no guarantees or shields from the perils, big or small (I'll omit matters of faith, for that's a private matter.) Though sought by all, security is never found; so it is with any secular quest for certainty. Thus, **your usual and best enthymemes are not irrefutable syllogisms—neither perfect logic nor unshakable truths**.

Clearly, probabilities and changeable circumstances mark all your interactions. Thus you seek practical enthymemes: imperfect but worth trying, chosen for their workability in the adventure of communication. **Probability is the communicator's rule**—your rule—in thinking and relating. As the perceptive old philosopher Joseph Butler said, "Probability is the very guide of life." That it must be. And it's the best you can expect to discover in your sending and receiving.

2. *GIVEN LIFE'S UNCERTAINTIES, NO ACT IS MORE URGENT THAN SELF-MAINTENANCE.* Put it this way: **Nothing is more urgent than caring for what you value most highly—the substance of your self.** The stakes are high in communication, with much to gain and lose; there's always that fragile self to look after and keep intact. Any threat must be countered with a strategy of protection.

Look below the surface to find what it is that you value so. While an impending loss may seem to relate to a material item like a car or money, at the bottom is an intangible, an abstract possession that in some way represents who you are or think you should be. Here we see the direct connection of self-concept to self-maintenance. Your chosen strategy is to protect those unseen but deeply valued self-perceptions. That's what moves you to fight or flee—or freeze. "It isn't losing the money that bothers me," he said; "it's because Sheila doesn't give a damn how I feel." Right! It's your feelings that hurt!

Below are some actual examples that show the power of self-protection and the kinds of urgencies that you face in your own life. What's the real issue in each instance? In other words, what might be the need lying behind each of these cases of self-protection? And, what are *your* real valuables that must be protected?

> Marsha had never been student body president in high school, but she told her new friends at college that she had been.
>
> James always left the room when the other guys started talking about girls they'd dated.
>
> Though last year her father had chosen to leave the family and remarry, fourteen-year-old Elizabeth "knew" that an illness forced him to be away now.

Let's take a longer example, one supplied by Pete, a former student of mine. Here's Pete's case, word-for-word, exactly as he wrote it for me. It's an intrapersonal dialogue, conducted on an occasion when he needed to talk to himself before taking action, as he agonized over a choice on exigence. Now, this case isn't about Pete losing his fortune or his dearest friend, but he's facing some kind of loss, and he's very upset about it. People don't feel pangs of self-doubt unless something precious is threatened. Answer the big question: What's that something of great value that motivated the intense communication of Pete's two inner voices?

> Violent Pete: That asshole scum! I offer him a beer and he laughs and says, "Give me a real beer!" Jesus Christ! How do you like that nerve? I'm gonna deck him.
>
> Peaceful Pete: Hold it! You can't just hit him. That is uncool. Besides, it doesn't matter.
>
> Violent Pete: Whadda ya mean it doesn't matter? He just laughed at our taste and if we let him get away with it, we'll be backing down like we usually do; this is getting embarrassing.
>
> Peaceful Pete: We're not backing; we're letting him believe what he wants to believe.
>
> Violent Pete: Yeah, and he's laughing at us, and you're letting him hand us this degradation. He probably thinks we're sissies, thanks to you.
>
> Peaceful Pete: Why do you care what he thinks, if I don't?
>
> Violent Pete: Of course you don't; you never do! You sit there and take it and pass it off, but you're passing it off on me, and I'm tired of paying for your mellowness. We've gotta stand up for ourselves.
>
> Peaceful Pete: Don't you understand! To fight him would be going down to his level of "being," a level where materialistic one-upmanship is mandatory and interpersonal understanding is nothing. I fought hard to leave that stage to get where we are now—at peace with ourselves and others.

With Pete's permission, I've used his dialogue in class discussions, facetiously suggesting that the basic issue is beer and its comparative qualities. But I'm happy to report that students don't buy that. They insist that the event has very little to do with beer. It's about Pete seeking to maintain himself; that's where the value issues lie. How would you explain that?

It's always about the self. That self of Pete's is the most important thing he has, and he must keep it intact. This case puts all essential elements together: We see Pete's vital narcissistic value system and personal ideology—*self-concept*—put at risk, and then we see his great internal struggle to choose an acceptable response to the challenge. What are Pete's options, as you read the dialogue? How many can you list? What would be the best thing for him to do, the best strategy for keeping the self intact?

3. *ACCEPT IT: GIVEN YOUR OWNERSHIP OF A "PRICELESS" SELF, YOU'LL ALWAYS BE WARY OF NARCISSISTIC INJURY.* We're all the same in that, notwithstanding our individual natures. It's true that there are varying personal and cultural expressions of maintenance, but regardless of kind or degree, everyone is inclined to be a keeper of the self. Getting on in this world requires that communicative function.

But let's assume that you want to reduce your "on guard" level. Fair enough, but at the same time you must acknowledge that growth as a communicator depends to some extent on knowing that self-maintenance behaviors are authentic choices. They are purposeful, narcissistic, and mostly good. If they were all bad, you and I and everyone else would be bad communicators all the time. **Caring for the self is a genuine way to communicate**.

Fundamentally, we are who we are. A leopard has its spots. And your spots—your self-maintenance strategies—are a prominent part of your *modus operandi* for living and communicating. They're ever-present reminders of your *human* nature. I doubt if King Midas with his golden touch could have done anything to eliminate his defenses. No, neither great wealth or world fame will give you the power to cap the well from which the self-protective impulse springs. Nor will changing jobs, spouses, names, life-styles, or residences. Your identity is not something to be pushed aside or snuffed out; you carry it with you. The story of wise Ralph Waldo Emerson is relevant here.

He once believed that he could change himself by travelling. But he came to know the folly of that.

> At home I dream that at Naples, at Rome, I can be intoxicated with beauty and lose my sadness. I pack my trunk, embrace my friends, embark on the sea and at last wake up in Naples, and there beside me is the stern fact, the sad self, unrelenting, identical, that I fled from.

The self goes with us wherever we go, as Emerson learned. Travel may be broadening, as they say, but it can't be used to escape from the real world of living with your narcissism. No, you'll have your self with you wherever you go and when you return.

Would you want a different Emerson? I certainly wouldn't. Without the existence of his sensitive and sometimes depressed self, that great writer's legacy would have been different, probably scant. Emerson communicates with us from personal loss and self-deficit. That's an essential key to explaining his inventive genius and extraordinary ability to identify with us over time. **Emerson's marvelous insight grew from a sensitivity sharpened by narcissistic pain and a keen need to create meaning for his audiences.** Knowing that, I'm not ready to advocate restructuring his nature. We are the beneficiaries of this man's life-long effort to maintain himself.

Think of what you'd lose without the promptings of narcissism. Who wants to give up life's excitement and uncertainty? How boring a world it would be with full security, blandness in attitude and absolute stability of behavior, absence of personal conflict, energy for competing, and goals for glory. For most who have made significant accomplishments in life, it was their striving to overcome self-deficits that gave them the edge.

Admit your narcissistic vulnerability. Like Pete, Ralph Waldo Emerson, and all other humans, you and I are vulnerable. In general terms, I'm sure that you're able to accept this truth about yourself: that those with whom you communicate, operating as they do with their needs and strategies, can reach that tender center of your self and have considerable effect, at times painful. For example, the major premise of another's enthymeme may clash with one of yours and trigger a defensive response. More often than not, this happens when the other's ideology threatens yours, particularly as related to a premise of your self-concept. Think of a time when someone in a lecture said something that seemed to discount your religious or moral orientation, going right to the heart of your soul. When that unwelcome premise touched a concept of yours, your very essence was endangered. Can you remember how it felt?

Vulnerability is essential to your relating and communicating. The fact of human vulnerability explains why some people are afraid to free themselves to express warm feelings. So, before you decide to rid yourself of vulnerability, look at the positive side. Interestingly, it's when you're the most vulnerable that you're able to care deeply and feel love. I bring this up to put the sharpest of points on the fact—and the thrill—of this narcissistic fragility of ours. **To offer an open, accessible self is to soften detracting self-protective measures and make a big target of oneself.** Take loving as the supreme example. To love is to take a chance. When Kathleen Turner in the movie *Prizzi's Honor* said to Jack Nicholson, "You can't protect yourself when you love somebody," she admitted her vulnerability—and a truth of life. She knew that the potential for hurt is great, but she seemed willing to risk it all. That's real love! Holding back is not.

Identification with others in interactions depends on your being open to them and they to you, revealing parts of your respective identities: points of entry allowed and premises of self illuminated. **The most effective communicators are those most willing to take a chance on communicating.**

4. *LOOK FOR INDICATORS OF YOUR VULNERABILITY.* What kinds of "interpersonal hits" are the hardest for you to take? What specific cues put you off balance and motivate you to protect who you are or want to be? These are the triggers of self-maintenance strategies, some functional but others maladaptive.

Try This. Check the following conditions that can put you on guard. in the spaces following add two or three other familiar conditions that come to mind.

I get defensive when I am . . .

_____ wrongly accused

_____ denied deserved praise

_____ criticized

_____ in a dependent position

_____ unfavorably compared

_____ talked down to

_____ not in control

_____ verbally attacked

_____ abandoned

_____ left out

When I feel . . .

_____ that I don't belong

_____ different or apart

_____ dumb

_____ untrusted

_____ neglected

_____ humiliated

_____ unappealing

_____ unneeded

_____ unappreciated

When . . .

_____

_____

_____

Before leaving this exercise, try to determine the general narcissistic sources from which these common conditions arise. That is, what specific fears lie behind them? What in your self-concept is put in jeopardy? What's on the line? Why are you so concerned about not being in control? What do you fear losing if you appear inadequate? What are the costs to you in feeling humiliated? Again, the goal isn't to make a major change in perception, just to learn more about who you are.

5. *THOUGH NARCISSISTICALLY VULNERABLE, YOU'RE ADAPTABLE.* Human adaptability is a true marvel. Most authorities on child development now agree that infants are born ready to respond to people.[1] They're amazingly resilient, and, more than we realize, forms of resiliency continue into adulthood. Looking back on your life, probably you can recall a social situation that you never thought you'd be able to endure—but you did, somehow making the necessary adjustments and surviving.

You have that power to adapt now, if and when you need it. We saw signs of this kind of power in Pete's case a few pages back. Instead of jumping into violence, he silently discussed the trying situation, using his intrapersonal skills to decide on the exigence and determine a fitting response.

No better evidence of human adaptability exists than in the experiences of people who have been incarcerated for long periods and under horrible conditions: those in prisons or death camps, for example. In his writing on life in Nazi concentration camps, Viktor Frankl gives us an inspiring view of human capability to accommodate to conditions and maintain dignity in daily functioning.[2]

There's always an alternate way of responding. One point here is that we really don't have to react in the same old defensive manner every time we're provoked. She doesn't *have* to shout back at him as she always does when he's critical. The *topoi* offer multiple self-maintenance options. In preparation for better communication, I suggest that you review those eight *topoi* now. Then single out one of them and list ten different kinds of strategies that you might draw from it, just to see some of the many alternatives. Then do the same with other *topoi.* Adaptability is the issue.

Try This. Here's an outline to use in analyzing an experience in which you were not adaptable.

a. Describe the event: with whom you communicated, where and when, and the exigence as you perceived it.

b. Note your problem in adapting: what you unfortunately said, verbally and nonverbally—or unfortunately didn't say.

c. Describe the result.

d. Describe your subsequent feelings about it all.

But there's one more line of analysis to carry out; it relates to the problem. Was what you said or didn't say your only possible response? Of course not. What better communicative adjustment might you have made? What would you do differently next time?

The fact is, you had a choice; there are at least eight *topoi*, and each one is laden with self-maintenance alternatives.

6. *LEARN TO ANALYZE YOUR SELF-MAINTENANCE PATTERNS.* In moments of vulnerability, how good are you at monitoring your procedures for sustaining and safeguarding yourself? Can you say why you care for yourself as you do? Are you aware of your chief strategies? What *topoi* do you rely on in the work of self-maintenance?

Try This. Name one *topos* (*Control, Achievement, Opposition, Attribution, Anger, Denial, Withdrawal,* or *Prevarication*); then conduct a brief analysis of your use of it, exploring specific strategies or roles that serve you. Let's say you've chosen *Attribution.* With whom and under what circumstances are your typical strategies of blaming or determining accountability likely to appear? What specific kinds of behaviors are involved? Soft judgments? Hard?

Now, since you choose these strategies purposefully, it's likely that you have expectations on results. What *are* your usual expectations with this kind of maintenance strategy? What do you want to accomplish in judging or blaming? **If you can give a clear answer to the question of intent, you'll be a lot closer to understanding yourself as a communicator**.

It's also certain that regardless of smart planning you'll occasionally be surprised by unwelcome results on choice of *topos* or specific strategy. What are some examples of such results? That, too, is a key question in coming to understand your ways of interacting. I hope that you'll work with personal issues like those in this section, for in doing so you'll turn up important information about your communicating self. No characteristic of your self is more basic than your patterns for maintaining the self.

7. *LEARN TO INTERPRET THE FEELINGS ASSOCIATED WITH YOUR SELF-CARE NEEDS.* Let's take what's called a "bad mood." Sadness or bitterness may be part of it, or hostility, apprehension, or suspicion. The feelings range from general uneasiness to rage. But whatever the emotional states, they'll spark strategies to maintain the self in communication.

How will knowledge about the emotional content of your messages help you. First, increased interest in learning about communicative responses to ordinary narcissistic pain, will increase your chances of maintaining adequacy in communication. That will build. Also, much immediate help can come from realizing what's happening to you in a moment of self-maintenance. As you find yourself choosing a message fortified by obstinacy or indifference or animosity or whatever, can you understand that the message was motivated by a need to care for your injured self?

Try This. Take yourself out of interpersonal communication for a few minutes and identify your feelings. Accept those feelings as useful symptoms; let yourself know that they're from hurt. That's why you're into that self-maintenance mode; that's why you needed those strategies of exaggeration, resentment, excessive perfection, or any other.

Are your bodily sensations related to your emotional state? Do you sense the secretion of adrenalin inside? Do your muscles start to tense up? Do your eyes get glinty? Do you find yourself gritting your teeth or putting on a funny secret smile? For some people, the first daily indicator of an unsteady mood occurs in the morning, when they know that they "got up on the wrong side of the bed."

Regardless of shape or form, signs of imbalance will appear in your intrapersonal circuits of communication, giving you internal evidence of self-maintenance strategies getting ready. And very soon they'll find their way into in*ter*personal circuits of communication, to be experienced by those with whom you relate.

What do your feelings regarding the audience tell you about yourself at the moment? Use your view of the other(s) to help you sense how you're relating.

Try This. Think back to a specific disturbing interaction that happened recently and ask yourself, "What was stirred up in me as I talked to him, and why?" As you learn to describe your reactions to others and their messages, you'll gain self-knowledge that will be useful in all communicating.

Note that the issue is not what they did *to* you. It's about what happened *inside* you as you interacted with them. It's *your* self that I ask you to focus on: how you felt with them and how you cared for yourself. It's about what that means, not what you thought was done to you. We'll return to this topic in Chapter Six, when we get into the topic of communicators' responsibilities.

What does your role adoption tell you of your feelings? After coming to some realization of how you're affected by others, bring role dynamics to your analysis. Let's say that in a given situation, you begin to have certain mental and bodily sensations that tell you your audience is evaluating you. Correctly or incorrectly, that's what you begin to sense. Perhaps you come to feel on trial and cast in the role of *defendant.* In taking that role, you find yourself viewing the audience as *jury* or *judge*—even *executioner*! You respond accordingly. In maturity, we have the choice of using roles assigned by others *or* creating personas from our own sources. In the latter case, we take charge of our invention and assume responsibility for our communicating.

Awareness of the way you adopt your roles can be extraordinarily effective in monitoring maintenance reactions and in increasing self-knowledge and readiness.

Consider the kinds of roles that you assign others as they interact with you. Those role assignments carry much meaning regarding your feelings about yourself and your relationships. Some of them are good for you; others are not. For example, as an adult relating to another adult (to a friend, sister, team member, etc.), it will usually be better for you to give that audience the status of *peer* rather than *superior* or *father* or other authority figure. In the interest of your communicative health, it's ordinarily more fitting to take others as your communicative equals. Now of course, it may be smart to select different strategies when relating to bosses as opposed to very close friends. But usually, good communication does not depend on self-subordination. **In accepting yourself as an adult, "peer" is the common and right role for you—and for the "equal" others.**

8. *EXTEND YOUR INTROSPECTIVE POWERS.* Here's another procedure that can increase your sensitivity to communication dynamics.

Try This. When you sense that something's out of kilter with yourself (The feeling may appear after an upsetting experience. Or it may be more difficult to locate—only a hazy feeling that's not easy to grasp.), the trick is to put a name to the feeling. It may be the cranky sign that you name "Grumpy" or the gloomy sign named "Sadface" or the angry sign named "Stormy" or the I-don't-want-to-face-those-people-today sign. Applying a name to a bad feeling may help you get a hold on it and know it for what it is.

One very common name that belongs to a lot of us is "You-do." This one is traceable to maladaptive use of *Attribution* (blaming or seeking to make others the cause of one's feelings). Here are two examples: "*You* make me feel dumb" and "*You* are ruining our relationship." Communicators use *Attribution* in this way to dodge responsibility, to make others accountable for their emotions. Whenever you hear yourself falling into "You-do," look out; you're asking for distracting anger, withdrawal, or other interpersonal trouble. I'll say more about "You-talk" in the next chapter. Meanwhile, learn to watch for it in your message-sending.

Trace it back. After naming a "noisy" feeling, ask yourself what happened recently that may suggest some kind of threat to your well being. Did you feel injured at some point in an interaction? Even very subtle slights and hurts can alarm the self-concept and set off feelings of insecurity. Understanding your emotional overcast for what it is can reduce its threatening power. What a personal victory that can be! And having nailed it down once, you know that you can do it again.

Karen has discovered an enviable personal tool. It's a warning device that she uses to sense her current emotional condition. Operating in*tra*personally—from inside her mind, she employs this technique to alert herself when she's psychologically and communicatively "off key." For example, one morning at work she began to perceive that just about everything she said had a mean edge to it. She was critical of others and quick to snarl. She noted an inner feeling of contempt for Roz and an urge to hurt her. Clearly, something was wrong, something that related to how Karen felt about *herself.* From this awareness, she realized that she was being terribly defensive! "What's behind it?" she asked herself.

To find an explanation to her distress, Karen talked to herself, going back to events of yesterday and before. And then the critical memory popped up: Ted had promised to arrive at eight the night before, but he never came. With the help of her intrapersonal *historian,* she re-experienced the disappointment and discovered that Ted's letting her down had played havoc with her self-esteem. With this insight, she began to feel better with herself, which improved communication the rest of that day.

Work on it. Be the persistent detective. Keep the self-awareness game simple. Just name the feeling and try to connect it with an event. Often it's an *interpersonal* event that led to the upset. **Rarely will you be able to get to the bottom of your bothersome condition without discovering who else is involved.** Who is casting a shadow on your sense of pride, on your reputation, qualifications, or intentions? You're affected by people because you need them, and you care about their feelings for you. You're an interdependent being—tied to others, and that makes all the difference.

Ultimately, you must look to your *own* shadow, to your in*tra*personal communicating: to those self-doubts about adequacy and self-worth. As you communicate with others, you're constantly communicating with yourself about yourself: praising and blaming, supporting and indicting, encouraging and discouraging.

Still, remember that you can't expect to understand the intrapersonal and interpersonal dynamics of every interaction; some clues are buried deep and are impossible to unearth, except with the help of a professional.

Keep a record. Again, some people find it helpful to record significant experiences in a journal, focusing on situations and signs of vulnerability that typify and kick off distracting self-maintenance strategies. Then they review their journal entries occasionally, to check on progress and to learn more about their interpersonal and intrapersonal communication patterns. That's how to get greater insight, and from that, better communication.

9. *BE PRACTICAL IN USE OF SELF-MAINTENANCE MEASURES.* In your preparations for improvement, remember that communication is functional. To illustrate this, let's take an occasion when someone must decide whether to be subtle or make a direct statement. We know that directness is often thought of as an honest, respected mode of address. But we also know that communicating well with others may require a more oblique or less than pure expression. In other words, we know that *on occasion* a tall or proud—direct or bold—stance will defeat our purpose, and so we invent an indirect strategy: for example, a euphemism from the *topos* of *Prevarication.* A euphemism is a less offensive substitute for plain words, for those that may provoke too much anger. For instance, "No, I'm not saying 'Get out of here,' but I do want to be alone right now." A soft-pedaling may be useful when emotions are high. We want to be effective in our choices of self-maintenance expressions—but not inhumane and offensive.

Practice constructive use of maintenance strategies. When you accept yourself as a communicator needing and using methods of self-care, you come to the question of how to master them. How can these behaviors, some of which are problematic, be carried off profitably? The answer is through meaningful trial use. **Conscious practice in directing your resources effectively—converting their power productively—can lead to greater ease in your choices**. Practice, for example, the strategy of conscious and purposeful withdrawal from an interaction to let emotions subside. You'll learn how acts of will can benefit your communicating. Though I'll treat the question of conscious choice more fully in the next chapter, I do want to introduce the idea here and have you start thinking about it.

Appraise your self-maintenance choices. Let's approach your prospects this way: Do you have favorites among the eight strategic *topoi*? Which do you choose most often? In what situations and with whom? How do they serve you? Are they ever counterproductive? On what kinds of occasions might they backfire? Which specific strategies from any one of the *topoi* do you wish to keep in your repertoire? Which have you ever thought of abandoning or replacing?

Try This.

a. First, you may need to turn back to Chapter Four and quickly review the eight *topoi.*

b. Name one *topos* and particular strategic parts of it that you use now and then.

c. Describe an occasion in which some strategy drawn from that *topos* worked well for you. In what way was your strategy a good one? Include details on the situation and person involved, your self-maintenance purpose, responses of the other, and results.

d. Describe an occasion in which a strategy drawn from that same *topos* did not work well. Why was your choice not a good one? Include details on the situation and person involved, your self-maintenance purpose, responses of the other, and results.

e. Why was your communicative goal well served in one instance and not in the other? Contrast significant conditions.

f. What's your reaction to this suggestion?—"Since you are a self-protector, do it well."

Self-actualized people know how to use their protective strategies well. I find that one of the attributes of the self-actualized people whom Abraham H. Maslow wrote about is that they cared well for themselves. Maslow might not say it this way, but with all their normal imperfections, his people serve as models of constructive self-maintenance. You may want to read the Preface and Chapter 11 of Maslow's book, *Motivation and Personality.*[3]

10. *THOUGH YOU WORK HARD IN BETTERING YOURSELF AS A COMMUNICATOR, YOU WILL REGRESS.* But don't despair when reversals occur. Even a well-established Communicative Disposition doesn't guarantee success in every interaction. On some occasions you'll revert to an unwanted self-maintenance pattern that was established in infancy. That's a part of what "being

childish" means. Virginia thought she was over "the business of pouting like a child whenever I felt hurt by someone." She thought she had learned "how to be adult" in all situations. But the fact is, no matter how adult she's become, she'll never entirely "get over" her beginnings. Nor will you or I.

Bad things happen. A happy childhood is the best provision for success in communication, but it doesn't mean that you won't slip back sometimes. The healthiest of individuals are hard pressed to function comfortably under highly stressful conditions, for example, in a relationship with a person too immature to show ordinary respect. Even in stable environments, threats do rear up and trigger "noisy" messages. We can't always tell how near the surface the sources of personal sensitivities lie.

Remember the story of Othello? From the information that Shakespeare gives, we can assume that Othello had an adequate rearing, but his story is one of catastrophic defensiveness arising from regression: Unable to handle the continued manipulations of the evil Iago, Othello eventually yielded to primal forces that rose from within himself.

There's hope for us. With increased knowledge about ourselves, awareness of the dynamics of communication, and growth in self-esteem, we regress less often.

CLUSTER C: YOUR FUTURE AS A COMMUNICATOR

We've been discussing your future all along, but here I'll fine-tune some of the most critical concerns, all of which relate to your communicating for the rest of your life.

1. *KEEP IN TOUCH WITH YOUR NARCISSISM.* Understanding your narcissism is quite challenging—and basic. Nor is it a new concern to you. You've been pondering it for years, asking, "Who am I?" and "Why can't I be more objective in making big decisions?" Though weighing such questions is a task that never ends, I can tell you that answers do appear along the way, sometimes as surprises. It's the continued effort that's vital, along with being patient and open to information.

Analyze your narcissism. Let's get specific and connect your pursuit of self-knowledge to personal elements that relate directly to communication. I have two questions for you.

First, how would you characterize the level or form of your narcissism? Now, I'm not asking for a negative emphasis here. If your connotation of the word is negative, you'll have to work on that bias before you can come to appreciate your narcissism, as you must. **Remember that narcissism is the great force of self: the source of motivation to be up and doing, though at times it can also be a drag on functioning well.**

Yes, narcissism can be favorable or unfavorable. As a communicator who functions in many different scenes, you are capable of acting maturely *and* childishly, being energetic *and* lethargic, being optimistic *and* melancholic, showing kindness *and* meanness, being open *and* closed off—and being both adequate *and* inadequate when interacting with others. Though narcissism is the seat of hurt and sadness, it also provides a necessary base for happiness and accomplishment.

Second, what's the nature of your self-occupation?

Try This. Set aside some time to focus on yourself. Ask these questions: When and how is self-occupation useful to me; when and how is it a hindrance? How does concern about myself affect my communicating with others? Think of some examples. In analyzing them, what features of self-interest facilitate communication? Often these are needs that motivate you, thus contributing to rewarding communication. On the other hand, do any features of your self-occupation detract from communication? These you sense as kinds of self-absorption that prevent you from caring about others and interacting satisfactorily with them (being unwilling to listen to them or identify with them and confirm them).

Below is a list of narcissistic conflicts. Since relating to audiences is the most basic function in communication, I'll put that issue first.

- Appreciation of audience characteristics perceived as different from your own *versus* immature, fearful reactions
- Ability to delay gratification *versus* the urgency for immediate satisfaction
- Healthy feeling of self-respect in interacting *versus* an exaggerated sense of individuality

- Adult and fair view of personal rights and privileges *versus* obtrusive feelings of entitlement
- Acceptance of ordinary communicative responsibility *versus* neglectfulness or indifference
- Flexibility in interacting with others *versus* rigidity
- Civil restraint in being effective *versus* manipulation and control
- Expression of true interest in others' life involvements *versus* inattention and disinterest

These are some of the issues of narcissism that relate directly to communication. Any determination of your Communicative Disposition—strengths, weaknesses, and potential—involves self-analysis along these lines. Questions on narcissism bear directly on your self-concept and on your identity as one who communicates with others. Remember that the self you bring to others, revealed in your narcissism, is the self they'll come to identify with *or* push away from. The quality of your narcissism is fundamental and critical in communication.

Rewarded communicators are those who are able, when appropriate, to subordinate the self graciously and to give of self generously. They're the most contented as well as the most effective senders and receivers; they're the best deciders of exigencies; their chosen roles are most fitting; and their enthymemes are the most validated by audiences. Thus, they experience identification and confirmation.

2. *BECOME CLOSELY ACQUAINTED WITH YOUR SELF-CONCEPT.* Your self-concept is a set of principles regarding who you are and believe you ought to be; signs of it appear in expressions of your narcissism and in your methods of communicating. One major theme of your self-concept may relate to idealism versus realism. Another may be about your sense of personal justice and entitlement: what's right and what's due you. Pervading the whole are notions on self-worth.

Look to your communication strategies to learn more about the principles of your self-concept. This is a good approach because personal principles (or essences of the self) can be discovered in your patterns of self-maintenance.

Try This. Start by reviewing your usual choices of strategic *topoi.* For example, contrast the view of yourself that you see reflected in choices of *Withdrawal* with the view of yourself reflected in choices of *Control.* What features of your self-concept seem to be present in the first instance, and how do they contrast with features present in the second *topos*? How are controlling and withdrawing consistent with the principles of your self-concept? You can continue the investigation by putting yourself in all sorts of situations and noting your strategies. From close observation of your typical communication strategies, you'll be able to get a sense of what you think of yourself and how you want to be seen (your vision of your ideals and expectations of yourself).

In your personal investigation, look for the workings of shame. When you feel that you don't measure up or when you catch yourself departing from your self-image, you'll invent communicative strategies of self-justification to put yourself in the right light and to counter humiliation—to avoid shame. It's avoidance of shame that motivates the excuses, fibs, controls, certain forms of depression, and all of the other means of self-maintenance. What's the sort of shame that you try to avoid? And which *topoi* serve you in meeting those face-offs with your self-concept? Which *topoi* don't serve you well? Working with these questions about meeting shame will put you in the vanguard of the quest for self-knowledge as a communicator. I hope that you'll keep at it. Little by little, you'll have the chance to chip away the thick casing that covers the self and thwarts your becoming acquainted with your identity as communicator.

Go back to the beginning. Let's do some more probing, attempting to follow your self-concept back to its origins.

Try This. First, name one characteristic or trait that you'd like to have (maybe *do* have), or that you think you *should have*: for instance, courage, cheerfulness, physical strength, sexual attractiveness, good moral sense, or decisiveness. How did you come to value this ideal, "ought-to-be" quality? Endorsement of any one such characteristic probably relates in some way to the early influences of significant others and cultural forces. Nan, who viewed herself as physically unattractive in a culture that values physical beauty, needed to develop strategies to save herself from the hurt of not being what she thought she *ought* to be. Bentley, a boy with an average IQ, was reared in a family with keen emphasis on intellectual accomplishment, so he needed to discover strategies of protection from the shame he felt. Given favorable conditions at home and among friends, both Nan and Bentley discovered means of self-maintenance that turned out to be positive and appealing personal attributes.

Do these cases ring true? Do their stories in any way remind you of the beginnings of your own self-concept and defenses that guard it?

Consider parental need as a factor in your development. Can you discern parental forces at work on the establishment of your self-maintenance modes? An instance that comes to mind is that of Jeff who is mechanically minded but who became an elementary school teacher like Mom. Mom may honestly deny it, but she was keenly inclined to make it happen that way. She needed Jeff to follow in her professional footsteps. He sensed her need—perhaps unwittingly—and, not wanting to be a disappointment, went into teaching. He did it *defensively* and subconsciously, to protect himself against anticipated rejection. Later in life, when more self-assured and ready to act *for himself,* Jeff studied auto mechanics and eventually opened a car repair shop.

Another case is that of the woman—ordinarily responsible and self-reliant—who experiences much internal dissonance at those rare times when she's unable to live up to her standards on responsibility and self-reliance. Why would a momentary departure from her self-concept upset her? In the simplest terms, it's because her dad, from the day of her birth, persistently promoted a code of responsibility, personal independence, and high values. The result is a fixed pattern of self-defense. Her high expectations are usually beneficial to her, but any deviation from her standards leads to a letdown. When preoccupied with "faults," she loses power as a communicator.

Relate your self-concept to your patterns of self-maintenance. I've asked you to do this before, but this time we're ready for a different approach.

Try This. First, name a specific feature of your self-concept that stands out: perhaps the belief that you're a considerate person. What maintenance strategies—good or bad—stem from it? When a person says something that seems to raise a doubt about your concept as a considerate person (or as a comedian or brave guy or good father or good driver or pretty lady), how do you act to protect your self-status? Coming to grips with origins of your "ought-to-be" constructs and learning something about how your self-concept connects to your protection of self will move you toward a more realistic perspective on your personal history. Among the benefits of your study will be increased freedom as choice-maker and greater satisfaction in communication.

Get practical! In the negotiations between your ideal self of "oughts and shoulds" and the functioning self that doesn't always measure up, you may need to strike a compromise. That's what famous pediatrician and psychiatrist Donald W. Winnicott found to be the most healthful resolution of the conflict between those two parts of one's self.[4] You do have alternatives. The old favorites from your stock of maintenance strategies will continue as first choices in communication until you become aware of additional options.

3. *APPRAISE YOUR COMMUNICATIVE DISPOSITION.* The Communicative Disposition (laid out in Chapter Four) is a standard comprised of six categories, by which you can gauge your knowledge and skill in communication: other-awareness, capacity for intimacy, situation awareness, inventional strength, sense of personal power, and acceptance of yourself as a communication strategist. It's a practical guide for making a smart accounting of personal attributes that either facilitate communication or detract from it. Here are recommendations from the six categories, accompanied by a few quiz questions.

Work toward greater other-awareness. This is about sensitivity to audience characteristics and needs, and here is the fundamental question: How attentive are you to receivers' interests, points of view, backgrounds, and problems?

In what situations or under what circumstances are you able

to be more sensitive in regard to others' feelings? In which are you less sensitive? How does your self-maintenance activity help or hinder your sensitivity?

Try This. Use the 10-point scale below for making personal assessments of situations, particularly those in which you're likely to be intent on safeguarding the self. Take a specific situation or event, and note on the scale your level of sensitivity to others. Examples: when a co-worker excitedly describes the great pleasure she gets in going to dog shows; when a visitor from Central America wants you to understand the weight of his tax burden back home; when you're involved in preparing for an important meeting and a colleague comes in with a personal problem.

1 2 3 4 5 6 7 8 9 10

quite sensitive so-so not very sensitive

Expand your capacity for intimacy. The main issues here are trust and willingness to share thoughts and feelings. Interpersonal courage and the need of confirmation and identification with others are also relevant.

When asked about their levels of intimacy in communication, most people answer, "It depends." In your own case, on what does disclosing parts of yourself depend? Let's have a thirty-word answer to that. You may want to share your answer with another person or group.

Here are other questions to ask yourself. How does effort to protect yourself in communication increase or decrease your capacity for intimacy? How does maintaining yourself in communication affect identification with others? Do the two goals ever conflict? If so, how have you resolved the conflict?

Increase your situation awareness. Any communicative situation includes time, place, emotional climate, purposes of participants, and related constraining conditions. Key variables in situational awareness are one's attentiveness to the dynamics of interactions and perceptiveness on goals and strategies.

Try This. Describe a communicative situation in which you recently participated successfully. How much of your success is attributable to your awareness of relevant situational elements? What specifically were you aware of? Which of your personal attributes contributed to that awareness? How did you use your awareness to facilitate communication? How did self-maintenance interests add to or detract from your situational awareness?

Build your inventional strength. To invent is to discover message content, preferring and selecting this thought or piece of material over that. You invent strategies at every second of every communication, no matter where or when or with whom. Knowledge about choosing strategies and awareness of choices lead to greater freedom and effectiveness. You need to appreciate processes of invention.

Your communicative choices are rhetorical, in that you invent purposefully; your inventing comes from your perception of an exigence, when you determine that something must be said; your purpose is to bring about identification with your audiences, to confirm and be confirmed. Included in invented content are roles assumed, for they're parts of the message. They function for you in the confirming process, and you want them acknowledged.

Here are some questions for you on invention. Generally, are you satisfied with your effectiveness in exploring issues, ideas, and feelings related to your interactions? What's your evaluation of your levels of curiosity, inquisitiveness, and imagination, as these qualities bear on inventing message content? Do such qualities work well for you in communication? Are you good at weighing alternatives in putting a message together? These are difficult questions, but they're important. See what you can make of them, as you think back to selected instances of communication with others.

Try This. How do self-maintenance tendencies facilitate or hinder your productiveness in invention? Recall two specific events, the first when arousal of self-protective feelings motivated the right message and the second when it motivated the wrong one. Take *Anger* or *Opposition* as an example of the *topos* relied on. You may want to prepare an answer to this question over time, maybe during free moments today or during the week.

Try This. Let's do a bit more with invention, a very important area of communication. First, bring to mind a particular good or bad experience in communication, either one for which you have a happy memory or one that you'd rather forget. Were you sufficiently objective as you participated? Do you imagine that you should have been more detached? Less detached? Explain. Were you relatively secure as you interacted? Explain.

Further, did your level of security promote any moments of courageous expression—taking chances? How does courage relate to inventional strength, in your view? And, it must be asked, isn't it sometimes the better part of valor not to be so courageous (foolhardy, I mean) when inventing message content? When?

In this experience you've selected, how do you evaluate your inventional judgment? Was it appropriate? Inappropriate? Mixed? Clarify your evaluation. How did your self-protectiveness contribute to or detract from your invention?

Again, remember that you always have a purpose in looking after the self. Choosing safeguarding strategies is a part of your invention, a central part of preparing messages. The secret is to chose *adaptive* strategies, those likely to facilitate communication. Though to you this may be a new way of thinking about communicating, it's essential to effectiveness. It's a realistic perspective that will heighten your awareness of vital rhetorical and interactive dynamics.

Add to your sense of personal power. Faith in your communicative effectiveness inspires actual effectiveness; a vision of confidence provides a good feeling and hope for future success. The process is circular: It moves from a belief in yourself to successful outcome and from that to reinforcement of belief in yourself. Thus do personal attributes work together productively: your self-knowledge, sense of well-being, skill, faith in ability, and self-acceptance.

Try This. To experience this growth process, answer the following questions. What descriptive words (two or three adjectives) would you place after each item below as it applies to your sense of power as a communicator? For example, does "sufficient" apply to your level of self-knowledge? Or is "considerable" more accurate?

level of self-knowledge

sense of well-being

level of communicative skill

faith in ability

level of self-acceptance

What descriptive words would you want to be applicable one year from now? How does your self-maintenance activity add to or detract from your sense of personal power?

In adding to personal power, consider the benefits of participation in groups and adoption of models.

Among the types of support groups are those whose members share gender concerns, professional interests, age concerns, parenting situations, and various psychological interests. Support groups often have an obvious interest in facilitating communication. Nearly everybody thinks about success in communicating, as group dynamics will reveal. Networks, too, are structures of communication.

Look also to models for support. Of your acquaintance, who are the best models of communication? What is it about them—e.g., in their attitudes and strategies of interaction—that explains their effectiveness? How do they gain others' respect? Think specifically of friends, relatives, teachers, and professional people. You can learn much from observing their movements and messages, if you look closely. They'll show their tried and true strategies and communication methods, not to mention their shortcomings. Both their strengths and their less appealing attributes are enlightening.

There are also distant models, those whom you may never meet directly but whose careers and general personas offer inspiration or lessons on communicating. The images they reveal may be more idealistic than those of people closer to you. Entertainers are prominent models for some, as are persons in the worlds of business, politics, athletics, and religion. Consider also figures in the arts, education, and social betterment. In your life, what leaders stand out as reliable sources of support? On my personal list would be Martin Luther King, Jr., for his communication of an unswerving dedication to universal brotherhood; former president Jimmy Carter and his wife Rosalynn Carter for their gentle but steady persuasion as they work tirelessly for human betterment throughout the world; Madeleine Albright, who acts effectively with admirable composure, intelligence, and clarity as Secretary of State; and Tiger Woods, professional athlete and mature communicator.

When feeling connected to suitable models, our own sense of self is fortified; we feel strong. As genuine models, as real people who are fallible and not entirely free of distracting narcissism, they suggest that we don't have to be flawless to interact well with others. A possible benefit of recognizing our models' fallibility is greater self-acceptance and from that a reduction in excessive striving for perfection and control. Thus models help to guide our communicative behavior.

Another means of enhancing self-assuredness and personal power is support from a professional such as a counselor or therapist. Most communities and many colleges offer these services.

Accept yourself as a communicative strategist. Will you admit to being a person who makes purposeful choices regarding what to say and how to say it? These are your choices that depend on time, place, and audience—on situations, attitudes, and emotional climates, and so forth. Occasionally, I meet a person who claims to reject any strategic function. Some years ago a man told me that he gives not the slightest attention to how he says things when talking to people: "I just say what's on my mind." Do you believe him? Doubtless he was sincere, but I've always wondered whether he really was that oblivious to others—and how he gets along with them.

Once when we were discussing this topic in a communication class, a young man boasted, "My sister never varies her statements to people; she speaks the same way to everyone." Did I believe him? I'll answer that question this way: Not wanting to challenge the proud brother's opinion, I ignored the issue (defensively perceiving no exigence) and moved the class discussion on. But if we assume that the sister is an interpersonally successful individual, it follows that any messages she has for Person A will be designed specifically for A, and those for Person B will be designed for Person B. Social maturity and realities of human variability *require* communicative tailoring.

What's your view? Do you admit to being a strategist, one who recognizes differences in audiences and communicates accordingly? Does knowing that you devote much energy to maintaining yourself in communication help you to accept yourself as a strategist? Isn't to care for the self to be strategic?

Does your knowledge of practical theory influence your view of yourself as strategist? Recall from prior chapters the explanations of communication theory: theory regarding the functional interactions of senders and receivers, including the perception of exigencies, assumption of roles, cooperative construction of enthymemes, and goals of identification. All these relate to strategy in communication. They are rudiments of *your* life as a choice-making communicator. Since exigencies and audiences vary, so must you adapt your roles and enthymemes. Identification depends on your being an adaptable communicator.

4. *TAKE STEPS TO STRENGTHEN YOUR COMMUNICATIVE DISPOSITION.* In this section, I'll suggest a number of ways to fortify your communicative foundations.

Learn self-talk. To implement your improvement program, try a method called intrapersonal dialogue. You talk to yourself all of the time, of course, but let's make it purposeful.

Here's the rationale. Your self is composed of many "subselves." Some are adult, like the one who urges you to meet responsibilities, and some are more childlike, such as the one who insists that you take a day off for play. Some are assertive, some submissive. Some hold up the values of thrift, progress, hard work, and good diet, while some don't worry much about those sorts of things; some stand for frankness in expression, while some will avoid frankness. The variety is great. When you appear in public, your inner selves are reflected in personas, in your communicative roles. Their character depends on the situation, whom you're with, how you're feeling, and what you're thinking or seeking at the time. Your options are wide.

That's the general idea of subselves, a way of visualizing the various parts of you. But let's give one of them a special role.

You have a vital inner person who might be called "Wise One" or "Best Guide." That's your well grounded, always supportive self, who offers good sense and correction when you need it. I want you to think now about contacting that always reliable subself of yours when you face a big decision, when you want counsel and gentle soothing—whenever you require the feedback of a trusty listener. This person is always there to provide helpful messages, if you're ready to engage him or her. We'll call this facilitator your intrapersonal "Good Audience," the subself whose guiding feedback represents the sum of all your accumulated knowledge and common sense on communication: all the good ideas, lessons, and advice that you've stored. Much of your accumulated information has come from relationships, from those thousands of interactions with parents, other relatives, friends, neighbors, and teachers. Also contributing have been the many books, films, and other media from which you've learned. Add to these the countless other rich experiences you've had over the years. You've seen and done more than you may realize.

That treasure of a lifetime is collected inside of you and is available from your intrapersonal "Good Audience."

Here's an illustration. One morning, Cathy, as she faced a day of interacting with others, felt a great need for nurturing and confirmation. It involved her "Little Child," a prominent subself who needed help. Something nice happened that morning. Instead of staying unhappy, Cathy had her "Little Child," call on her "Good Audience," a supportive listener.

Little Child: I feel uneasy today—kinda sad and lonely.

Good Audience: Tell me about it.

Little Child: It's just a vague feeling; I don't feel like going out into the crazy world today.

Good Audience: Well, I'm here with you, and I'll be here as long as you want me; I'll listen to you and comfort you.

Little Child: I want someone to take care of me. I want to cry. Can you help me?

Good Audience: Yes. Here, Cathy, let me hold you. You can

trust me with your feelings. I want to hear all about it. Let's talk.

Little Child: OK. That's nice. It's just that I . . .

On went the conversation, for two minutes or so. Cathy's "Good Audience" listened patiently to "Little Child," and that's all that she needed this time: to express her feelings safely and be comforted by a warm, caring part of herself. Cathy does have a faithful and empathic friend there. And you can take care of yourself and confirm yourself in the same way, making you feel good about yourself. In confirming yourself, you become mellower and more responsive to others, less needful of defending obtrusively.

On another occasion, Cathy consulted her "Good Audience" on how to approach her employer about a raise. In a dialogue that centered on possible approaches, her "Professional Woman" and her "Good Audience" talked and came up with a promising plan to try with the employer, one that Cathy felt she could carry out confidently. In purposeful intrapersonal communication with that useful subself, Cathy can retrieve all sorts of alternatives, stored ideas, and supportive material for a whole range of communicative contingencies. And so can you. **In caring for yourself, you prepare yourself to accept and confirm others**. That's a truth of living and interacting.

Learn to play better. Here's another area to explore. Playing and playfulness are important, not only for their contribution to your general growth but also as key factors in development of a Communicative Disposition. Those who know how to play are better communicators than those who do not. You see, both communication and play require the freedom to release the self—to take a chance, to enter in freely, to feel assured and be imaginative. And the same negative forces that restrict us in communication restrict our play. In both play and communication, we are hampered by excessive self-concern and insecurity. **In a sense, communication IS play**. You'll see what I mean.

Here's another intrapersonal dialogue, involving David's "Good Audience" and one of his subselves whom we'll call "Stiff Stanley."

Stiff Stanley: No, I don't do very well at playing social games and such; it's hard to unfreeze yourself, if you're a controlled type like me.

Good Audience: You mean you hold yourself back? Why?

Stanley: Ya gotta keep yourself in check, you know. I'm afraid to let go, really.

Good Audience: Afraid of what?

Stanley: What if I let myself go, cut loose. Think of the embarrassment—everything out in the open for all to see.

Good Audience: You mean exposed and defenseless?

Stanley: Yes, that's what I mean! Never let yourself be that unguarded, man!

Good Audience: Yet, you seem to be a person who realizes that unless you do something about those rigid defenses, you can't play freely and well.

Stanley: Yes, I've heard that said, like in communicating with people. I kinda know that.

Right! David seems to have learned that his subself "Stiff Stanley" can be helped in intrapersonal conversation by his "Good Audience." On another occasion, they had this exchange.

Good Audience: I'm pleased that you're getting better at recognizing those bothersome defenses of yours, Stanley. What will it take to get you to "lighten up" even more?

Stiff Stanley: That's easy. It'll happen when I'm sure that I won't be caught off-balance and look foolish or dumb. I need assurance that my way is OK—that I'll be liked and respected. See, when a guy messes up—when he shows his stupid or klutzy side—he becomes humiliated. I don't even want to think about that! I guess I need to be a more mellow game-player!

Good Audience: And mellow communicator?

Stanley: That, too; I'd go for mellow.

Thanks, Stanley—er, David. You've grown, and you've said something that many aren't ready to say.

These pieces of intrapersonal dialogue suggest that reinforcing your Communicative Disposition takes self-awareness and effort. Actually, the work never ends. My hope for both David and Cathy is that they'll continue the self-talk, allowing their "Good Audiences" to engage their inner people who have roles to play in solving problems. In talking it over together, they'll come to understand better their uncertainties and fears; they'll learn to loosen up a little and play easier. They'll have more fun, and they'll do better in the game of talking to people. You, too, may want to try self-talk, as you work to improve your interplay.

What about rules? Extending the subject of play as it relates to communication, we ought to mention adherence to rules. But what does that have to do with communicating? The fact is that both playing and communicating require acceptance of rules, those agreed-upon codes and conventions of fair, proper, and productive interaction: what's allowed and what isn't. Some communication rules are culturally imposed. For instance, in Hispanic cultures, it's generally not acceptable to be as direct with eye contact as in Anglo cultures, but lots of *abrazos* (hugs) and backslaps are fine. Bragging is not approved in most communications within Asian cultures.

When I lived in New Zealand for a few months, I noted a leveling force appearing occasionally in people's ordinary messages. It seemed to be an act of effrontery to display signs of wealth or to converse about valuable possessions or to tell of big money-making plans. I talked to one person who felt considerable internal conflict in admitting he owned an expensive Jaguar automobile. Though the car was a pleasure to him, he seemed to feel that the fact of possession was a potential liability in communication. On another occasion, a neighbor confessed to me that people of his country were sadly deficient in taking advantage of economic opportunities; they didn't want to appear aggressive in matters of making money. "No poppy is to stand taller than any other" is the way he expressed the rule. Interestingly, it was because he was talking to an American that he felt safe to be critical of his people. He thought he knew his audience, that I would appreciate success in financial "wheeling and dealing."

Cultural rules—often unwritten and merely assumed—are imposed for the general good and to meet specific needs (though some become outmoded and decline in usefulness). Rules are adopted by members of large and small groups, as they function together; by friends as they define their relationship; by spouses as they build a marriage; by employee and employer as they relate in doing the work at hand; by salesperson and customer as they make transactions. Set up to facilitate and regulate communication, rules ordinarily are beneficial, often necessary. Given the vicissitudes of living and interacting in this world with others as we find them, rules provide a mechanism for relating effectively and civilly. When good rules are violated, whether in play or communication, a breakdown is likely to result.

Let's clarify rule observance. What are the rules on use of names in a certain job interview? Is it Mr./Ms. or Ron/Sue? Is it OK for the interviewer to be informal but not for the interviewee? When applicants ignore the rules on communicating in the interview or are unwilling to set aside personal and private rules, the interaction may not go well. In a public speech to the Lion's Club, what are the rules on use of light profanity such as "damn" and "hell"? On heavier profanity? In the nonverbal message category, what are the rules relating to a professor patting a student on the back during an office hour while saying, "Fine work with that term paper!" I'm sure you'd agree that gender is a variable. What other variables come to mind? Rule adherence can get complicated.

Why are rules violated? Quite often, deviations are expressions of unmodified narcissism: of indifference to the situation's requirements, of choices to give ourselves advantage or protection, or of a general lack of communicative sensitivity. Certain "out of bounds" strategies may be chosen in order to "beat the game," to dominate in communication and "win out," to save face after "fumbling."

But in the game of communication, when good rules are violated, big penalties are marked off. When conflicts between individualism and the social good arise—when you put yourself and your special rules above others and community rules—you'll face problems in communication. A prospering community—or any functional social unit—involves individuals willing to set aside individualistic demands that detract from the general welfare. In itself, such restraint will not ensure good communication, but it will decrease dysfunctional defending.

Moreover, in adhering to basic social rules, you can still be self-expressive. The solution lies in finding an acceptable personal level of playfulness with others—a comfortable way of functioning *with mutual satisfaction* in the give-and-take of the game of communication. Given ordinary self-interest, you can reach the optimum level in relating to others through heightened awareness of rules—and being willing to adjust your narcissistic need to the requirements of the moment.

See the funny side. Here's one more promising topic to consider. It's about your sense of humor, and it fits well with the discussion about taking things easier. A few pages back when hearing from David's "Stiff Stanley," I did detect a brief show of humor. That's a good sign. It indicates that David can see the funny side now and again—not easy for defensively controlled people. There's nothing funny about feeling shame! Oh, yes, onlookers may see the humor in it, but not the person who experiences the shame. In any event, those who communicate with David will be much happier when he can laugh at his defensive acts more often. To be sure, the corrective work must be on David's terms. First, he needs to know that added communicative sophistication is possible for him. It's possible for most of us.

Think about what makes people and their ideas appealing. I refer mainly to a communicator's character and ways of dealing with audiences. We know that personal attributes are inseparable from ideas and behaviors; audiences tend to connect them. But what makes communication strategies acceptable and messages believable and appealing? The main topic here is credibility: the highly significant variable that Aristotle called *ethos.* Good playing, rule awareness, and appreciation of humor often are a part of *ethos*, but more must be said. People like people who are not inflexibly on guard. Why? Because **people who are relatively adaptable, stable, and accessible—easy to reach and relate to—are those who don't threaten us.** We feel comfortable with them and are able to be our best with them (ways that our vulnerable selves don't always "get" to be in this uncertain world).

Relatively self-assured people, with their mature self-maintenance strategies, are able to provide what we want most: acceptance and confirmation that accords with our vital self-concept. Even though some of our characteristics and premises may differ from theirs, these people help us to be tolerably congruent—to act as we think we are, as often as possible. Thus favorably self-maintained people cool our impulses to deploy our big defensive weapons and act in ways we really don't want to be. That's something special because such respectful treatment isn't an every-moment occurrence for anyone.

Do you ever read that section in the newspaper where a reporter on the street tells about the opinions of passersby on a topic of the day? Reading newspapers in cities around the country, I've noticed that when reporters ask people to name admirable traits of others, the respondents always name qualities suggestive of relative nondefensiveness. Some of the listed qualities of so-called "nice" people are trustworthiness, openness, ability to take criticism, considerateness, willingness to accept others and their differences, and the ability to overlook their faults. Of course, these are some of the very qualities in others that make communication possible and rewarding. Nice people are nice to communicate with! One thing they have in common is the freedom to rise above personal preoccupation, to be genuinely interested in others.

It takes a good measure of self-assurance and courage to be minimally—acceptably—defended out there in communication, and isn't that what we'd all like for ourselves? Think of times when you've felt safe enough to give your very best. With knowledge, new experience, and real self-acceptance you can be that way more often. **To the extent that you can learn to choose facilitative self-maintenance procedures, your *ethos* will**

be bolstered. You'll be seen by others as a credible communicator; you'll be liked better and listened to with greater interest.

THE COSMOPOLITAN MODEL

We're reached an extremely important point here, where everything comes together. I wish that we were face to face so that we could talk together with the benefit of our respective nonverbal cues and spontaneity. The reason for seeking closer communication is that I want very much for you to know about a vital communicative model called the COSMOPOLITAN: one whose respect for self and others, potential for real satisfaction in communicating, and future good prospects are exceeded by no one! This wonderful *master* role is yours, if you want to work for it. All that's needed is a commitment to continue on the road to betterment in communication.

There's one criterion, though. **You need to endorse the idea of "becoming," to recognize that we humans never reach perfection in communication** (or any other growth goal, for that matter). Can you fit the discipline of "never-done" into your self-concept? Will the level of your narcissistic need allow it?

And what about the discipline of "never-certain"? Are you to the point of allowing principles of probability to rule in your reasoning as a communicator? As much as we like to talk about conclusions that are inevitable, proof that is absolute, and plans that are infallible, we have no guarantees. The fantasy of certainty is as unrealistic as the fantasy of perfection.

Endorsing the Model

As a COSMOPOLITAN, you progress in building a Communicative Disposition.

You do it by:

- actively deepening your *other-awareness*: acknowledging priority of the audience, sharpening your sensitivity to benefits of mutual respect and accommodation,
- actively expanding your *capacity for intimacy*: learning to

trust others with your situation-appropriate feelings and ideas,

- actively developing greater *situational awareness*: increasing your appreciation of the exciting dynamics of different scenes of communication,
- actively increasing your *inventional strength*: enhancing your sophistication in deciding on message content,
- actively adding to your *sense of personal power*: coming to place greater value on your qualifications as a communicator, and
- actively learning *to accept yourself as strategist in communication*: rejecting the false notion that you ever are innocent of persuasive intentions.

As a COSMOPOLITAN, you continue to try new growth strategies for greater communicative expertise.

You do it by:

- actively engaging in purposeful *self-talk*: solving problems in communication and inventing useful data and perspectives,
- actively discovering and releasing your *playful side*: removing the chains that restrict your comfort and freedom in speaking,
- actively utilizing situation-specific *rules*: being the "Roman in Rome," the one who knows the codes of conduct needed to communicate satisfactorily in given scenes and to get on well,
- actively seeking to communicate from the *funny side*: occasionally trying—and enjoying—messages carried by humor, and
- actively studying models of *ethos*: identifying human qualities to which communicators respond affirmatively, thus adding to your understanding and acceptance of safeguarding methods.

As a COSMOPOLITAN, you are moving forward in freeing yourself of ignorance and fear.

You act to be free of the ignorance that prompts inexpedient self-maintenance: ignorance of normal human narcissistic deficiency and fragility, vulnerability, and motivation. Your aim is to counter ignorance with knowledge of the enormous power of personal ideology and self-concept in communication and the human urgency to look after the self. Your aim is to know about the variety of choices people make in approaching communicative situations, as well as characteristics of self-maintenance strategies (both useful and dysfunctional) and human adaptability.

A COSMOPOLITAN is unblinded by fear, though fully aware that ours is a bustling world—sometimes frightening—of variety, ambiguity, and change. Though we want to say things to each other, to function well together and successfully, we need a measure of personal safety. A sense of well-being provides us an opportunity for real communication: for appreciating, respecting, and accepting others' strategic selves and interacting accordingly. When we develop self-assurance, our self-maintenance needs intrude less. Out of that come willing and wise disclosures of thoughts and feelings—and mutual pleasure in communication.

Though not free from normal apprehensions, the COSMOPOLITAN seeks to avoid fearful reactions to the myriad personas of pain that people bring to scenes of interaction: to communicators' neglectfulness of others, rejecting, controlling and manipulative behavior, and attempts at domination. In growth, the COSMOPOLITAN communicator's maturity and knowledge will help to moderate personal fears and allow for humane recognition of others' narcissistic circumstances and their efforts to protect and maintain themselves against shame.

As a COSMOPOLITAN, you are coming to relate maturely with diverse audiences.

This qualification is fundamental. It's basically what characterizes civility in communication. But for the differences in audiences and situations, our lives as communicators would be decidedly uncomplicated. We wouldn't need to exert ourselves in communication (and we'd need fewer books on communicating better). But the truth is that every person is a bit foreign to us, even friends and relatives—enough so that we must make strategic accommodations in order to communicate with them. Differences among people range from age to occupation, skin color to region of birth, economic status to voice quality, gender and sexual orientation to personality and attitudes, life style to body size, and personal habits to aesthetic standards.

The COSMOPOLITAN recognizes human apartness as the instigation for rhetorical action. You don't want to be alone, but you are. Necessarily separate and distinct, and therefore moved to discover grounds of identification with others, you take on formidable tasks as a communicator. Included in that is a graceful handling of ordinary interpersonal fears when perceptions of dissimilarity or strangeness are factors. The manner of dealing with perceived differences will depend on your sophistication and maturity. Though at times even the healthiest communicator will fall to error in audience prejudgment, the narcissistically balanced COSMOPOLITAN functions with a self-concept that is stabilized by reliable premises of self-regard and confidence, providing a force against regressive reaction to feeling alone.

The COSMOPOLITAN is your trustworthy model for sterling *ethos* and success. I recommend that you continue wholeheartedly and without reservation in the directions suggested by this model. Adequate communication in this world requires no less of a commitment from you.

Now we move to the last chapter, from preparing yourself to communicate better to doing it with others.

Chapter Six

Communicating Better

FIRST THOUGHTS

My students frequently suggest ways to prevent problems when maladaptive self-maintenance enters an interaction. I take notes on their ideas and find that some are as good as those in communication textbooks. Take, for example, their thoughts on delaying an "overheated" interaction:

"Stand back and think about it."

"Take a moment to see the whole picture."

"Cool down; talk about it later."

"Wait until the time is right."

Such responses tell me that it doesn't take long in life to gain a lot of knowledge on dealing with protective behavior, our own and others'. Some of my students' advice emphasizes understanding and accepting others, for example:

"Explore the other person's feelings."

"Don't misunderstand others; see where they're coming from."

"Empathize with others."

"See where they are insecure."

"People should accept others as they are."

Some common suggestions are stoical, requiring personal toughness when we feel threatened:

"It's no big deal."

"Ignore it."

"Don't take it more seriously than it's worth."

"Don't overreact."

Others suggestions are varied, relating to everything from invention of messages to posture:

"Stay on the issue."

"Don't personalize everything."

"Give positive feedback."

"Be honest and open."

"You can avoid bad defending by conscious choice."

"Use good manners."

"Don't be a threat."

"Change the subject or direction of the conversation."

"Sit down face to face, and talk about the problem."

Those are excellent recommendations. Incidentally, one of my favorites is "Don't add words to the fire." I always like doing that exercise in class because of the great variety of practical remedies that turn up. Of course, applying them is another matter, and that's what we work on in communication classes.

Also, most of the students' suggestions put the main focus where it must ultimately go: on the audience. I'll illustrate that with another classroom-related story.

Once in a bookstore in Mexico I picked up an interpersonal communication book titled *Tu y los otros,* which in English is *You and the Others.* While liking the title, I thought of a possible improvement, and, as an exercise I brought the book to class and asked my students if they could think of a better title. Several recommended *Los otros y tu.* That's what I wanted to hear! The new title puts the audience first. **When it's time to say something to others, it's they—*los otros*—whose needs and interests should be uppermost in your mind**. That will be a main theme of this chapter: meeting the others where *they* are and adapting to *them* accordingly. In fact, if you've come to the point where you can put aside personal preoccupations and attend to others' welfare, you have no need to read this chapter. And you're ready for sainthood as well.

While the previous chapter's main theme is on *preparing* yourself to communicate better, the main theme of this chapter is actually *doing* it. I've organized the contents into clusters of related steps. Each cluster highlights several recommendations. You'll note some unavoidable overlapping, but that will be useful.

CLUSTER A: AUDIENCES AND SITUATIONS

1. *AS YOU INVOLVE YOURSELF WITH PEOPLE, NOTE THAT ALL ARE HIGHLY MOTIVATED TO MAINTAIN THE SELF.*

Narcissistic safeguarding, including attainment of personal justice, is a constant behavioral element in the chemistry of communicative give and take. The act of self-maintenance cannot be removed from the functions of communicators. Sometimes strategies of maintenance are hidden, hardly breaking the surface of their sending and receiving, but you've got to assume their existence *all the time.* I stress this because I know that when wrapped up in ourselves we can become oblivious to the fact that **others' self-maintenance is as vital to them as ours is to us**. We must always remember this universal condition as we communicate.

Try This. Select the most secure person you know, and observe his or her strategic communicative behaviors closely for a day. If you don't want to scrutinize someone you know, select some prominent figure and read the best biography available on him or her. You may learn that self-maintenance behaviors of people you know or read about are chief marks of their character. One notable mark of Franklin D. Roosevelt's communicating was the effort to keep his physical paralysis under cover. Strategies vary, but all people are motivated to care for themselves in communication. You'll be dealing with them for the rest of your days.

2. *KNOW YOUR SPECIFIC AUDIENCE AS WELL AS YOU CAN.*

Sense unmet needs of the audience, whether it's one person

or fifty. Abraham H. Maslow's lesson that people always function with unsatisfied needs will help us relate to audiences whom we engage in any setting. **When you don't take their needs into account, your chances of satisfaction are diminished.**

Try This. Before approaching your next major experience in communication (for example, asking the boss for a day off from work), raise this question about that audience: Which needs will I be competing with when I meet with her tomorrow? Imagine what's going on in her mind. What might her personal burdens be? Besides the pressure of departmental duties, she'll have other worries, such as a bad back, a pending divorce, or weight control. Of course, this kind of inquiry into communication variables also applies to groups as audiences, but probably in less precise terms.

Consider Richard who, works under you in the company. Sitting there on the other side of your desk at 11:45, he may be distracted by hunger, or he may have an urgent need to visit the restroom. Yet ultimately more critical are Richard's unmet needs regarding self-esteem and safety. What are his immediate narcissistic concerns? Take his sense of adequacy or inadequacy in your office; behaviors may come out in any number of ways, ranging from lightheartedness to overt aggression. If he's unsure of his status with you or of his role (and therefore feels uneasy with you), his participation will be constrained accordingly, and the outcome of your interaction with him may be unfavorable. But with discernment and appropriate action—especially with good listening and patience—you can respond appropriately.

Remember that Richard has social fears, as does everyone with whom you communicate. And don't leave yourself out. Some people have learned to be pretty good at handling their apprehension. How about you with yours?

Use your fears to get an understanding of others' fears. One way is to make use of your projective skills.

Try This. Name one feeling of fear that you have in communicating with others, a feeling that you think might be experienced by others. It may be a feeling that arises when you're with an authority figure such as a police officer, or when you're in certain situations such as meetings at work or interviews. You can use data about yourself to learn about others, for your fears will apply to some of your audiences some of the time. If you as an adult human have these misgivings, millions of others do as well. We are not that unique.

But your current audience differs from all others. It's possible, for instance, that one person's moment of uncertainty or travail will be another's welcome adventure. You've noticed how someone you know will jump right into a situation that you'd never enter, at least not as freely or as fast. Or another may avoid what you thrive on. Though both of you sometimes feel insecure, your individual thresholds of narcissistic pain are different, as are your ways of perceiving conditions. **The character of any event is as felt and viewed by the participants.**

I know a woman with delightful chutzpah; I see it as a splendid combination of freedom and courage to say what she thinks. It's defensive, she once told me. But while I find it constructive defensiveness, not everyone likes her kind of interplay. As she says, "I have to be careful with some people; they think I'm 'brassy.'" Yet as that lady knows, and A.G. Sertillanges confirms, "It is futile to linger endlessly over differences; the fruitful research is to look for points of contact."

Consider the other's self-concept and personal ideology. In communicating with Richard, this point can't be exaggerated. A basic question (in the nice sense) is "Who does he think he is?" Let's say that in comparing himself with you, he feels less important. But does he want to be less important? No. And does he not resent himself for feeling less adequate? Probably. And resent you, too? Possibly. So to identify with Richard the adult, you need to discover a more positive perspective on his view of himself. A more basic question about Richard might be "Who does he *want* to be?" Or "How does he *want* to be taken?" Or, more specifically, "Where is he proud to stand—or does he *need* to stand—on issues relevant to my interaction with him?" **Can you appreciate his self-concept, particularly as he ideally envisions it? What factors of his personal ideology are closely tied to his identity as you communicate?**

Have you noticed how much others want to be shown respect? "Of course!" you say. But don't pass it off too fast. The need for respect is part of all communication, and it's apparent in any kind of verbal and nonverbal language. The "I-want-respect" message is imbedded in *every* enthymeme of *all* communicators; it's a significant fact of their sensitivity. Look for the signs and then act on the evidence. Whatever your responses, remember that it's useless to expect favorable results in communication, if your message suggests a lessening of the other's dignity. Showing respect is an essential base for communicating with people.

Remember, then, that everyone with whom you communicate can be hurt. That explains apprehension. I think this has been amply treated in prior chapters, but we tend to suppress it in our communicating, blinded by our self-concern. "Heck, Tracy can take anything," someone said to me. "She's an indestructible fortress!" The heck she is! Now, Tracy may be known as a very strong person; for instance, she never says no to people who need a shoulder to cry on, and she always seems so sure of herself. We like that in her. But the very fact that she wants to act as though she's invulnerable may testify to her sensitive side. Those with unquestioned self-assurance have no need to "wear it on their sleeves." To appreciate others, we need to know and respect their vulnerability. You'll make a big mistake with Tracy if you relate to her on terms that overlook her human fragility (even if it's rarely seen). I'm not suggesting that you need to burst her bubble. But one day when you've been less than considerate and she shows her hurt, you may be sorry about your faulty perception of her. And why all these years have you been unaware of Tracy's vulnerability, making her the exception to a rule of human nature? Is it because you *need* her to be "Ms. Invincible"? If so, why?

The topic here is awareness of tender dimensions of everyday narcissism. The advice is to respect another's self-concept and fears and to recognize vulnerability. This applies to any type of narcissistic bruising that your audience might anticipate or feel in interacting with you. You have to be careful with that self of theirs.

Look for their roles. A specific strategy for getting information on your audience is through figuring out the roles played. Remember Richard a couple of pages back? What seems to be his dominant role in that communication in your office? Can you put a name to it? Naming is a key act in analysis. Let's say that both his words and his actions suggest pride and loyalty regarding the company that employs the two of you. That's important to know. Would you call Richard a "Company Man," then? If that's an apt name for a big role of his, you'll be able to extrapolate numerous other related traits and characteristics that will help you to communicate better with him. For instance, you may be able to conclude that he's punctual, willing to put in extra time in a pinch, and generally quite reliable. Remember, too, that he takes on other roles of which you'll want to be aware. Yes, he's dedicated and true-blue, but he has additional dimensions that you should appreciate. Keep your sensory faculties active.

Look for role as a reflection of self-concept. You can get information on what a person is guarding—maybe guarding against—by seeing roles as reflections of self-concept. We can't go very far with this in hypothetical terms, for individuals vary in their narcissism. But let's say that Richard's behaviors suggest to you the role and ideology of "Faithful Son." Further, sensing that those behaviors stem from a self-concept that requires respect for parental behaviors, you'll have some idea of major premises to expect from Richard as you communicate with him. You might anticipate that he'll base some of his enthymemes on parental values and a related sense of commitment.

When a person is blocked in adherence to key values, frustration will show up in self-maintenance behaviors. Recall the analysis of Hamlet in Chapter Three. Protective strategies of that particular "Faithful Son" arose out of his sense of inadequacy in living up to parental demand. Shamefully, he was unable to carry out his father's wishes.

3. *TO COMMUNICATE WELL, YOU NEED TO ACCEPT CERTAIN TERMS OF YOUR AUDIENCE.*

Abandon what you think others *should* be and acknowledge what really *is* with them. Let me put it in the framework of roles.

Acknowledge others' roles; accept them in those roles. You can apply this to Richard. It's somewhat like saying, "Acknowledge and accept his self-concept." To withhold acknowledgment of role choice is to ignore the very substance of his being—his ideology—and to risk negative operations of his shame-producing mechanism. **I can think of no more certain way to get a return of destructive protectiveness from anyone than by rejecting a favored role.** If you can't let Richard have his role, you need to examine your relationship very carefully, for there's real trouble ahead. Yes, the fullness of Richard's roles contains protective components. Nonetheless, unless the cost is too great, you must let Richard protect himself as he chooses.

Don't try to change a person. Some of the saddest mistakes follow from believing that you can change your friend, lover, or co-worker. Now, Richard *himself* may be able to make a change, if he chooses to and works at it, but *you* can't be the one to bring it about. OK, if Teddy loves you, he'll do anything for you—almost, maybe this time. But believe me, he is who he is, and if you can't live with that, he's not for you. Maybe I'm too harsh. If so, it's because I want to be sure that I communicate this point to you.

Again, the consequences of rejecting others' established behaviors will appear in their messages as strategies of self-maintenance, some of which may disturb communication. The bitter fruits will range from mild frustration to resentment, from annoyance to hate. **If she thinks that you want to change her, she'll resent it; and if you've tried hard to change her, you'll resent yourself for failing.** She may come to dislike you; you may come to dislike yourself.

4. *LOOK FOR VARIABLES OF THE SPECIFIC SITUATION.* Communicative elements such as time, place, and purpose vary greatly, and their relevant features may be significant in given interactions. Choices that you make in adapting to the situation can be the most critical in any communicative interaction.

Time may be a critical factor. The best time for the parents' important conversation about a family financial predicament may be after the kids have gone to bed. Being able to talk freely, without having to deal with distractions, might be vital to being rational with each other at that time.

And then there's time as it relates to peculiarities of the people involved. Some people communicate better in the morning. But with a colleague of mine—a night person—it was the opposite. Walt let his department chairperson know—but with good humor—that if he were ever asked to teach a class before 10:00 in the morning he would resign. Now, Walt may have been kidding, but he knew that it would be a struggle for him—a self-maintenance struggle, perhaps—to face a class when at odds with his nature. Knowing himself, he hoped to avoid a bad situation.

Some of us are negatively affected by seasonal events: Christmas festivities, Fourth of July celebrations, and certain anniversaries, for instance. Do you know anyone who has a hard time on specific occasions? As communicators, we need to remind ourselves of human peculiarity. What other time-centered variables should we keep in mind?

Place can be a critical factor. I know a person who gets tense in confined places: for example, in the conference room in the building where she works. She feels uneasy there, constricted and unable to keep her mind on topics of discussion. Another friend tries to avoid visiting her mother-in-law's home. As soon as she walks in—even when no one is home, she begins to bristle and put her guard up.

Purpose is always a situational factor. Many people, if perceiving that the purpose of an event is to solicit donations, will deploy safeguarding systems immediately and keep them active throughout the proceedings. Their strategies can cut across all *topoi*, from *Prevarication* ("I gave at the office.") to *Withdrawal* ("Let me out of here.")

Impossible though it is to be aware of all situational forces affecting communication (and I've barely scratched the surface here), you can appreciate the fact that all sorts exist. Actually, your experience may be the best teacher in this.

Try This. Think back to a situation in which you or another person unfortunately overlooked a variable in time, place, or purpose? What was it? What was the outcome? Looking back, what could you have done to prevent that outcome?

CLUSTER B: ANALYSIS AND PRACTICE

1. *BE THE COMMUNICATION ANALYST.* Now that you're well acquainted with basic communication theory, put it to use as analyst of communication.

Be a "participant observer." That is, as you take part in communication, use your analytical powers at the same time. Join two primary communicative roles: first, in active participation in the give-and-take, and second, in sensing what's happening in the interaction as it moves along. Look for cues on thought and feeling as you monitor your participation. Are you being understood? How can you tell? What seem to be the truest and most reliable messages coming back to you? And what of your feedback? Do you sense that it's helping the other? Are you fully (at least reasonably) responsive to the other?

In your observations, give particular attention to how your self-maintenance strategies are affecting the audience. And never forget that **your powerful narcissism interacts with your receiver's powerful narcissism at every moment**. You and the others relate as custodians of your respective *vital* selves. Listen and look for signs of that interplay.

Most of the suggestions that follow apply to you as participant observer.

Check the level of your self-absorption as you interact. One of the main obstacles in adequate sending and receiving is excessive self-absorption. When attending to yourself excessively, you neglect others. That's a fundamental "no-no" in communication. **A neglected person will let you know, in one way or another**. The message may be difficult to interpret, but you've experienced the typical responses: the sharp verbal retort, a show of annoyance, or an awkward silence that says, "Hey, I don't feel good talking to a guy who's all wrapped up in his own life and doesn't give a hoot about mine."

When you receive feedback that suggests, "You're really into yourself," can you recognize the message for what it's doing to communication? How do you answer such feedback? Do you feel defensive? Are you able to make good use of the information? For the sake of productive communication, what are your options?

Grasp the theme of the sender's message. What's its central idea? Almost all messages have a dominant thrust, of which we can make a good determination much of the time. What's the theme of Sandra's message to Art?

Sandra: I'm not going to the ballgame today.

Art: Got something else to do?

Sandra: Yes, my sister's coming down.

Art: You haven't seen her for quite awhile, have you.

Sandra: It's been several weeks, and I've missed her.

Even though a lot of Sandra's message is impossible to represent here, especially the nonverbal indicators, the main idea seems obvious. Simply put, Sandra has decided on a visit with her sister—a significant person in her life—instead of going to the game. She has a need to do that.

Sense the feeling content. In the dialogue above, we got a glimpse of Sandra's feelings for her sister and their relationship. Let's continue the dialogue, to see what nuances of feeling enter into the conversation.

Sandra: My sister and I were very close all through school, and then . . .

Art: Something happened?

Sandra: Things changed after she got married.

Art: What did . . . ?

Sandra: It's a long story—enough for now.

The objective theme is that the sisters' close relationship declined when the other sister married. But that's not what stands out in the conversation. We sense strong feelings: first of Sandra's joy in early years with her sister, followed by deep disappointment. And then we see a definite withdrawal to take care of the self, which, while not a fully explicit message, tells a sensitive receiver to back off.

Note nonverbal components in your interaction. Again, all we have in these dialogues are printed words. Not being there, we don't have Art's advantage. He saw physical signs of sorrow and helplessness: moistness and constriction in the eyes, an obvious frown, and tension in Sandra's shoulders. A person's eyes and movements, their fix on the receiver, or their wanderings can speak eloquently about the sender's feelings. Such behaviors can also tell how it is with the person in that specific place, while communicating on a specific topic with this specific person. They tell of Sandra's level of comfort and sense of safety with Art on this topic.

2. *PUT YOUR SKILLS TO GOOD USE.* You may need to make a conscious effort to do the right thing.

Give her breathing room. That would seem to be good advice for Art as he responds to Sandra's withdrawal. Patience and forbearance are two virtues that pay dividends. Like the rest of us, Sandra needs time and space—relief from pressures of interaction, a chance to collect herself and find balance. **Sometimes, there's too much verbal activity**. Theodor Hecker has a valuable bit of advice for us: Too often a person is "far more likely to talk where he ought to keep silent." More communication mistakes arise from too much speaking than from too much listening. *Know when to ask questions.* Eventually, it may be appropriate for Art to probe a little, showing interest in Sandra's situation. That might be a good way to give her an opportunity to say things, if she chooses. Of course, his strategy will depend on the nature of his relationship with her. In any event, if he feels that Sandra wants to share more with him but is reluctant to initiate it, he may assume the role of initiator. But it bears repeating: Silence has its uses.

Yet, you don't want silence to be misinterpreted as disinterest or indifference. **Knowing when a person needs help in opening up is a marvelous interpersonal attribute to acquire**. It's the skill of sensing when a thoughtful inquiry is the appropriate course to take.

Be a functional responder. Responses range from merely being there to saying something. Unless you mutually agree to end an interaction and go your separate ways, communication will continue. And that means there'll be activity, even in silence. **When you're with another, you never stop sending messages; all of them give information about your thoughts and feelings**. To succeed, you'll have to show each other the respect of a goodly presence of self—making yourselves available and letting yourselves be known. With that spirit, you'll have a chance to exchange clear and unequivocal messages. This doesn't mean always agreeing and never disagreeing. Your presentations of self depend on circumstances, purpose, and so forth. Later, in discussing confirmation, I'll expand on this important topic.

Watch your language. Without doubt, clarity is the primary preventative to distractive self-protection. Without clarity, other means of getting along with someone may be of little help.*

Various other qualities of verbal and nonverbal language are desirable. Particularly valuable are those practices that facilitate communication when issues of character and self-concept are critical. And that's very often. For example, **be alert to defensive strategies that might be taken as slights or indignities, as diminishment of self**. Especially demeaning is language that assaults identity: such as defamation by a colleague, racial slurs, ethnic or gender jokes, or an uncomplimentary reference to a person's sexual orientation. In addition to the moral unacceptability of such offenses is the narcissistic injury that's likely to be inflicted. What's more threatening to communication than a discounting of someone? It's been called "dissing," showing disrespect. Harmony can't be sustained when any participant's identity and basic worth are put forth as issues in evaluation. Achievement of identification and social unity require sensitivity and skill in selection of language, in all interactions.

Check your categorizing. True, we do group people, as we must. Classification is necessary; it's a defense against chaos. But when it's a strategy of hard defending, like stereotyping (often a defense against feelings of inadequacy), everybody loses. The target of the message is wronged, while the sender operates from a delusion that his or her self will be protected. It just doesn't work. The greater one's need to classify others meanly, the deeper is one's fear (and the greater is one's loss of freedom). Stereotyping is self-entrapment; it never meets its purpose of providing personal comfort.

---

* While advocating clarity, I must admit that some moments call for vagueness: for instance, when full transparency in an idea may be too much for another to face at that time.

Let's consider difficulties in the stereotyping of nonverbal messages. Take, for example, perceptions of bodily and vocal characteristics. What tone is carried by a big and deep male voice? That depends on a number of variables, including the situation. In one situation, it'll be scary and responded to with awe, as in the case of the big, menacing voice that James Earl Jones gives to Darth Vader in "Star Wars." But when the same James Earl Jones plays the role of Mufasa the Lion King—a kindly and protective father—the same big male voice sounds reassuring; it's perceived as supportive and warm.

Audience responses show that the James Earl Jones big type isn't the only commanding voice. Witness the political success of former New York City mayor Fiorello LaGuardia, who though of small stature and high voice, was a notably powerful and effective public speaker. Standard conclusions on the effects of body size, vocal pitch, and other nonverbal characteristics are unreliable. Each instance must be taken individually, from a sense of rhetorical value, rather than from a handy stereotype.

Watch your "YOU" language. The pronoun "you" is one of the most explosive and dangerous words in English. Actually, I'm referring to a problem that goes much deeper than the use of one little word, but we'll start with that. Here's some direct advice: **Stop saying "You . . ." all the time**. Maybe you don't overindulge in confrontational use of that "fighting" word, but you definitely talk with people who do. Consequently, you may know that one of the surest ways to bring out unhappy defensiveness in another is to thrust forward a pointy "You" sentence. Look at these.

"*You* make me angry!"

"*You* make me sad!"

"*You* always blame me!"

What's the common response to such declarations? Here's what we can expect. "No, I don't" or "You're the one who . . ." or some other comeback that perpetuates the unnecessary exchange of defensive barbs and jabs. Thus, the interaction becomes a fruitless debate over who's responsible for what. A lot of narcissistic heat is generated but not much light.

The issue is *responsibility* or *ownership*, and there's a solution: Take responsibility for "you and yours": **Own your feelings.** What you feel *is* yours. Your anger is yours, not forced on you by the other person, and you'll have to accept that. As David Augsburger advises, when you're free to own your own thoughts, feelings, and words, you become free to choose your actions and reactions. Your actions are yours; mine are mine. "No one can make another angry. . . . *I* make me angry at you." Moreover, anger is never your only alternative.[1] For example, you could decide to be indifferent, even agreeable.

What *is* advisable when you're moved to come back with "You . . ."? The answer is to say it right: Say it as *the owner* of the feeling. Instead of saying "You cause me to feel . . .," charging the other with responsibility for your emotional reaction, tell how you feel as receiver of the message. Follow this model: "I feel this way about that." Or specifically, "I am angry" or "I feel sad" or "I feel I'm taking too much blame." While "you" statements provoke harsh retorts, "I" statements are unchallengeable. Think of it logically: You *feel* your feelings, and with an "I" statement, you say they're yours, which they are. As *your* possessions, your feelings are not to be disputed. When you take responsibility for your feelings and don't try to assign causation to someone else, you end the ownership dispute, right there.

Try This. The following "You" statements are overly accusative and likely to evoke counter-attacks. Can you convert them to "I" statements? Reword each so as to show real ownership of relevant feelings and provide a promising base for good communication.

"*You* make me feel ashamed."

"*You* are driving us apart."

"*You* always control everything."

I have known cases in which replacement of "I" for "you" did wonders for communication. Once after we had discussed this strategy in a class, a woman came up to me and asked if I could recommend any material on making "I" statements. I gave her a copy of a two-page article on the subject. Well, we finished the course, and a few weeks after that she came back to see me and reported, "You saved my marriage. My husband and I have learned how to make 'I' statements with each other." Wow! Though she gave me credit that wasn't due, I was pleased and very happy for her and her husband. Their hard work paid off; they learned how to take ownership of their feelings and thereby were able to decrease unfavorable defending.* **Saying how you feel rather than giving someone else the responsibility for your feelings can become a valuable communication strategy.**

Choose your roles wisely. We've discussed your awareness of audience roles. But what of *your* role-playing? As you know, some of your roles do not turn out well with given audiences. In particular, I mean roles that they perceive as threatening. Like questionable language usage, such roles are likely to set off strategies of unfavorable self-maintenance. Whether your audience's perceptions are right or wrong is not the issue. It's what they sense that counts.

Here are a few roles that are likely to be sensed by audiences as threatening:

"Critic"—one who will put me down

"Monarch"—one who will try to boss me around

"Schemer"—a conniver, one who will use tricks to persuade me

"Elitist"—one who thinks he's better than I am

"Fence-sitter"—one who never tells me where she stands

I'm sure that you have examples of the effects of such threatening roles.

---

* Incidentally, did you notice her use of "you" in thanking me? In this instance, it was ok because she was not denying ownership of her feelings. But can you think of an example of a complimentary "you" statement that's problematic?

Sharpen and use your sense of exigence. An exigence prods you to speak up (or, on given occasions, prods you to shut up). Can you distinguish between favorable and unfavorable exigencies, between one that may lead to satisfactory communication and the one that's likely to cause problems? The latter should be ignored. If you agree with my former student that sometimes another's insult is "no big deal," then you can let the affront go by without making a direct response. Frustrating though turning away may be, the satisfaction gained from withholding a powerful counterattack often outweighs the satisfaction gained from launching it. Remember the good cowboy who was strong enough to walk away from a fight? While retreat is not always the best strategy, you can learn to pick and choose among potential rhetorical moments.

The secret is in being careful about perceiving exigencies; **sometimes "no communication" is the best communication**. Or the best move may be to perceive an exigence, yes,—but as an opportunity to confirm instead of disconfirm. For example, you could respond to someone's incivility with disarming humor, genuine forgiveness, or other non-belligerent message.

"Dear Abby" recently got a letter from "Secure in Wisconsin," a newly married woman who came upon a box of pictures, letters, and cards that her husband had once received from a woman he'd known. Enjoying a good marriage, the secure wife "rationalized that they were long forgotten," left them as she found them, and never mentioned the subject. The husband eventually threw them out. Abby responded, "Dear Secure: You are a very wise woman. And your husband is a lucky man." This rhetorically mature and smart woman chose not to find an exigence in her discovery of the material. Of course, such maturity isn't achieved by everyone, especially at those moments of terrible insecurity when the temptation to act is so pressing. But even people with distracting defensive tendencies can make admirable strides in coming to distinguish between worthy and unworthy exigencies.

Find the enthymeme. Focus on the chief enthymemes of messages, to discern essential themes and patterns of logic in an interaction. In this way, you'll also locate key values, interests, goals, and purposes, as revealed in others' premises. Let this theory, coupled with appreciation of the identification process, be your practical guide. Listen for the basic premises of messages (and yours in response). You need that information in deciding on how to hold up your end and select communication strategies that decrease the distance and appreciate difference.

Be the communicator who pays attention to structural elements of the event, to what's happening and what works and what doesn't.

CLUSTER C: INTERPERSONAL POWER

1. *IN COMMUNICATION, YOU ARE A FACTOR IN OTHERS' FEELINGS OF COMFORT AND SAFETY.* When you care for the needs of others, you increase your chances for effectiveness. For example, it's smart in any interaction to be aware of the four prevalent "A's" discussed in Chapter Three, those key circumstances that lead to self-protective behavior: being *alone, afraid, aidless* (helpless), and *angry.* When you can be sensitive to these circumstances, you're likely to be trusted by your audiences. And **from trust comes strong ethos:** credibility, the communicator's most valuable asset. Your sensitivity will show that you welcome the opportunity to communicate and that others can be secure and at ease with you. Each of the main points below relates in one way or another to trust and *ethos.*

Look in the mirror. What you see is a person whom some may perceive with worry or uncertainty. Can you accept that perplexity about you? Among possible concerns of theirs are your educational level, bearing and manner, background or race, age, or gender; not to mention attitude, language use, dress, personality, and so forth. Some see you as *different*—and don't forget that. To counter uneasiness arising from others' perceptions of your dissimilarity, you will seek grounds for identification with them and then build from that. Establishment of trust is a necessary goal. Moreover, trust is an earned treasure, coming only from continued effort—genuine and generous—to cooperate in creating structures of common interest, compatibility, and unity.

You and the others have two ways to go in dealing with differences: you can let your mature sides lead, adopting self-maintenance strategies that are likely to facilitate trust, or you can fall back on regressive patterns of defensive discrimination, dominated by dogmas of difference.

Look in the mirror again. There you see a communicator who can influence the direction of an interaction. In the simplest terms, **your words and manner can promote ease and openness, or they can promote stiffness and greater distance**. Of course, this varies according to your audiences and specific situations. As you look in that mirror, it might benefit you to think about the influence you have in communicating with various people. Whatever your opinions on that, I do know that who you are and what you say are major influences in establishing the climate of an interaction, in determining whether it's to be open and inviting or closed and forbidding.

You can alter your communicative behavior if the situation requires it. Remember a time when you felt resentment or bitterness during an interaction with a boss, police officer, judge, or other authority figure? Very likely, you chose not to clash head-on with that powerful one. No, you sensibly chose a strategy calculated to avoid unnecessary conflict, such as a form of *Prevarication.* Or you may have decided on an acceptable strategy of *Withdrawal,* to cool off. Usually these choices make rhetorical good sense, and if such sensible choices can be made with bosses, why not with friends or spouses? Why not defer to *them?* It's a matter of adapting and accommodating, of coming forth with a positive reorganization of a dubious interaction.

Keep in mind that there's no law requiring you to define any situation as an opportunity to get even! Or to run away! Or to be the special one! After all, **the best strategy is one that works for both parties**. Taking an opposing position may not imperil the relationship; indeed, that may be what's needed. Or it may be the worst choice. Your best options are those that further good communication and build strength into your relationships: those cushions of accord that will help you and the others to weather the storms that blow through from time to time. The main issue is function: Will a given strategy facilitate communication? Let the adage "Form follows function" be your guide.

Look into your individualism. How do audiences react to others' needs to be special? Now, we're all individuals, with our particular personalities and behaviors, and I'm not recommending that you suppress your individuality. But then there is individualism, which in contrast to individuality is the extreme of self-interest in behavior. It's "me-centered," a narcissistic doctrine of indifference to others and the general good. As such it works against the flexibility required in communication.

A historian once referred to a prominent nineteenth-century individualist as one who had a habit of "capitalizing on capital I's." He had the political power and social position to get away with his individualism, and the culture allowed it. But while anyone of us might revert to an individualistic state upon occasion, we're more aware these days of communication as a "we" and "us" enterprise. At our best, we interact accordingly.

Clearly, you have options regarding how to be and how far to go in adapting to others—when to give up something of the self and how much—and knowing when to compromise. **Relating successfully demands harmonization of interests**; identifying with audiences is basic to communication.

Look out for co-dependence, the flip side of individualism. Remember the story of the mother and daughter who, dedicated to protecting themselves, came to be excessively dependent on each other? In so doing, they denied themselves the opportunity for personal growth and individuation (becoming "their own persons"). Not all that uncommon, co-dependence is an unfavorable narcissistic condition that might be seen as just the opposite of extreme individualism. The dysfunction of co-dependence stems from excessive togetherness and the resulting loss of independence. In contrast, individualism is dysfunctional in its absence of connection, with the individual standing apart from others. In terms of communication theory, co-dependence and individualism are problems of identification: too much and too little.

Sometimes referred to as narcissistic collusion, fusion, or symbiosis, co-dependence can be an easy trap to fall into. Though it's a cooperative arrangement of reciprocal help and providing for each other, it's ultimately crippling. The loss of self-identity and freedom of choice exceed the gain in comfort and protection. What's the solution? Work things out to have both interdependence and freedom—optimal degrees of closeness and expression of individuality. That may take a lot of honesty, courage, and hard work.

To get, you have to give. Let's return to our discussion of individualism. What's it worth to make an effort to communicate with her? How much should I give in adjusting to his mood? What are the costs of going the second mile with him? What are the rewards? To what extent should I persist in satisfying my narcissistic needs, when I know that success in communicating hinges on the issue of my (and the other's) individualism?

Other cultures offer useful models in this regard. For example, we can learn from Asian cultures that there are alternatives to obtrusive individualism, choices that will strengthen our interactions. Imbedded in Asian cultures, with their notable Confucian emphasis on maintaining social relationships through interdependence, are structures for softening immoderate expressions of individualism. Asian avoidance of excessive directness and harsh "no" responses are cases in point. One of North American society's strengths is the openness that allows us to learn from the many cultures that thrive here and to incorporate attractive qualities from various sources.[2]

Always be aware of your self-maintenance function. This suggestion applies to all means of caring for the self, but let's start with defensiveness and find relevance to all strategies. Gershen Kaufman believes that making *conscious* choices in defending is a very important early process in growth. We might say the same about all self-maintenance strategies. Kaufman's plan for continued growth involves being aware of when you defend, noting what activates a particular response, and noting how you defend. Further, to be able to choose a particular defense implies being able to let go of it when trust is established, when protection is less urgent. Kaufman also suggests naming the defense, a step he believes leads to greater awareness and control of its use.[3] When you can name your defensive roles and see them as communicative strategies, you highlight your behavior and understand it for what it is. Once you come to recognize a given mode and accept it, you can use it more constructively.

2. *ACT TO SET A PRODUCTIVE CLIMATE IN COMMUNICATION.* Communication is a *transaction*, an event in which people exchange messages and affect each other *simultaneously* and *together.* Joined in communication, you and I are interdependent. When relating, you and I tailor our strategies to fit our immediate purposes and—when rhetorically competent—to fit the specific conditions of our interaction. This applies, of course, to our use of maintenance strategies: You are protective with me to affect me and I with you for the same reason.

Be rhetorically smart in inventing your self-maintenance methods. In making decisions on whether to say it this way or that way, you try—or should try—to avoid counterproductive strategies. And though caring for the self in communication is normal and unavoidable, remember that some forms do not work well. You can learn a lesson on choice from the two farmers in Robert Frost's poem "Mending Wall." They'd meet at the property line each spring to replace the stones that had fallen during the winter, "to set the wall between us once again." It was their custom to make this annual repair of the boundary. But, said one farmer, "There where it is we do not need the wall." And,

> Before I build a wall I'd ask to know
> What I was walling in or walling out,
> And to whom I was like to give offence.

Keep in mind the possibility of defensively walling others out and giving offense. Purposes, situations, and audiences vary, and, as David Augsburger said about emotions, we do have alternatives. For instance, in no situation is showing contempt or blaming or any other strategy the only choices available; in your sophistication, with your breadth and social experience, you have options. "But what if she deserves to be put in her place?" you ask. OK, but what do you want in return, reconciliation or continuation of bad times? If you hope for reconciliation, you might consider the biblical advice: "A soft answer turneth away wrath; but grievous words stir up anger." There are various self-maintenance *topoi* and many, many strategies in each *topos.* For instance, in the *topos* of *Control* there are countless roles, including those of leading, helping, conducting, organizing, controlling, restraining, facilitating, managing, overseeing, equalizing, coordinating, and reconciling. Which of the great assortment will facilitate the kind of communication you want? That's the question.

The "less likable" persons in your life need special attention. Can you accept them in communication with you? Here's a perspective that will enhance your *ethos,* if you're willing to go forward with it. On occasion you may be held back by the view that she should take care of herself this time; you're reluctant to support someone who doesn't care that much about you. I'm sure that you've felt this way—that she doesn't deserve the time of day from you. Right? Maybe she doesn't deserve it, but it's to your benefit to have her doing her self-maintenance enthymemes *with* you rather than throwing disturbing premises *at* you. Helping her to stay balanced narcissistically is mutually advantageous.

Help them feel unthreatened by you. The way to make a "bad guy" into a willing communication partner is to let that person know—honestly and truly—that he will be safe with you. It helps to remind yourself that security is a necessary foundation of trust, and **trust is as sure a preventive to obtrusive narcissism as you can find**.

What's true with less than lovable persons may have even greater meaning in regard to those you love and whom you want to love you. Psychologist Carl Rogers said, "We can love a person only to the extent that we are not threatened by him."[4] The best thing you can do to get on with any audience—of one or many—is to give them good reason to feel safe with you.

Try This. Take one of your relationships with a family member or friend. Name one specific self-maintenance strategy of yours that seems to disturb the communicative climate when you're with this person. Perhaps the person finds your strategy threatening and must resort to "saving face." Look to the eight *topoi* in Chapter Four to categorize your questionable means of self-maintenance (*Control, Achievement, Opposition, Attribu-*

tion, Anger, Denial, Withdrawal, or *Prevarication*). Then answer these questions.

a. How would I describe the strategy?

b. When did I last choose it with this person?

c. What were the circumstances? What motivated me to make use of this strategy? What was I protecting against; what in my self or self-concept was I caring for or justifying?

d. How did I make use of the strategy?

e. Why is it a questionable choice? How did it prevent achievement of my communication purposes? Did it evoke hard face-saving from the other?

f. Name a strategy that would yield more favorable results for both of us. Why not try that one next time?

After you've had an opportunity to try an alternate strategy, evaluate the results. Determine how well it worked. Include pluses and minuses and a recommendation for the future. There's always a tomorrow and a chance for improvement.

3. *CAREFUL NOW, A SELF-MAINTENANCE STRATEGY MAY HAVE A "BUG" THAT'S "CATCHING."*

Since self-maintenance runs through all communication, this statement can be interpreted simply and correctly as saying that communicators affect each other. It can also mean that communicators carry "bugs," that their behaviors may be contagious. Thus, interpersonal influence ranges from healthful to unhealthful, from wholesome to diseased. The quality of any strategy will depend on factors related to the situation and purposes of the communicators. But so often the main factor is the narcissistic condition of the individuals themselves. **Unless the narcissistic health of all involved is good enough to handle a strategy with bugs, it will contaminate communication.**

Take walling off the self, as an example. While a common and sometimes useful choice in self-maintenance, your overguarding can trigger another's defending—and with negative results. For one reason or another—from early learning or regression—a person perceiving a threat from you may respond with self-protective strategy that turns out to be dysfunctional. Thus your maintenance behavior can adversely affect another's behaviors, influencing the person to lash out or hold back on identifying with you.

One often-suggested source on handling threat is Jack R. Gibb's catalog of defensive problem conditions and correctives.[5] Studying group interaction, Gibb identified six behaviors that increase defensiveness. They are especially useful when seen as reminders of contagion in self-maintenance. Here are the six points.

Check your strategies that appear evaluative. Have you ever considered the possibility that certain of your maintenance strategies may be taken as judgmental? People put themselves on guard and become inhibited when they feel that others are critically appraising them. Gibb suggests replacement of evaluation with *description,* to avoid arousing uneasiness. Description, as a non-judgmental statement, is acceptable because it doesn't ask for a change in behavior or attitude. Note that this caution on evaluation relates to the dangers of "you" language mentioned earlier (when someone shouts, "You're always criticizing me," instead of *describing* how she or he feels at the moment).

Check your strategies that seek to control. Examples are messages that appear to have the purpose of restricting others' choices or directing their behavior. As we've seen, they tend to suggest inadequacy in others. Replace controlling strategies with a *problem* orientation and show a genuine desire to relate as a peer, attending to the topic or problem at hand instead of trying to do things *to* others.

Check your strategies that may suggest a hidden motivation. Others resent it when they suspect they're being used or worked on with gimmicks or techniques. Replace such methods with *spontaneity,* with straightforward and open messages.

Check your strategies that appear as neutral. Neutrality in speech can appear to show lack of concern for others. Reflecting an attitude of detachment, it precludes clear acknowledgment of others' importance. Replace "clinical" and unfeeling maintenance messages with *empathy,* with reassuring messages, or other clear indications that you identify with the receivers' problems and feelings. I'll have more to say later about confirmation and empathy.

Check your strategies that give a tone of superiority. Messages showing that you want dominance in power or position evoke a defiant or other intrusive response. Replace suggestions of self-supremacy with respectful messages that recognize areas of *equality* and promote mutual trust. You'll note that superiority is related to the individualism that we looked at earlier. Also, individualism is often connected to certainty, the last of Gibb's points.

Check your strategies that show an attitude of certainty. Behaviors that reveal dogmatism and a need to be right and to win out arouse counterproductive defensiveness. Replace certainty with *provisionalism*: a willingness to experiment and search for answers *with* others, rather than adamantly holding to a one-sided, individual view.

Can you acknowledge the one who doesn't acknowledge you? Here's another perspective on contagion. As you know, we need to be confirmed by others. When a person comes along who doesn't confirm you in your kindest overtures, you'll tend to be scornful of that person: "I did everything for her, and what do I get in return? Nothing!" Very likely she was controlled by her narcissism—absorbed with self-concern—and therefore was incapable of appreciating your support. From her inability to confirm (and possibly infected by *your own* narcissistic ache of the moment), you caught a bad case of defensiveness yourself. Susceptible to slight, and thus unable to understand and accept her as an injured or temporarily weakened person, you repudiated her for not meeting your confirmation needs. Here's another good example. Heinz Kohut, the founder of self psychology, tells how depression can be a communicable defense.

> The depressed person's inability to respond to us—our incapacity to infect him with even a minimum of joy in response to our presence and to our efforts in his behalf—inevitably creates a lowering of self-esteem in ourselves, and, feeling narcissistically injured, we react to it with depression and/or rage.[6]

Sometimes the injured one becomes one who injures; the infected one infects.

Try This. I'd like you to recall a time when you transmitted your "contaminated" defensiveness to another.

a. What were the circumstances? Where? When? With whom?

b. What did you say and do that unfortunately "infected" the other?

c. Describe the quality of your "diseased" behavior, noting verbal and nonverbal elements.

d. Describe how your "communicative illness" was "caught" and returned by the other person. Classify it using one or more of the eight self-maintenance *topoi.*

e. Why did the event occur in the first place?

f. What would you do differently next time? Write yourself a prescription for communicative health.

4. *VALUE THE PROCESSES OF CONFIRMATION AND IDENTIFICATION AS YOU COMMUNICATE.* For me to confirm you is to acknowledge your existence. It's to say to you, with words or a mere flicker of an eye, "You're somebody; I hear you." Such an act, whether obvious or nearly imperceptible, gives you that wonderful feeling of being validated; it expresses appreciation of your dignity or sense of pride and status.

This preeminent need to be acknowledged is our master exigence. In a real sense, we might call the yearning for confirmation the communicator's "primal cry." It's what motivates our invention of the "Confirm me" message. Indeed, the need for confirmation can be all-consuming, and to be unresponsive to another is to deny that need. That hurts. When disconfirmed by someone whose response is important to them, people will suffer a loss in self-esteem. And you know what follows: narcissistic imbalance and subsequent acts of self-justification, ranging from noisy anger to quiet retreat. On the other hand, a recognized and accepted person is unlikely to fall back on unfavorable defenses.

In the past few years, we've come to know a new word,

"dissing," which I mentioned earlier in the chapter. It's the act of saying or doing something that another takes as a show of *dis*respect. Dissing is communication felt as an injury to the self. Dissing is disconfirmation. It often results in a hard defensive response.

Before suggesting ways to confirm another, I'd like to point out the importance of the process by naming several ordinary strategies of relating that *disconfirm.* Note that each of these avoidable strategies is unfavorably self-serving and neglectful of the other.

Shifting responses. Charles Derber wrote about what he called "conversational narcissism." One form is the "Shift-Response."[7] When using this strategy, people put attention on themselves and overlook others' interests. Here's one of Derber's examples:

John: I'm feeling really starved.

Mary: Oh, I just ate. (shift-response)

How would people you know react (either overtly or inwardly) to this kind of disconfirmation from you? Name two probable reactions.

In contrast to the shift-response is the support-response, as shown in this exchange from Derber:

John: I'm feeling really starved.

Mary: When was the last time you ate?

Make a side-by-side analysis of John's feelings when he was shifted and when he was supported.

Making impervious responses. Like shifting, the impervious response ignores the other's message, as if nothing was heard or seen. It's a real put-down. I recently heard someone say, "He looked right past her, seemingly unaware of her plea or her tears. To him, she didn't exist." How does it feel to be treated in this way, to be unnoticed or slighted? How is the impervious response likely to affect the climate of an interaction?

Another impervious response is not returning a telephone call. How does it feel to be alone and waiting for that call? Why do people neglect to return calls?

Interrupting. It's often not good communication to interrupt people, but I have to admit that some people don't seem to mind. Also, the rules of certain cultures permit free interrupting. Nonetheless, you've got to be careful. Some people become quite put off when not given a chance to finish sentences, especially in public where their dignity or sense of adequacy is threatened. One reason for their unwillingness to let the affront go unanswered is that, in their minds, others will think them ineffective or weak. Drawing on your experience, what are the hazards of interrupting? When or with whom is it OK and when not?

5. *TAKE ACTION TO CONFIRM.* Now, let's go to the positive side and see what can be done to confirm others.

Hear the person out. Let her have her say. Not only will you learn something useful about interacting with her, but you'll also give her a chance *to be somebody.* And only *somebody* can confirm *you.* Think about that. Isn't that what you want in communication?

A little may mean a lot. You know, so often all that people need is a gesture of support—just a warm word perhaps—or a wink or wave! Or some indication they are needed. To be needed warms the heart and feeds the soul. It reinforces our sense of our worth. When audiences are denied recognition, it's no wonder that they stiffen up or slump down, lapse into arrogance, or slam the door and take off. Such acts should tell us our significance to them. **A significant person is one whose confirmation is valued.**

Bring forth your empathic best. First, we need to distinguish empathy from sympathy; these capabilities are different but frequently confused. Sympathy is the capacity for sensing another's feeling and is often associated with pity. Empathy is deeper. It's your capacity to experience another's feeling, thought, or attitude *as your own.* To empathize is to pull away from your customary narcissism and "catch the flame" of the other's state of the moment. It's to be extraordinarily attuned. Note that I didn't suggest the impossible: abandoning your narcissism. Since no one can do that completely, no one can ever become fully empathic. For most of us, empathizing with another is not an everyday happening. For some people it's rather rare. In communicative terms, a precondition of empathy is a comfortable relaxation of ever-ready strategies of self-maintenance. It's an easing off of self that allows you to experience the other's state of being. Who is the most empathic person you know? A teacher, perhaps? Some teachers are able to be empathic, to the extent that they experience the ideas, emotions, and points of view that their students bring to the classroom. In this regard, I think that ideal preparation for teachers' everyday work would include visits to their students' neighborhoods and homes. Think how that would increase the teachers' powers of empathy at school. Directly or vicariously, we need to put ourselves in others' territory, to learn how it feels to be there.

Like other interpersonal powers, your empathic capacity can be increased. Rely on it in its current state of development, yet expect it to increase as you grow. As your sense of self-adequacy increases, you'll spend less energy in the kind of maintenance that detracts from communication; and **the less energy you spend doing it the HARD way, the more you'll be free to empathize with and confirm others**. That's the best reason for learning about your self-maintenance patterns and for working toward greater self-assurance. Take it as a life-long personal project to enlarge yourself with a keener empathic sense. You'll be a more effective communicator in all areas of your life.

Show that you care. It's not enough to experience the other's feelings and ideas; you must act on the experience. In other words, assume that a necessary step beyond empathy is *showing* it: communicating in accord with your sensitivity to another's state. Make your empathic self available to the other.

While some people will need more constant and direct expressions of your caring, none can ask more of you than you're prepared to offer. The advice then is to seek mutual accommodation, yes, but to relate sincerely on your terms, knowing and respecting your needs and limitations as well as the other person's. In the long term, real sincerity (albeit subtle) has a greater chance for success than dramatic behavior that's forced.

And the *sincere* you has more resources available for communication than you sometimes think. When the odds are favorable on being appreciated, that responsive part of you has good words to bring forth, an amiable smile, and a cordial nod by which to send a validating message.

Find areas of common ground. With empathy and real caring, there's a chance that he'll respond in kind. If he does, whether the topic is controversial or innocuous, there's a chance that together you can create the trust for going forth and discovering enough shared interest to carry your moment of communication. That's the great faith of well-meaning communicators everywhere. Even in disagreement, the two of you can stand solidly on your respect for each other. And if you don't have that, you can start by talking about that.

6. *TAKE A RISK.* Difficult though it may be to perceive, there's peril in most of your communicative situations, even the ordinary. When you make yourself available to others, you can be hurt. **To communicate is to chance loss, and that's why we're self-protective.** It's a real bind because to over-protect is also to lose. Heavily defended participation curtails effectiveness. Such is your dilemma: If you open up, you might get hurt, but if you don't open up, your gains will be limited. Is there a way to handle the dilemma? Consider the following perspective as you try to answer that question.

There are many people who've lived for years—twenty, even fifty or more!—earnestly believing that it's always prudent and necessary for them to keep the guard up high, even though the original reasons for doing so have long vanished. Much of that vigilance isn't beneficial any more. They have grown some since childhood, and they ought to reflect on the wisdom of their years of living, recognize their maturation, and give themselves credit. "Maybe you can drop some of your armor now," I'd advise. "Shouldn't you be presenting messages that are more congruent to who you are *now* and how you actually feel *now*? Isn't it possible that as you take chances in communication the feedback from others will not be as devastating as you once imagined? Very likely you're now a stronger and readier communicator than you think. Listen, **'being real' is the issue you have to face: it's about taking a chance on be-**

ing 'up front' and letting your feelings and opinions be known."

I once came across a movie review with much relevant wisdom for us here. "To live is to risk," observed the reviewer. Not risking is to refuse life itself. "We can never ask too much of life, but can easily ask too little of ourselves. And by asking too little we give too little." There's still time to make changes, urges the writer: "it is never too late to accept life's gambit."[8]

Reflect on new ideas. Check yourself on being too comfortable in your ideological provincialism. Maybe narcissistic isolationism is a better term because what I'm referring to is a kind of defensive walling off of oneself from others' ideas or experiences. It's a self-defeating strategy, since it imposes a drastic curb on rewards of interpersonal interaction. If you are now able to risk engaging others' minds and entertain varieties of intellectual perspectives, you know of the satisfactions, in spite of the risks. Test new strategies. Why not treat others to fresh ways of relating? This may call for courage, but it's also a call for expansion of your self. Your experimentation will put you in the role of innovator, encouraging you to discover stimulating rhetorical perceptions and new methods of interacting. You need that now and again. **Dare to drop rusty self-maintenance gear; substitute underused but promising strategies for those that are ready for the rhetorical junkyard.**

A primary recommendation, then, is to endorse your personal role of courage as you relate to people. Find that courageous part of you and acknowledge that it's there and available. Once acknowledged by your conscious gesture of acceptance, the brave one will make a public appearance. This is what it takes, then: *acceptance* of this courageous part of yourself, then *validation* of that part by applying a name (perhaps "The Lion") and then *talking* to him or her as a real person, as someone who will step forward as your best representative.

7. *ABANDON THE WIN-LOSE MENTALITY.* Conflict and competition run through almost all communication. People have differences, and people seek power. Those are facts. We all have narcissistic needs, and we must function with our human nature. But **we don't have to live with behaviors that get us nowhere and harm relationships**.

Work to have everybody succeed. One of the obstacles to satisfactory conflict resolution is the premise that only one person can win. The win-lose way of thinking is sometimes called the zero-sum game, a situation in which one person's gain always leads to another's loss: The sum of gains equals the sum of losses. That's necessary in an athletic contest or political election, and in those true win-lose games, the winner takes all. But interpersonal communication need not be that dire or falsely framed.

Get rid of the economic model in communication. In applying the winner-take-all theory to interactions or conceiving of situations in which the store of "goodies" is limited, you must conclude that somebody will end up disappointed. Yes, scarcity is a harsh reality in certain areas of life. We know that if there are only so many job openings down at the plant, some applicants will not be hired. Since there's only one remaining ticket for the performance of *The Magic Flute*, either you or I will stay home and watch television.

But very few interpersonal conflicts and competitive interactions are about shortage, and even though there's much "trading" in ordinary interaction, it's not controlled by severe laws of economics. In other words, each participant can be rewarded—and amply. That's because the prized "commodity" in the enterprise is *confirmation*, sometimes referred to as validation. The law of supply and demand does not operate in that market. Interpersonal "goodies" are not in short supply. **There's always enough confirmation to go around, if you and I are liberal enough in its manufacture and distribution**.

Then what's the real issue in conflict, as discussed here? Fundamentally, it's stingy narcissism—being miserly of self. It's interpersonal "tightness." Even in arguing or competing, I *can* confirm you, if I will. I've got plenty to give and nothing to lose, if I dare abandon my constrictive economic model of scarcity and convince myself to be interpersonally generous and risk giving something of my self.

Yes, I *can* bring myself to confirm you, if I'm able to see my defensive resistance as *self*-defeating—whether it arises from some specific kind of pride or a general sense of shame. In analysis of my narcissism, will I be able to see that winning out over you is losing for me—losing something more valuable? It's up to me to be smart enough and big enough at that critical moment, to help both of us to confirm ourselves as winners. And when compromise is necessary, it's up to me to do my part to shape it as a "win" for both of us.

CLUSTER D: THE COSMOPOLITAN AND THE ROLE OF GOOD AUDIENCE[9]

1. *FOLLOW THE COSMOPOLITAN MODEL.* I want to end this book by bringing back the COSMOPOLITAN, the model representing all communicative virtues we've been exploring. **Put maturity, effectiveness, and civility together and you have the basic shape of the COSMOPOLITAN.** Further, the COSMOPOLITAN, progressing steadily in development of a Communicative Disposition, is free of distracting provincialism and able to function humanely, even in a threatening interpersonal climate.

A COSMOPOLITAN, perhaps akin to the self-actualized person described by Maslow, confidently welcomes the differences that distinguish us, and is not incapacitated by social fear or an urgency to defend anxiously against cultural, racial, educational, age, gender and other human distinctions.

Communicating with an adequate sense of security, the COSMOPOLITAN acts as a force for increasing the level of others' security. **Not faultless but growing, the COSMOPOLITAN is a communicator who respects both self and audience, who interacts for both personal and social good.**

2. *LEARN THE FUNCTION OF THE GOOD AUDIENCE.* In day-to-day interaction, the master role played by the COSMOPOLITAN communicator is that of "Good Audience." In Chapter Five we discussed the intrapersonal "Good Audience," the internal good listener who provides guidance and correction when you engage in self-talk, drawing on your personal store of experience and good sense. For instance, through the process of self-talk, your own "Good Audience" can react to issues regarding your communicative planning and strategizing, thus helping you to function well. Now, we'll take this idea to the social realm, to understand it as a role in communication with oth-

ers. First, I'll need to set the scene with a comment on social guidance and purposes of an audience.

What is social guidance? To maintain a functioning society, humankind has built up over centuries a host of behavioral standards and corrective systems. We can call them social guidelines, many of which are unwritten. We use these standards and systems in monitoring activity in a community or culture, to let us know how we're doing, whether we're on the right track in our social functioning or veering off. Among the instruments on which we have come to rely are moral codes, sets of spiritual and social values, cultural constraints, practical guidelines, personal commitments, laws, and so forth. The forms are numerous, and the variety is great. Of course, communicative interaction is a part of social functioning, and it too is monitored and constrained. In communication, we call the corrective messages "feedback," a familiar term.

What's the basis of this feedback on messages? Feedback that keeps an interaction on track originates in those same places: codes, values, standards, and norms of society. Central in the ideologies of audiences, these constraints guide the behavior of interacting senders and receivers. Take for example, an instance of destructive rage flaring up and disturbing communication. In practical terms, such a violation can be checked. But it can't be controlled by vague laws or arbitrary criteria. What guidelines will set things straight? Or better, *whose* guidelines will set things straight?

There's only one answer, and you know it well: the *audience*, a microcosm of society and the only agency with appropriate standards, with a real investment in the situation, and with adequate power to take action. An audience *is* powerful, even in an interaction involving so-called equals. It's peer power. The audience—of one or many—can help to facilitate or correct an interaction and guide events toward good results. At every moment in your daily communicating, you have occasion to relate as a "Good Audience." Though welcome by others, it's not an extraordinary function.

Can you envision an audience as an active speaker? This question may seem strange, but it's from sound theory. A communicator assumes two fundamental roles simultaneously, at once sending and receiving. The roles can't be separated. So in a real sense, we don't have speakers *and* listeners. All participants send and receive—constantly. When we listen actively to another, we respond all the time, verbally and nonverbally. On this point, Maurice Merleau-Ponty wrote, "I am not passive while I am listening; rather I speak according to what the other is saying."[10] In the interplay, audiences speak with and without words, and they influence accordingly.

What's the nature of audience power? It's the power to confirm and disconfirm that gives the audience—the other—status and position. To confirm is to endorse, to validate or support. To disconfirm is to deny endorsement—to withhold permission for unsocial, unsatisfactory communicative behavior. **Therein lies the power of the audience: to influence interaction toward mutual effectiveness and reward.** That's the work of the "Good Audience."

But how good is the "Good Audience"? The answer is good enough. **The "Good Audience" is good enough for the communicative moment.** It's nonsense to expect perfection and unfailing responsiveness from any audience. Adjectives like *faultless* and *noble* aren't of much use in describing communicators in ordinary interaction. The right words are *practical, functional,* and *adequate.*

3. *ADOPT THE ROLE OF GOOD AUDIENCE.* As a communicator—a receiver-sender—the "Good Audience" draws on its COSMOPOLITAN nature. When doing well, you and I fill that role. Our verbal and nonverbal responses convey messages, saying "Tell me more" or "Don't go too far" or "Repeat that" or "Be kind to Teresa" or "I don't like that" or "Nice going." Of course, that's similar to what various guidance systems and controls of society say to us. People in our lives need those messages, and they count on us to say such things. And we need *their* beneficial messages; we need them as good audiences.

Let's look closely at the practical work of a "Good Audience." *The primary function is to provide feedback.* This is the business of supporting and correcting that I have discussed above. Aware and able communicators let others know how things are going, helping to determine the status of the exchange and locate relevant issues. Adequate communication requires this information. To give useful feedback is to be a "Good Audience."

As a seeker of its own ends, the "Good Audience" accepts the fact that there's at least one opposing view in any significant deliberation. Communication thrives on differing opinions. And who has the burden of presenting another view, providing needed interpersonal and ideological balance?

Remember the destructive Bernarda Alba whose story we examined in Chapter Four? Who was more responsible for the disaster befalling those people in that house, Bernarda herself or those around her who did not assert themselves and stand up as a "Good Audience" to her dysfunctional communication? Or must we conclude that oppressive forces of culture determined the end? Asked another way, can you conceive of the women around Bernarda being able to use the *topos* of *Opposition* in defense of themselves against her chosen *topos* of *Control*? That's asking a lot. Why? Like Bernarda, the others were culturally oppressed. Only the sufficiently healthy and mature—good audiences—will have the courage and ability to support others who are under the sway of detrimental forces.

The "Good Audience" mediates the clash of narcissism and the social good in daily life. The force exerted by unrestrained narcissism opposes general interest and community need. The "Good Audience" works from practical wisdom and in a functional role, appreciating the truth that **altruism has no natural advantage over narcissism; anyone's social sense is less well-established than primary self-interest**. That's why we need the power of the "Good Audience" helping the communication along.

The "Good Audience" works for civility in communication. Civility counteracts distracting self-interest. That vital quality of human interaction relates directly to much of what we've been discussing in this chapter. As we conduct our lives in this fast and furious world of uncertainty and change, we occasionally grate on one another—*if we don't watch out.* **Civility is "watching out.**" It's your sensing that your acts may be received as a threat. A threat to what? To another's self-esteem, background, status, personal sense of justice, or cultural identity.

Civility means being comfortable with diversity, with another's economic status, educational level, religious choice, ethnicity, and so forth. It means being aware of another's "face" and helping him or her to "save" it gracefully. That's one of the nicest—most civil—things you can do for anyone. It shows your carefulness in monitoring your individualism, e.g., when tempted to relate from a "high and mighty" narcissistic role or "survival of the fittest" mentality. It's being secure enough to be a peer and not to need another's diminishment. **Civility means making the best communicative use of your best nature.**

And in that regard, a mark of maturity and sophistication in communication is civil—tactful, fair and considerate, often deferential—regard for others in choosing your self-maintenance strategies. **Watching out for yourself need not conflict with watching out for others.**

Like your sense of well-being and most other personal characteristics, your civility is never a finished product; it's ever growing. As developed, it's there now to support the persona that you'll call up to represent you in your very next communicative act.

The "Good Audience" keeps to personal purpose. The "Good Audience" is self-interested, necessarily narcissistic. With its own ends to meet, it seeks to be effective, to exert power, and to be acknowledged. As with all communicators—motivated by personal intent to affect and influence—it's "after something." Of course! Any other posture would be false. And only in serving its own purposes can it be a *real* person to others.

"Goodness" in an audience is not necessarily "niceness"; further, "nicey-nice" behavior suggests a deception. That's a hazard in any communicative event. Indeed, **you'll receive more reliable feedback from an act of obvious self-service than from an act that's seemingly innocent and disinterested.** No one is innocent of narcissistic need. Nor should one feel shame about it.

The "Good Audience" is self-respecting. A sense of dignity is a great comfort in communication. To be a self-respecting communicator is to be one's own person and to maintain oneself confidently in communication. **It means taking care of oneself**

while meeting obligations to others involved. Though constrained by social reality and requirements of unity and identification in communication, the "Good Audience" is healthfully self-assured and relatively free from harmful fusions with others and stifling dependencies.

The "Good Audience" is rhetorically mature. By this I mean communicatively "grown up," responsive to the fact that to reach others, one must take appropriate *action.* **To communicate satisfactorily with people is to be purposeful, to choose ways to be effective with them—and to get rid of ways that don't work.** It's to be realistic, sensible, and practical. It's to be the level-headed communicator who can distinguish between certainty and probability—and to know that in life the latter rules over the former.

The "Good Audience" has a functional grasp of communication theory and practices. Suffice it to say that included in our model is a sound understanding of the processes of sending and receiving messages, perceiving exigencies, taking roles, building enthymemes, and identifying/confirming—particularly as these elements apply to the all-important task of maintaining the self. Cognizant of relevant issues in an interaction and of choices available, the model communicator is prepared to act: to speak up, support, confront, agree, counter, and deny, as indicated. In this sense, behavior of the "Good Audience" will conform to the general principles of communication found in basic books on the subject.

Of course, this model of maturity and skill is able to make wise choices of self-maintenance *topoi* for given situations, noting whether a form of *Attribution* or *Anger* would be more useful than *Control* or *Prevarication.*

In sum, the "Good Audience" is a useful standard of excellence in communication. This communicator is smart enough never to forget that forms of narcissism will always challenge the social good, and at the same time, is aware that an audience not acting in its own interest can't be trusted to tell us the truth about ourselves, including our unfavorable individualism when it arises. By respecting itself, the "Good Audience" will not fall into the trap of giving unlimited license to others' destructive behavior. With positive *ethos* (though only human after all and "good" only to a relative degree), the "Good Audience" is civil and concerned, rhetorically mature and competent. The "Good Audience," society's only source of guidance for behavior in communicating, is our first and last great hope.

If you read the **Dedication** when you first opened this book, you may have wondered what it meant. Take a second look; I know it'll make more sense now. It's for you.

DEDICATION: TO THE GOOD AUDIENCE

> When they are good, they are very, very good, and when they are bad, they are horrid. Audiences, I mean. This, then, is to salute the "Good Audience": the communicator who, with competence, compassion, courage, and civility, cares enough to let us know when we're doing well and when we're not.

All I ask of you is that you continue working at it: toward becomimg the COSMOPOLITAN in communication, toward becoming fit in the role of "Good Audience."

Notes

Introduction

1. "Social Insecurity," *America West Airlines Magazine* April 1996: 74, 76–77, 79–80.

2. "Historical Perspectives on the Presented Self," *The Self and Social Life*, ed. Barry R. Schlenker (New York: McGraw-Hill, 1985) 33–64.

3. "Two Questions about Psychoanalysis and Poetry," *The Literary Freud: Mechanisms of Defense and the Poetic Will*, ed. Joseph H. Smith (New Haven: Yale UP, 1980) 113–18. To demonstrate the ubiquity or prevalence of the defensiveness that Edelson notes, I can't resist quoting a line from a recent film version of *Shadowlands* (a story about the relationship of C.S.Lewis and Joy Davidman): "People read to know they're not alone." The quotation suggests that to be alone is to be unprotected, an unacceptable condition, and to read is to guard against that.

4. *Man's Aggression: The Defense of the Self* (Boston: Gambit, 1973) 216.

5. "Toward a Meaning-Centered Philosophy of Communication," *Journal of Communication* 12 (1962): 197–211.

6. *Ego Defenses and the Legitimation of Behavior* (Cambridge: Cambridge UP, 1988) 2.

7. *Ego Defenses*, 24.

8. See Heinz Kohut, *The Analysis of the Self* (London: Hogarth Press, 1971) 108–9 and Kohut, *Self Psychology and the Humanities: Re-*

flections on a New Psychoanalytic Approach, ed. Charles B. Strozier (New York: Norton, 1985) 12–13, 110, 198–99.

9. *The Restoration of the Self* (New York: International Universities Press, 1977) 290. For an important comment on Kohut's belief on shame as the central affect in narcissism, see Andrew P. Morrison, "Shame and the Psychology of the Self," *Kohut's Legacy: Contributions to Self Psychology,* ed. Paul E. Stepansky and Arnold Goldberg (Hillsdale: The Analytic Press, 1984).

10. *Theories of Human Communication,* 5th ed. (Belmont, CA: Wadsworth, 1996) 167–68.

11. Though Burke did use synonyms for the term guilt in a sense that may seem to bring it close to meaning "shame," e.g., the imprecise term "embarrassment," he did not in these instances have reference to the condition of felt inadequacy that we now understand to be the basis of shame. On shame versus guilt and Burke's position, see Harold Barrett, *Rhetoric and Civility: Human Development, Narcissism, and the Good Audience* (Albany, NY: State U of New York P, 1991) 8–10.

12. In this regard, I recommend David Zarefsky's thoughtful (and rhetorical) exploration of the problem relating to the current conflict in the United States on diversity and community interests: *The Roots of American Community* (Boston: Allyn and Bacon, 1996).

13. Kohut, *Analysis of the Self.*

14. My principal source of information on Japan is Takie Sugiyama Lebra's *Japanese Patterns of Behavior* (Honolulu: UP of Hawaii, 1976), an excellent book. It should be noted that over time behavioral adaptations do occur in cultures. On the May 16, 1995, broadcast of "The MacNeil/Lehrer Newshour," Sho Shioya, Japanese journalist, discussed psychological changes among Japanese children of the 1980s, those entering adulthood. He pointed to a certain sense of deprivation, insecurity, and anxiety among them and a resulting attraction to cults, to groups offering meaning in life and a purpose. He traced this behavioral phenomenon back to absent, neglectful fathers who are preoccupied with their work, creating a condition that leaves a void in family life.

Chapter 1

1. Harry Guntrip, *Schizoid Phenomena, Object Relations and the Self* (New York: International Universities Press, 1968) 175.

2. Besides relying on my catalogue of extensive observations of human interaction and responses of focus groups, I have found two books particularly useful as sources for developing the eight *topoi*: Merle A. Fossum and Marilyn J. Mason, *Facing Shame: Families in Recovery* (New York: Norton, 1986) and Gershen Kaufman, *Shame: The Power of Caring*, 2nd ed. rev. (Cambridge, MA: Schenkman, 1985).

3. On the topic of choice in selecting maintenance strategies, defenses in particular, turn to George Vaillant, *The Wisdom of the Ego* (Cambridge: Harvard UP, 1993).

4. See Gershen Kaufman, *Shame*, 71.

5. Inner speech is not a newly discovered phenomenon. Plato, in the *Sophist*, asked, "Are not thought and speech the same?" What is called thought is a dialogue with oneself, "unuttered conversation with the soul."

6. Lloyd F. Bitzer, "The Rhetorical Situation," *Philosophy and Rhetoric* 1 (1968): 1–14.

7. In Aristotelian theory, enthymemes are units of thought based on probabilities, not certainties. There's no need to prove a point or try to be convincing or persuasive if the conclusion is certain and uncontestable. It's not certain that everyone wants to advance in his or her employment, and some do advance without giving constant attention to deadlines. Some engineers will succeed without having had a course in trigonometry, and an outstanding fielder at third base for the Armadillos may be kept around for his glove. Communicating on all of the above themes will center on degrees of probability, as developed by the communicators.

8. See, for example, his *Rhetoric of Motives*. See also the explanation of Burkeian theory in Philip K. Tompkins, *Communication as Action: An Introduction to Rhetoric and Communication* (Belmont: Wadsworth, 1982).

9. The term "being with others" is a good informal synonym for identification. It's the principal theme in my book, *Daring to Be: Love and the Art of Rhetorical Intercourse* (Chicago: Nelson-Hall, 1982).

10. Daniel N. Stern, *The Interpersonal World of the Infant* (New York: Basic Books, 1985). See Chapter Seven.

11. For an important article on confirmation, see Kenneth N. Leone Cissna and Evelyn Sieburg, "Patterns of Interactional Confir-

mation and Disconfirmation," *Rigor and Imagination*, eds. Carol Wilder-Mott and John Weakland (New York: Praeger, 1981).

Chapter 2

1. George Vaillant shares this immature vs. mature qualification to distinguish behaviors: *The Wisdom of the Ego* (Cambridge: Harvard UP, 1993).

2. For a more complete treatment of child development as it relates to communicative competence, see Harold Barrett, *Rhetoric and Civility: Human Development, Narcissism, and the Good Audience* (Albany: State U of New York P, 1991).

3. Willard Gaylin, *Feelings: Our Vital Signs* (New York: Harper and Row, 1979) 32.

4. Daniel N. Stern, *Diary of a Baby* (New York: Basic Books, 1990) 60–61.

5. Barrett, *Rhetoric and Civility*, 33. Confusion often arises when "narcissism" is defined as "self-love." "How can narcissism be about 'loving' yourself?" we might ask. "Isn't it true that severely narcissistic people do not love themselves?" Those are proper questions because some expressions of narcissism relate more to reduced self-esteem than to love.

6. See Mario Jacoby, *Individuation and Narcissism: The Psychology of the Self in Jung and Kohut* (London: Routledge, 1990).

7. Arnold H. Modell, "Self Preservation and the Preservation of the Self: An Overview of More Recent Knowledge of the Narcissistic Personality," *Narcissism, Masochism, and the Sense of Guilt in Relation to the Therapeutic Process*, Bulletin 6, the Psychotherapy Research Group, Department of Psychiatry (San Francisco: Mount Zion Hospital and Medical Center, June, 1983) 2. The second source is Alan L. Grey and John Fiscalini, "Narcissism, the Self, and Interpersonal Psychoanalysis," *Narcissism and the Interpersonal Self*, eds. John Fiscalini and Alan L. Grey (New York: Columbia UP, 1993) 1.

8. Sophie Loewenstein, "An Overview of the Concept of Narcissism," *Social Casework* (March 1977): 136–42.

9. For further study of shame and its influence on human behavior, consult Gershen Kaufman, *Shame: The Power of Caring*, 2nd ed. rev. (Cambridge, MA: Schenkman Books, 1985; Andrew P. Morrison, *The Culture of Shame* (New York: Ballantine Books, 1996) and his essay, "Shame and the Psychology of the Self," in *Kohut's Legacy:*

Contributions to Self Psychology, ed. Paul E. Stepansky and Arnold Goldberg (Hillsdale: The Analytic Press, 1984); and Francis J. Broucek, *Shame and the Self* (New York: Guilford Press, 1991).

10. On the connection of creative work to shame, see Broucek, *Shame and the Self*, xiii.

11. Readers who want to study the theory of socialization further should go to Donald W. Winnicott's pioneering work, *The Maturational Processes and the Facilitating Environment* (London: Hogarth, 1965). For an enlightening interpretation, see also Stephen M. Johnson's *Humanizing the Narcissistic Style* (New York: W. W. Norton, 1987).

12. See Johnson, *Humanizing the Narcissistic Style*, 39f and 44.

13. Gershen Kaufman, *Shame*, 28–29.

14. *Japanese Patterns of Behavior* (Honolulu: UP of Hawaii, 1976). This an excellent book for anyone who wishes to learn about the culture of Japan. Another is Takeo Doi, *The Anatomy of Dependence*, trans. John Bester (Tokyo: Kodansha International, 1973).

15. Luigi Barzini, *The Italians* (New York: Atheneum, 1964) 166.

16. "Why We're Losing Sight of the Common Good," *Washington Post National Weekly Edition* 4–10 March 1996: 29.

17. *The Wisdom of the Ego*, 331.

18. *Darwinism in Human Affairs* (Seattle: U of Washington P, 1979) 126–28. On xenophobia, see also Vernon Reynolds, Vincent Falger, and Ian Vine, eds., *The Sociobiology of Ethnocentrism: Evolutionary Dimensions of Xenophobia, Discrimination, Racism and Nationalism* (Athens: U of Georgia P, 1987).

19. For a useful view of the condition of helplessness, see Martin E.P. Seligman, *Helplessness: On Depression, Development, and Death* (San Francisco: W.H. Freeman, 1975).

20. Deborah Tannen, *You Just Don't Understand* (New York: Ballantine Books, 1990).

21. For a clear statement on the integration of masculine and feminine attributes (attributes in androgynous combination), see Ronald B. Adler, Lawrence B. Rosenfeld, and Neil Towne, *Interplay: The Process of Interpersonal Communication*, 6th ed. (Ft. Worth: Harcourt Brace, 1995). Regarding a gender model for professional suc-

cess, Alice G. Sargent writes convincingly that "an androgynous mix of behaviors" provides "the most effective management style." Most of her observations apply to communication. See *The Androgynous Manager* (New York: AMACOM, 1983).

22. On the question of communication patterns arising from the conflict between self-perception and cultural rules, I recommend Jill Ker Conway's book *True North: A Memoir* (New York: Vintage Books, 1995). Among notable thoughts is her valuable insight on the rhetorical choices made by exceptional women who though wanting to use their power and influence in society repress that part of "their story," as they function in their marriages and family lives. Incidentally, what she calls repression, we might understand as denial, a communicative strategy for self-maintenance.

23. See Guy E. Swanson, *Ego defenses and the Legitimation of Behavior* (Cambridge: Cambridge UP, 1988) 1–25.

24. Kenneth E. Boulding, *The Meaning of the Twentieth Century: The Great Transition* (New York: Harper and Row, 1964) 159–63.

25. For an intriguing and relevant view on the motivation of terrorism, see John W. Crayton, "Terrorism and the Psychology of the Self," *Perspectives on Terrorism*, ed. Lawrence Zelic Freedman and Yonah Alexander (Wilmington: Scholarly Resources, 1983) 33–41.

Chapter 3

1. Harold Barrett, *Rhetoric and Civility: Human Development, Narcissism, and the Good Audience* (Albany: State U of New York P, 1991) 25.

2. See Merle A. Fossum and Marilyn J. Mason, *Facing Shame: Families in Recovery* (New York: Norton, 1986); Stephen M. Johnson, *Humanizing the Narcissistic Style* (New York: Norton, 1987) and Lynne Layton and Barbara Schapiro, *Narcissism and the Text: Studies in Literature and the Psychology of the Self* (New York: New York UP,1986).

3. See *Motivation and Personality*, 2nd ed. (New York: Harper and Row, 1970), especially the Preface and Chapter 11; see also Maslow's *Toward a Psychology of Being*, 2nd ed. (Princeton: D. Van Nostrand, 1968). This note covers all references to Maslow's ideas in this section.

4. Gregory Rochlin, *Griefs and Discontents: The Forces of Change* (Boston: Little Brown, 1965) 3, viii.

5. For a full and informative study of helplessness and its origins, see Martin E. P. Seligman, *Helplessness: On Depression, Development, and Death* (San Francisco: W. H. Freeman, 1975).

6. In reference to the definition of dysphoria, see S. R. H. Beach, E. E. Sandeen, and K. D. O'Leary, *Depression in Marriage: A Model for Etiology and Treatment* (New York: Guilford, 1990) 9–10. On incidence and interpersonal dysfunction, see the same authors' article, "Dysphoria and Marital Discord: Are Dysphoric Individuals at Risk For Marital Maladjustment?," *Journal of Marital and Family Therapy* 19 (1993): 355–68. In introducing the topic of depression, my purpose is to suggest effects on communication, without reference to causes. For an enlightening view on personality sources and biochemical sources of depression as well as the relevance of shame, see Andrew P. Morrison, *The Culture of Shame* (New York: Ballantine Books, 1996).

7. Alice Miller, *The Drama of the Gifted Child*, trans. Ruth Ward (New York: Basic Books, 1981) 38.

8. Gershen Kaufman, *Shame: The Power of Caring*, 2nd ed. (Cambridge, MA: Schenkman, 1985) 76.

9. Fossum and Mason, 85.

10. Mario Jacoby, *Individuation and Narcissism: The Psychology of the Self in Jung and Kohut* (London: Routledge, 1990) 166. See also 171–75. For an informative book-length treatment of the subject of rage, see Willard Gaylin, *The Rage Within: Anger in Modern Life* (New York: Simon and Schuster, 1984).

11. Heinz Kohut, *Self Psychology and the Humanities: Reflections on a New Psychoanalytic Approach*, ed. Charles B. Strozier (New York: W. W. Norton, 1985) 125, 252.

Chapter 4

1. *Feelings: Our Vital Signs* (New York: Harper and Row, 1979) 26, 40, 35.

2. Called a "rhetorical disposition," this is one of the main topics of my book, *Rhetoric and Civility: Human Development, Narcissism, and the Good Audience* (Albany: State U of New York P, 1991). The keys to a Communicative Disposition are adapted and extended from material on pp. 27–32.

3. See Heinz Kohut, *Self Psychology and The Humanities*, ed. Charles B. Strozier (New York: W.W.Norton, 1985) 12–13, 110, 198–99.

4. For a clear and convincing argument on our roles as rhetorical strategists in interpersonal communication, see Gerald M. Phillips and Nancy J. Metzger, *Intimate Communication* (Boston: Allyn and Bacon, 1976).

5. One good source on the topic of optimal frustration is Heinz Kohut, *The Restoration of the Self* (New York: International Universities Press, 1977).

6. Guy E. Swanson, *Ego Defenses and the Legitimation of Behavior* (Cambridge: Cambridge UP, 1988) 18–19.

7. Merle A. Fossum and Marilyn J. Mason, *Facing Shame: Families in Recovery* (New York: Norton, 1986) 101.

8. "Working With Anger," *Bridges Not Walls: A Book About Interpersonal Communication*, 5th ed., ed. John Stewart (New York: McGraw-Hill, 1990) 343–46.

9. *Narcissism: Denial of the True Self* (New York: Macmillan, 1983) 74–75.

10. See Phebe Cramer, "The Emperor's New Clothes," *The Development of Defense Mechanisms: Theory, Research, and Assessment* (New York: Springer-Verlag, 1991) 39–40.

Chapter 5

1. For a convincing discussion of infant sociability at birth, see H.R. Schaffer, *The Child's Entry into a Social World* (London: Academic Press, 1984).

2. *Man's Search for Meaning* (Boston: Beacon, 1963).

3. *Motivation and Personality*, 2nd ed. (New York: Harper and Row, 1970).

4. "Ego Distortion in Terms of True and False Self," *The Maturational Process and the Facilitating Environment* (London: Hogarth, 1965).

Chapter 6

1. David Augsburger, *Caring Enough to Confront* (Glendale: Regal Books, 1980) 46–48.

2. On American individualism, see Robert N. Bellah, et al., *Habits of the Heart: Individualism and Commitment in American Life* (Berkeley: U of California P, 1985). For a clear contrast between North American individualism and the Asian emphasis on the interpersonal arts in communication, see June Ock Lum, "The Impact of Confucianism on Interpersonal Relationships and Communication Patterns in East Asia," *Communication Monographs* 55 (1988): 374–88.

3. Gershen Kaufman, *Shame: The Power of Caring,* 2nd. rev. (Cambridge, MA: Schenkman Books, 1985) 150–52.

4. *Client-Centered Therapy* (Boston: Houghton Mifflin, 1951) 159.

5. Jack R. Gibb, "Defensive Communication," *Journal of Communication* 11 (1961): 141–48.

6. Heinz Kohut, *Restoration of the Self* (New York: International Universities Press, 1977) 188.

7. Charles Derber, *The Pursuit of Attention: Power and Individualism in Everyday Life* (New York: Oxford UP, 1979) 24–35.

8. Review of the film "A Sunday in the Country," *Films in Review,* 1985.

9. I have written of the good audience in other books. See *Rhetoric and Civility: Human Development, Narcissism, and the Good Audience* (Albany: State U of New York P, 1991) and *Speaking in America* (Ft. Worth: Harcourt Brace Jovanovich, 1993).

10. Maurice Merleau-Ponty, *The Prose of the World,* trans. John O'Neill, ed. Claude Lefort (Evanston: Northwestern UP, 1973) 143–44.

Glossary

A

absolute a certainty; *contrast with* a **probability**

Acceptance of Oneself as a Communicative Strategist one of the six keys to a Communicative Disposition: acknowledgment of the fact of one's human function as inventor of messages to influence others

Achievement one of the eight strategic *topoi* of self-maintenance: characterized by purpose and action to accomplish and succeed; ranges from adequacy in performance to pursuit of "perfection"

adapt to adjust to new or changed conditions

adaptability capacity to change or adjust to conditions

adaptive value worth of a strategy as measured by usefulness in a given circumstance; *see also* **functional strategy**

alienation condition of detachment from an audience

androgynous incorporating both female and male gender traits in an individual's makeup; *see also* **gender characteristics**

Anger one of the eight strategic *topoi* of self-maintenance: characterized by expressions of ire or wrath; ranges from indignation to rage

attention the act of directing or keeping the mind to an event, person, or object

Attribution one of the eight strategic *topoi* of self-maintenance: characterized by aims to discover cause or origin, to censure or blame; ranges from noncontentious assignment of responsibility to bitter accusation

attunement a condition of accord or unity; communicative harmony; *see* **identification**

audience the person or persons addressed in communication; the other, the listener, or the receiver

B

blame *see* **Attribution**

C

Capacity for Intimacy one of the six keys to a Communicative Disposition: the ability to experience genuine kinship or closeness with another, to share and trust

choice an option; basic to the process of invention in communication, i.e., to discovery of message content appropriate to purpose, audience, and occasion; *see also* **invention** *and* **strategies**

civility respect in meeting perceived differences between self and audience, beyond courtesy and politeness; basic mark of communicative maturity and sensitivity; *contrast with* qualities of unsocial demand, e.g., individualistic narcissism; *see also* **maturity**

co-dependence state of mutual and excessive dependence in a relationship; narcissistic collusion; *see also* **symbiosis**

common ground a basis of common interest or like-mindedness in a sender-receiver relationship; *see also* **identification**

communication interactive process of symbolic influence in effecting audience response to a message—in securing confirmation; more than the act of informing or transmitting thoughts and feelings

Communicative Disposition a standard of qualification for adequacy in communication; a set of criteria for communicative health and success used to evaluate strategies of self-maintenance in communication; *see* the six keys: **Acceptance of Oneself as Communicative Strategist, Capacity for Intimacy, Inventional Strength, Other-Awareness, Sense of Personal Power,** *and* **Situation Awareness**; *see also* **COSMOPOLITAN model** *and* **"Good Audience"**

communicative identity those characteristics of self that are available to and perceived by participants in communicative interaction

communicative rationality sound thinking in interacting with others, specifically as pertaining to the act of relating to audiences without undue fear of narcissistic injury

confirmation the act of acknowledging or validating messages, and in particular, the self of the sender; a communicated recognition or gesture of endorsement or positive regard; a basic human need

Control one of the eight strategic *topoi* of self-maintenance: characterized by action to regulate and direct; ranges from ordinary and purposeful effort toward effectiveness to obstinate, authoritative intervention

cope to deal with problems in communication, e.g., in choosing useful, mutually acceptable self-maintenance procedures

COSMOPOLITAN model the exemplar sender and receiver (the latter in role of "Good Audience") representing acceptable standards of interaction; a standard of steady growth and maturity in communication; representation of a Communicative Disposition with attributes reflecting a level of functioning allowing for effectiveness and civility, especially in relating with others who differ in status, behavior, culture or race, interest, background, orientation, or any other condition; *see* **"Good Audience"** *and* **maturity**

courage attitude of assuming risks positively and willingly facing painful or threatening situations

credibility believability, trustworthiness; favorable *ethos,* a vital factor in communication

cultural interface interaction of representatives of contrasting cultures; *see also* **multicultural**

cultural scripts prevailing themes or forces of a culture, some of which suggest values, e.g., popularity and conformity

culture the acquired beliefs, values, customs, behaviors, ways of living, etc., of a cohesive social unit larger than a family

D

decode act of a receiver in determining or interpreting meaning in a sender's message

defending justifying or protecting the self against narcissistic injury, i.e., against disconfirmation; inventing a communicative strategy for the purpose of maintaining cohesiveness of self or self-concept; *see* **saving face**

defensive ethos marks of one's defensive character, giving distinctness to one's self

defensiveness self-protectiveness: preparedness to guard the self or self-concept against anticipated disconfirmation, against narcissistic violation

defensive strategy a purposeful communicative act in defense of the self or in self-justification, whether useful or problematic; *see* **hard** *and* **soft**

deficiency *see* **deficits**

deficits needs or lacks commonly acquired in ordinary development and revealed in personal attributes and behaviors: may function favorably as motivation in communication or unfavorably, e.g., as distractions; *see also* **losses** *and* **narcissistic injury**

Denial one of the eight strategic *topoi* of self-maintenance: the act of refusing to recognize or acknowledge threatening facts, conditions, ideas, or feelings; ranges from inattention to delusion

depression *see* **dysphoria**

difference reference to the highly critical factor of diversity in communication of sender-receiver; *see also* **human condition** *and* **separation**

disconfirmation ignoring, rejecting, or otherwise discrediting another's message or presentation of self; *see* **"dissing"**

"dissing" a colloquial term for disconfirmation; act of "putting a person down"

dysfunction communicative impairment, inadequacy, or maladaptation, e.g., inability to adjust to audience needs; *see also* **narcissism** *and* **"noise"**

dysphoria a general or ordinary form of depression: condition of low spirits, discontent, malaise, or "blues," associated with or reflecting self-criticism and reduced self-esteem; may function as defensive *Withdrawal*

E

economic model a concept of communicative interaction based on the false principle of limited availability of "commodities" for confirming others; *see* **zero-sum game**

empathy the quality that allows one to experience another's feelings, thoughts, or attitude

encode act of the sender in communication of choosing verbal and/or nonverbal message symbols; *see* **sender**

enthymeme [EN-thuh-meem] a unit of thought in communication, analyzable as an ordinary line of reasoning in a message; a practical syllogism based on probability and designed to accord with the sender's perception of receiver receptivity; *see also* **invention**

ethos mark of one's character or personal qualities that indicate credibility; has been named the most critical factor for success in communication with another; *see also* **self**

exigence a circumstance or condition perceived as requiring response; the reason behind one's decision to send a message, e.g., what prompts a response when one feels that one's truthfulness is questioned

exploratory mentality inventional strength in communication, characterized by creativeness, curiosity, imagination, will, and energy, etc., in discovery of roles, enthymemes, or other material for use in communication

F

facilitative that which advances communication, e.g., a functional defensive strategy such as timely *Prevarication*

fallibility human deficiency or imperfection; liability to make a communicative mistake or miscue

family system a family's organic structures that constrain thinking and behaving: codes, rules, rituals, values, etc.; bases of family self-maintenance patterns

fear apprehension relating to narcissistic injury and disconfirmation; *see also* **insecurity**

feedback verbal and/or nonverbal message of response from receiver to sender; *see also* **self-correction**

Freudian theory classical psychoanalytic formulations on conflict of drives leading to guilt and development of neuroses; *contrast with* theories on self that point to a sense of self-deficiency leading to shame and development of narcissism; *contrast with* **self psychology**

functional strategy communication strategy characterized by usefulness: mature, healthful, and mindful of receiver's needs; *see also* **adaptive value** *and* **strategies**

G

gender characteristics attributes classified as female or male; *see also* **androgynous**

gender plurality *see* **androgynous**

"Good Audience" the communicator as adequate receiver, who, with balanced interests of personal purpose and others' welfare, interacts effectively to confirm and disconfirm—support and constrain—thereby contributing positively to communicative outcome; *see also* **Communicative Disposition** *and* **COSMOPOLITAN model**; *note also* "Good Audience" as a major subself—one's idealized perception of a knowledgeable and caring part of the self that is available to offer guidance and support in intrapersonal communication

grandiosity full and relatively unrestrained self-expressiveness; a possible negative factor in communication, if perceived as excessive, e.g., as arrogant, pompous, or flashy

H

hard self-maintenance strategies that reflect heavy self-absorption and thus are likely to be maladaptive; *contrast with* **soft**; *see also* **narcissism**

health *see* **COSMOPOLITAN model** *and* **maturity**

human condition ordinary social circumstance characterized by factors of separateness among individuals (given their differences and marks of individuality) typifying the predicament of humankind and providing motivation for identification and communication; *see also* **difference** *and* **separation**

I

identification communicative kinship or point of unity in thought or feeling; act of affiliation or connection that is the essential basis of communication; state of "being with" an audience; *see also* **attunement**

identification with the aggressor defensive identification with an aggressive person or group, for status and security

ideology one's body of beliefs, values, principles, or specific doctrine; colored by narcissistic needs, self-concept, and sense of justice and reflected in chosen self-maintenance strategies; *see also* **self-concept**

individualism a guiding doctrine or principle of ideology that places individual or personal interest above social interest

individuality aggregation of one's needs, roles, goals, ideology, etc., distinguishing one person from another

innocence the condition of infancy characterized by absence of or indifference to personal rhetorical power and intent; with loss of innocence resulting as the infant becomes aware of personal individuality and rhetorical influence, i.e., of the power to affect others

insecurity feeling of uncertainty, lack of assurance, self-doubt, instability, etc., relating to problematic or unsettled status of self; *see also* **fear, shame, threat,** *and* **vulnerability**

interdependence a union or state of mutual dependence, as in a marriage or other close relationship; *contrast with* **co-dependence**

interpersonal communication ordinary interaction of senders and receivers exchanging messages

intimacy interpersonal closeness, a measure of which is necessary to communication (as constrained by situation, purpose, audience, etc.)

intrapersonal communication internal communication or dialogue, between or among one's subselves; *see* **self-talk** *and* **subselves**

invention process of selecting content for messages of communication, including roles, enthymemes, and supporting material, e.g., as suggested by a relevant self-maintenance *topos*; *see also* **choice, functional strategy, self-maintenance, sender, strategies,** *and* ***topoi***

Inventional Strength one of the six keys to a Communicative Disposition: ability in choosing favorable content of messages

issue a point of controversy; a debatable topic, e.g., the *issue* of taxation in a debate on educational reform

J

justice, sense of sense of right and wrong; a central element in one's personal ideology, relating to fairness, deservedness, equity, etc., with critical implications for uses in defensive and self-justifying strategies

justify to choose a self-maintenance strategy for personal vindication, support, or protection of one's behavior, name, status, or trait, etc.

L

losses narcissistic deprivation of infancy from ordinary understimulation and overstimulation of caregivers; specifically, from undue pressure, neglect, absence, death, and so forth, resulting in shame and with implications for invention of self-maintenance *topoi*; *see* **deficits** *and* **narcissistic injury**

M

machismo a strong or ardent sense of manliness, e.g., in exaltation of virility, power, and entitlement

maturity a condition characterized by adaptable, civil, sensitive, and effective behavior; basic to ability to accept and make accommodation to differences in audiences; *see* **COSMOPOLITAN model**, *and* **"Good Audience"**

message a unit of communication or the content thereof, e.g., a comment, question, request, meaningful gesture, or extended statement such as a speech

model a standard, paradigm, or representative pattern serving as illustration, comparison, or guide for imitation

motivation a moving force, e.g., for defending against self-diminishment, maintaining pride, achieving, and meeting other goals in communication

multicultural cultural variety or diversity: a condition of audiences; *see also* **cultural interface**

N

narcissism "the great force of self"; an individual's sense of self or "selfness" as developed from responses in infancy to environmental conditions of overstimulation and understimulation, and as enabled by an acquired sense of shame; represented in communication by two forms: **hard** forms foreshadowing dysfunction and **soft** or functional forms which provide the bases of useful self-maintenance procedures in communication; *see also* **self** *and* **shame**

narcissistic collusion *see* **co-dependence** *and* **symbiosis**

narcissistic injury emotional injury to the self, especially in infancy, from over- or understimulation, with consequent effect on one's sense of shame; *see also* **deficits, losses,** *and* **shame**

narcissistic motivation the prompting of communicative action to meet needs of self and perceived threats thereto, for justification or protection; *see also* **defensiveness, self-maintenance,** *and* **shame**

narcissistic reality the view that a communicator's subjectivity or self-interest may contribute to mutual success in sender-receiver interaction

needs urgent or basic narcissistic requirements, with security being fundamental; felt deficiencies that underlie the urgency to identify with others and be confirmed interpersonally, e.g., through acts of reassurance and respect; *see also* **confirmation, identification,** *and* **self-maintenance**

"noise" any interference in the processes of sending and receiving messages: physical, cultural, political, semantic, psychological, religious, and so forth

"noncommunicativeness" a receiver's non-responsiveness (actually paradoxical or ambiguous responsiveness) to a sender's message, e.g., as indicated by a blank facial expression

non farsi far fesso Italian precept: "not to be made a fool of"

nonverbal a message or message part presented without words, e.g., by facial movement, gesture, scent, dress design, and so forth

normal that which is regular, usual, or standard; used frequently in this book in reference to ordinary maintenance of the self in communication

O

objectivity a perspective characterized by relative freedom from the influence of self-needs and self-interest; *contrast with* **subjectivity**

Opposition one of the eight strategic *topoi* of self-maintenance: characterized by expressions of counteraction or resistance; ranges from dissent to contemptuous challenge

optimal frustration in child development, favorable level of deprivation in satisfaction of needs or deficits in yearnings, thus a level of injury and stimulation conducive to growth and narcissistic health

options *see* **choice**

Other-Awareness one of the six keys to a Communicative Disposition: sensitivity to others'—receivers'—feeling states, thoughts, and predispositions

overstimulation in an infant's experience, the excessive communicative presence of a caregiver; "being with" the infant "too much"; *see* **losses**, **narcissism**, **narcissistic injury**, *and* **stimulation**

P

participant observer a communicator who, while interacting, also takes note of the events and character of the interaction

perception a sense impression or discernment of a communicative event, person, or object, and so forth

perfectionism extreme or obsessive striving to adhere to a standard of perfection, e.g., as demanded by one's self-concept (one's personal view on adequacy in performance); *see also* **self-concept**

persona a part of the self that is represented interpersonally—"out there"—in communication

philotimo Greek cultural value that urges maintenance of dignity and social balance as well as avoidance of ridicule or social loss, e.g., that arising from financial failure or loss in a competition

play social interaction in a game, sport, conversation, or like event; good when entered into with an optimal degree of freedom, openness, self-assurance, and respect for others, thus a model for most communicative activity

premise a basic belief, axiom, or guiding principle; part of one's ideology as a personal point of view, value, or element of self-concept that directs thinking or doing (including communicating); *see* **ideology**, **self-concept**, *and* **values**

Prevarication one of the eight strategic *topoi* of self-maintenance: characterized by forms of explanation, evasion, equivocation, exaggeration, and untruthfulness; ranges from rationalization to lying

pride sense of personal dignity or self-respect and self-worth, ranging from healthful self-esteem to arrogance

probability likelihood or reasonable expectation, e.g., as related to judging the usefulness of a given role in communication; the basis of strategic invention and the stuff of enthymemes

productive narcissism useful self-interest; the force of self as promoter of sender-receiver satisfaction in communication; *see* **narcissistic reality**

protect *see* **defend**

purposeful directed toward a goal, not aimless or meaningless; a mark of sound rhetorical invention

R

receiver listener, audience, or the other

reciprocity a state of cooperativeness and mutuality in exchange, with sharing of benefits

regression a return to a state of infancy, represented in communication by immaturity or needs of a child, e.g., in childlike dependency or inability to postpone gratification

rhetoric the study of the art of influencing audience responses, with emphasis in this book on choices related to the attainment of the affirmative response called confirmation; *see also* **rhetorical imperative**

rhetorical communication that is audience-centered, purposeful, and functional; *see* **rhetorical energy**

rhetorical energy rhetorical strength or motivation directed to a rhetorical end, i.e., to affect an audience according to purpose; *see* **rhetorical**

rhetorical imperative suggests a premise of this book: that each human is possessed of a basic motive directed toward influencing others to respond favorably, i.e., to confirm one's messages and oneself; *see* **confirmation** *and* **rhetoric**

rhetorical value probable effective power of a given strategy in communication

risk the danger of experiencing injury, principally disconfirmation, in communication with another

roles specific behaviors chosen to meet given exigences in communication, e.g., "Tough Guy" to confront an audience; *see also* **invention**

role-taking strategic assumption of a role in communication; *see* **roles**

rules directives or codes of a given group—family, society, or culture—that constrain choice in communication, e.g., a rule that regulates a person's use of profanity or body scent

S

safety *see* **security**

saving face defending one's dignity, reputation or "name," or other self-conceived mark of value; a function of self-maintenance; *see* **self-maintenance**

security a relative sense of safety in meeting possible narcissistic injury or shame, especially in regard to the hazards of disconfirmation; *see also* **needs**

self one's identity or essential narcissistic qualities and character; in communication, as one conceives of one's self *and* as one is perceived by the audience; observable in communication by one's strategies of self-maintenance, e.g., means of self-justification

self-absorption inordinate preoccupation with personal needs and interests; unfavorable narcissism

self-acceptance acknowledgment of and respect for one's traits and behaviors; not only self-approval but also healthful recognition of personal traits of questionable communicative value; *see* **Acceptance of Oneself as a Communicative Strategist**

self-actualized in the theory of Abraham H. Maslow, the person able to achieve full potential in creativity, independence, spontaneity, and grasp of reality

self-concept one's set of personal principles or ideology of self: includes perceptions, beliefs, feelings, attitudes, and specific views on what one ought to be and do and ought not be and do, and so forth; *see also* **ideology**, **self**, *and* **shame**

self-correction adjustment of communicative behaviors to accommodate one's self-concept, purpose, and demands of the audience and occasion

self-disclosure the choice of making information on oneself available, e.g., personal concerns, feelings, attitudes, beliefs, and so forth; the act of presenting the self for identification with an audience

self-esteem one's level of self-respect and self-pride; *see also* **self-acceptance**

self-interest *see* **self-investment**

self-investment the nature and level of one's occupation with personal needs, advantage, prospects, and so forth, relative to one's attention to those of others; *see also* **self-absorption**

self-justification *see* **defensive strategy**

self-maintenance caring for the self and thus a fundamental communicative act; strategies to provide for personal support and security in communication, i.e., to protect and sustain the self against perceived threat of diminishment or injury; *see* **cope, invention, justify, narcissistic motivation, needs, saving face, self, shame, threat,** *and* ***topoi.***

self-perception *see* **self-concept**

self-protection *see* **defending**

self psychology psychoanalytic school founded by Heinz Kohut that names shame from felt self-deficiency as the motivator of self-acceptance; *contrast with* classical theory that finds guilt arising from transgression (e.g., breaking a rule or law) as motivator of the quest for forgiveness; *see also* **Freudian theory** *and* **shame**

self-talk interaction of one's subselves; *see* **intrapersonal communication** *and* **subselves**

sender creator and conveyor of a message, e.g., speaker; *see also* **encode** *and* **invention**

Sense of Personal Power one of the six keys to a Communicative Disposition: awareness of one's social strength as a confident, effective communicator, as a person of rhetorical influence

separation interpersonal disconnectedness or distinction, reflective of the human condition; *see also* **difference** *and* **human condition**

sex biological identity, not to be confused with gender; *see also* **androgynous** *and* **gender characteristics**

shame the powerful emotion related to self-doubt and self-deficiency: stemming from felt inadequacy in being or behaving; thus the enabler of one's peculiar narcissism and self-maintenance strategies, favorable and unfavorable; *see also* **insecurity, narcissism, narcissistic injury,** *and* **self-concept**

"Shift-Response" a strictly self-interested and oblivious response to another's message; irrelevant and nonconfirming feedback, called "conversational narcissism" by Charles Derber in his book *The Pursuit of Attention: Power and Individualism in Everyday Life.*

situation the scene of communication, including place (e.g., home, work, sporting event, or wedding), time (e.g., early morning, spring, birthday, Yom Kippur, or old age), emotional climate (e.g., happy, chaotic, inhospitable), and purposes of participants; *see* **Situation Awareness**

Situation Awareness one of the six keys to a Communicative Disposition: sensitivity to the nature or "requirements" of communicators in a scene of communication; ability to "get a feeling" for the dynamics of place, time, purposes, rules, and emotional climate that influence sending and receiving in an interaction

socialization process by which family, cultural, and other human influences work to shape the identity and social nature of a child, including the shaping of a self-concept, values, and behaviors; *see also* **culture** *and* **family system**

social sensitivity *see* **Other-Awareness**

soft adaptive self-maintenance communicative strategies; *contrast with* **hard**; *see also* **narcissism**

stimulation arousal of a response in an interaction, especially as pertaining to caregiver with an infant; *see* **losses, narcissism, narcissistic injury, optimal frustration, overstimulation,** *and* **understimulation**

strategies methods, procedures, modes or techniques; means of communicating with purposefully selected enthymemes or roles; approaches to a communicative exigence; *see also* **choice, functional strategy, invention, self-maintenance,** *and* ***topoi***

subjectivity a perspective characterized by the influence of self-needs and self-interest; *contrast with* **objectivity**

subselves inner persons or parts of oneself involved in one's intrapersonal communicating, e.g., "Ambitious One" or "Ms. Critical Side"; *see also* **intrapersonal communication** *and* **self-talk**

symbiosis interdependence of persons; in psychology and psychoanalysis, often used in reference to co-dependency or narcissistic collusion; *see also* **co-dependence**

T

threat a perception of danger to the self in a communicative situation, especially relating to anticipated disconfirmation, and as instigated or heightened by feelings of vulnerability and insecurity; normal and ordinary concern relating to social safety; a source of exigence and thus a prompter of self-maintenance strategy; *see* **exigence**, **fear**, **insecurity**, **vulnerability**, *and* **self-maintenance**

topoi (singular: ***topos***) self-maintenance categories suggesting approaches or kinds of communicative strategies from which to select in given situations; *see also* **choice**, **invention**, **self-maintenance**, *and* **strategies**

transactional the interdependent nature of a communicative exchange, with each participant's roles of sending and receiving assumed simultaneously; example: "Though she remained silent while he complimented her on solving the riddle, her message of pleasure was clear: her bright smile at first, and a second later a happy nod, and then a loving kiss."

trust confidence and safety of the self in interaction, derived from evidence of others' integrity, reliability, sense of fairness, good intentions, and so forth; to chance making disclosures of self in communication, necessarily giving up a measure of control and self-protection, in expectation of confirmation; a highly significant factor in communication; *see* **credibility**, ***ethos***, *and* **security**

U

understimulation in the infant's experience, insufficient communicative presence of caregivers; "being with" the infant "too little"; *see* **losses, narcissism, narcissistic injury,** *and* **stimulation**

V

validation *see* **confirmation**

values social or individual conceptions of the *good*; certain of the premises of one's self-concept; important influences on choices in communication, e.g., a value on community responsibility appearing in a person's strategic roles and premises of enthymemes; *see* **culture, family system, ideology, premise,** *and* **self-concept**

verbal the words of messages; *see* **encode** *and* **message**; *contrast with* **nonverbal**

vulnerability openness to narcissistic injury; includes one's relative helplessness, fragility, dependence on others for care and confirmation; *see* **fear, insecurity,** *and* **threat**

W

Withdrawal one of the eight strategic ***topoi*** of self-maintenance: characterized by retreat from communication; ranges from mental absence to physical absence

X

xenophobia fear of strangers

Y

"You" problematic use of language that places the responsibility for one's feelings on another, e.g., as seen in this kind of judgment: "You make me feel klutzy when . . ."

Z

zero-sum game an interaction in which one person's gain equals another's loss; *see* **economic model**

Name Index

Subject Index

J